FORKED TONGUE

SECOND EDITION

FORKED TONGUE

THE POLITICS OF BILINGUAL EDUCATION

ROSALIE PEDALINO PORTER

With a new epilogue by the author

TRANSACTION PUBLISHERS
New Brunswick (U.S.A.) and London (U.K.)

New material this edition copyright © 1996 by Transaction Publishers, New Brunswick, New Jersey 08903. Originally published in 1990 by Basic Books.

This book is printed on acid-free paper that meets the American National Standard for Permanence of Paper for Printed Library Materials.

Library of Congress Catalog Number: 96-10625
ISBN: 1-56000-881-4
Printed in the United States of America

Library of Congress Cataloging-in-Publication Data

Porter, Rosalie Pedalino, 1931-✓
    Forked tongue : the politics of bilingual education / Rosalie Pedalino Porter ; with a new epilogue by the author — 2nd ed.
        p. cm.
    Includes bibliographical references and index.
    ISBN 1-56000-881-4 (pbk. : alk. paper)
    1. Education, Bilingual—United States. 2. Education, Bilingual—Political aspects—United States. 3. Linguistic minorities—Education—United States. I. Title.
LC3731.P66 1996
371.97'0973—dc20   96-10625
                                                              CIP

To my beloved parents,
Lucy and Frank

Forked Tongue

———————— ◇◇◇ ————————

1551　"*What hath this actor won now by his forked question?*"
　　　　　　　　　　　　　　　　　　　　　　—Gardiner

1604　"*. . . a forked kinde of argument.*"　　　　　—Cawdry

1667　"*Hiss for hiss returned with forked tongue To forked tongue.*"
　　　　　　　　　　　　—Milton, *Paradise Lost* (X, 518)

1837　"*Mr. Hunt . . . charged them with talking with a 'forked tongue,' in other words, with lying.*"　　—Washington Irving

1867　"*The Great Father, as they* [*the Navajo*] *are wont to style the Government, speaks with a forked tongue.*"
　　　　　　　　　　—*Weekly New Mexican* (Santa Fe)

1990　"*To speak deceptively*"　　　　　　—Webster's Dictionary

Contents

———————— ◇◇◇ ————————

Acknowledgments

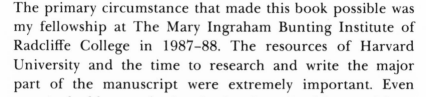

The primary circumstance that made this book possible was my fellowship at The Mary Ingraham Bunting Institute of Radcliffe College in 1987–88. The resources of Harvard University and the time to research and write the major part of the manuscript were extremely important. Even more valuable was the inspiration I received by participating in the Institute's impressive community of women scholars. Ann Bookman, assistant director of the Bunting, was assiduously helpful as mentor and friend.

The initial work on this project, in the form of a preliminary outline of the entire book, was done at the Rockefeller Study Center on Lake Como where, beginning in late November 1985, I spent a month in residence. I am grateful for the ideal working conditions and the intellectual stimulation that made up the life there.

Members of the Newton Public Schools who have my sincere thanks include former Assistant Superintendent Norm Colb, who gave me large responsibilities, trusted my judgment, and never wavered in his commitment to language minority children; former Superintendent John Strand, who stood consistently firm in Newton's battles with the bilingual bureaucracy; the Newton School Committee who demonstrated their earnest support for language minorities with public praise of the program and generous annual budgets;

and, with great affection, the teachers and teacher aides who have worked with me for the past nine years to develop the successful program described in chapter 5.

My three years on the National Advisory and Coordinating Council on Bilingual Education gave me the opportunity not only to gain a national perspective on my field but the chance to influence policy decisions on congressional legislation in this area. I thank former U. S. Secretary of Education William Bennett for the appointment. Among those in the U. S. Department of Education who were especially helpful for my work are Keith Baker, Adriana deKanter, Carole Pendas Whitten, Edward Fuentes, and Olive Wagner.

Christine Rossell and Robert Rossier are two professional colleagues whose contributions have been exceedingly valuable. Their rigorous readings of several drafts of my manuscript and their encouraging comments were essential. Other scholars and educators with whom I have had lively and useful discussions about the issues in this book, whether we agreed or not, include Nathan Glazer, Jill McCarthy, Catherine Snow, Esther Eisenhower, Joe Nye, Kenji Hakuta, Charles Glenn, Thomas Scovell, David Groesbeck, Marie Eberly, Gilman Hebert, Ed Lerner, Kay Polga, Judy Sandler, Russell Gersten, Bob Harrington, and Tony Torres. The contributions of Barry McLaughlin, Christina Bratt Paulston, and Bernard Spolsky are especially important in chapters 3 and 4. Martin Kessler, my editor at Basic Books, gave me early and consistent encouragement together with astute critical advice. Project editor Charles Cavaliere and copy editor Sharon Sharp were exacting readers and a pleasure to work with.

I must add a note of thanks to the Apple Computer Company in Marlboro, Massachusetts, which came through with a free loan of a computer when, halfway through the manuscript, I was suddenly and technologically bereft.

Thanks, also, to Apple Systems Engineer Scott Newcombe, who made the machine usable.

On a personal note, I am grateful to a host of friends and especially to my family for being understanding and encouraging throughout my intense preoccupation with this project. My sons, Steve, Dave, and Tom took obvious joy in my work as it progressed, and I am indebted to Tom whose panoramic mind produced the metaphor for the title. I reserve my special heartfelt gratitude for my husband, David, who knows well the depth of my appreciation for his unstinting support.

FORKED TONGUE

Introduction
The Bilingual Controversy

Not long ago at the Rockefeller Study Center on Lake Como, I sat at dinner next to a well-known American nuclear deterrence strategist who asked me what I was working on. When I answered, "Bilingual education," he asked me why there is such confusion about it and what a good liberal like himself should think about the education of children who don't know the English language. His reaction was typical—people *are* confused. My explanation of the issues and problems prompted him to suggest that I write on this challenging social issue for the general public, for other concerned citizens who would like to have a sounder basis for their opinions. On a similar occasion back home, in conversation with a notable American historian, I was alarmed to hear him say that he understands and is totally in favor of bilingual education in this country. He said, with great conviction, that he supports the teaching of Spanish to all schoolchildren so that we can quickly become a bilingual country!

The widespread lack of understanding of this controversial field ultimately convinced me to address this book to a more general audience and not only to educators. It really is time to present the issues clearly and dispel the myths, misrepresentations, and distortions routinely accepted by

1

people, like my academic friends, who are sensitive to social issues.

Why am *I* writing this book, and why is my personal perspective valuable in the national debate over the use of different languages in public education? I am neither a linguistics specialist nor a social scientist but a practitioner. I have worked in this field since it began in the early 1970s, first as a Spanish bilingual teacher, then as director of a program for 400 children from thirty different language backgrounds, and, most recently, as a member of the national council that recommends policy on bilingual education to the U.S. Congress. I have been involved daily with the consequences of applying some of the theories advanced in recent years to improve the education of children whose English is so limited as to make their schooling ineffective.

I *am* one of these children. I sat in the back of the classroom in the Elliott Street School, Newark, New Jersey, at age six, an immigrant child, not understanding a word being said by the teacher or other students. I experienced the pain and frustration of struggling to learn a second language unassisted and the difficulty of being accepted by my peers in an American classroom.

Rarely, if ever, do classroom teachers or immigrant parents write or speak out in any public forum. Community leaders and politicians make demands on behalf of language groups with whom they are not always in close touch. Researchers in linguistics, sociology, and psychology develop theories and hypotheses prescribing solutions to the serious problems of educating language minority children, and educational institutions implement these new ideas. Seldom is there a place in the public dialogue for what teachers actually see happening in their classrooms and for what the parents actually want for their children.

This book, then, combines for the first time concrete local, national, and international experience with extensive research to produce a firsthand view of which policies, practices, and programs actually succeed for the language minority children they are intended to serve. It reveals the failures of a twenty-year national policy based on an untested learning theory that, far from helping language minority children, actually impedes their progress. The consequences for our society are ominous and divisive.

The awakening realization came in the 1960s that the number of language minority children in our schools was growing rapidly and that they were not receiving an adequate education. A dramatically new and experimental approach, Transitional Bilingual Education (TBE), was proposed as the solution. It prescribed native-language instruction with English lessons gradually added to allow the student to learn subject matter while making the transition to English. This civil rights initiative was seen as a strong and necessary effort to correct a disgraceful situation. The insensitivity shown to language minority children is well documented: labeling limited-English students as mentally retarded; punishing, verbally or physically, children who used their native language in school; and neglecting students to such a degree that many simply left school. A number of federal and state laws, regulatory acts, and court decisions were passed to improve the educational opportunities for language minority children. The principal ones are Title VI of the Civil Rights Act of 1964, which prohibits denial of equal education opportunity on the basis of race, language, or national origin; Title VII, the Bilingual Education Act of the 1968 Elementary and Secondary Education Act, which provides funding for bilingual education and sets guidelines; and the U.S. Supreme Court decision of 1974 in *Lau* v. *Nichols,* which places an obligation on school districts to take action to remove language barriers that have the effect of excluding linguistic minority children from full participation in public education.

Just as these actions on the part of civil rights advocates, legislators, lawyers, and judges began to open up access to an equal education, another force began to grow to restrict the free exercise of educational options. The conviction was quickly and firmly planted that limited-English children must be taught in their native language if their educational needs were to be adequately met. Advocates argued categorically that through TBE, the children would learn English faster and would learn their school subjects better. Who could be against such objectives?

Because of the earlier discrimination suffered by language minority children, many educators, lawyers, and legislators were easily convinced that any program using only English-language instruction must be bad and any program that taught the children in their native language must be not only equitable but superior. Without any evidence to challenge the assumption, this view gained acceptance among the well-intentioned. There was an unequivocal mandate from the federal government and from the Supreme Court twenty years ago that special language programs *must* be provided in every school district with non-English-speaking students, but the order left the design of such programs to the individual communities. The political movement for recognition of the rights of linguistic and ethnic minorities, however, coalesced into a militant demand for native-language-based bilingual education as the *only* allowable option.

The original beneficiaries of bilingual education and its strongest advocates have been Spanish-speakers. When bilingual education began, 80 percent of the limited-English schoolchildren were Spanish-speakers. Bilingual education has been and continues to be an instrument in the movement for latino equality and power in U.S. society—a natural impulse of immigrant and migrant groups on the lowest rung of the economic ladder. However, the economic aspirations, natural as they are, have been cloaked in the guise of an educational program said to produce superior achievement for all language minority children—a proposition that is essentially false, as the years of practical experience with bilingual education are beginning to reveal.

Population changes in the past twenty years have greatly altered the character of American classrooms. Language minority children now account for 10 percent of all American schoolchildren, and in some districts these children constitute 25 to 60 percent of the entire school population. While a large majority continue to be Spanish-speakers, the rest represent 145 language backgrounds. The language minority population is increasing at a much faster rate than the rest of the population and is no longer contained only in urban schools but is present in suburban and rural districts as well. By the turn of the century language minority children could make up 20 percent of the total school population, with speakers of Asian languages accounting for the highest rate of increase.[1]

These changes in population define the complex cultural problem to be addressed: Given the number of ethnic and linguistic groups—among them, legal and illegal immigrants; native Americans; refugees from Southeast Asia, Iran, Afghanistan, and Central America; and others—who make up the 145 language groups now involved in bilingual education programs, it is only reasonable to assume that different groups have different objectives. Some groups are intent on rapid assimilation; others are more concerned with holding on to their language and traditions; all look to the schools as the agency that will support and execute their priorities. Even Spanish-speakers are not a monolithic group with agreed-on goals but comprise a variety of communities from over three dozen countries in Central and

South America, the Caribbean, and Europe, and from all economic and social levels.

The increasing diversity of our pluralistic society requires a variety of educational programs that respond to the objectives of different communities, but political agendas take precedence over educational innovation. Instead of learning from the experiences of other multilingual countries such as Canada, Germany, Sweden, England, and Israel, and trying different approaches, the bilingual education establishment has mounted a shrill campaign against any alternative programs. No amount of research evidence on the dubious value of native-language instruction for extended periods has had any effect on the campaign. Native-language instruction has become a goal in itself rather than one of the means to the goal of a better education for limited-English children.

The bilingual education establishment is fighting to maintain its primacy and prerogatives unchallenged, even though bilingual programs have, in the majority of cases, proven unsuccessful. Boston is one of the glaring examples of this failure (see chapter 3). In 1986 the Boston School Department revealed that several hundred students in the junior high schools had been in bilingual classrooms for seven years, despite the three-year legal limit for this special program. Yet even after seven years in the program they had still not learned enough English to be enrolled in a class taught in English.[2] The Boston bilingual program, it seems, is neither transitional in nature nor bilingual in outcome.

Beyond evaluating the successes or failures of bilingual education as it is currently practiced are the larger considerations of social equality and justice, of the effect of national language policies on many ethnic, cultural, and linguistic groups. The bilingual education model is essentially segregative because it is linguistically isolating. It promotes separate schooling for the major part of the school day, de-laying English-language development and the benefits of in-tegration of limited-English students with their English-speaking classmates. If there were convincing evidence that children learn their school subjects better if they are taught in their native language, then we could continue to ap-prove the temporary segregation; but that case has not been substantiated.

Language policy has powerful ramifications in the for-midable issue of social cohesion, even nationhood itself. At a time when we have made massive commitments on behalf of racial integration and equal access for our citizens, the demand for "my language and my culture" sets up warring tensions. Attempts to preserve ethnic neighborhoods, schools, and clubs for cultural maintenance run directly counter to the democratic rights of equal access in housing, education, and social institutions. In the 1970s latino par-ents in Boston, Springfield, and Worcester, Massachusetts, opposed busing, preferring to have their children enrolled in nearby schools that were largely segregated. Community leaders opposed busing also, fearing the loss of political and economic power that would result from this diffusion of their community. Alfredo Mathew, Jr., a hispanic civic leader, cautioned,

While bilingualism, from a political point of view, is meant to foster the Puerto Rican/Hispanic identity and consequently en-courages concentrations of Hispanics to stay together and not be integrated, one also has to be wary that it not become so insular and ingrown that it fosters a type of apartheid that will generate animosities with others, such as Blacks, in the com-petition for scarce resources, and further alienate the Hispanic from the larger society.[3]

Other latino leaders expressed even stronger concerns at the time. Dr. William Milan, a professor of Caribbean literature at New York University, feared that if this problem of segregation were not faced, it would damage hispanic children's prospects in the largely English-language job market. Dr. Thomas Carter, an early pioneer in bilingual education, had reached a similar conclusion: "Given only two polar choices—ethnic segregation with instruction in Spanish or desegregation without it—I would choose the latter as most beneficial to the child and society."[4]

The impassioned rhetoric for cultural maintenance through bilingual/*bicultural* education, as the program is sometimes called, comes almost exclusively from middle-class, advantaged individuals indulging in a nostalgic, romantic ethnicity. The responsibility of the schools, charged to prepare students for opportunity and change, is surely not to freeze the home culture and language in place. Evolution of language and culture, which has occurred naturally with every group that has come to this country, poses its own set of tensions between generations. Children growing up in a new culture want to shed their inherited identities, and parents want to hold on to old familiar ways. At the same time, other parents understand that their family ways will inevitably change as their children begin to participate in the larger society. Many parents are *not* committed to having the schools maintain the mother tongue if it is at the expense of gaining a sound education and the English-language skills needed for obtaining jobs or pursuing higher education.

The goal of preserving every linguistic and cultural variant is for anthropologists to address. It may not be the desire of new immigrants, however, to retain every feature of their language and culture but to adapt and modify them for the sake of social and economic advancement. An example of the wisdom of the community overriding the theories of linguists and the efforts of community activists is the case of Black English. The momentarily fashionable notion that teachers should be trained in this form of speech and that they should give classroom instruction in this dialect to black students was defeated by the parents of these very students.[5] They understood, as do many bilingual parents and educators, that it is a major responsibility of the public schools to expand students' language development, to give students mastery of Standard English so that, having a repertoire of language skills, they may use different dialects appropriately for different situations.

Richard Rodriguez, a Mexican-American writer, observes that as bilingual education has taken over the schooling for language minorities in the past twenty years, the separation by social class has deepened: "For the Spanish-speaking, especially, it is possible today to live a quasi-public life, apart from English. It is a tragedy and a luxury."[6] He fears that those who have the most to lose in a bilingual America are the foreign-speaking poor, who are being lured into a linguistic nursery, as he calls it, far from the power and opportunities in English-speaking America. The character of this "quasi-public life" is essentially a ghetto life, which Rodriquez himself rejected when he entered the mainstream of American life through the mainstream language. When one hears that Spanish-speaking children can get along without much English in some parts of the country, one must then ask if being restricted to one neighborhood need be the highest aspiration for Spanish-speaking children. The wrong-headed notion that Spanish-speakers are the only group that cannot be expected to learn English for mastery of school subjects is patronizing and demeaning to all latinos and should be forcefully denounced.

Bilingual education advocates consistently oversell the importance of native-language instruction. No doubt some use of the home language in the classroom when non-English-speaking children first arrive in school may be helpful, but the bilingual bureaucracy draws no boundaries on this introductory stage. They promote the notion that *all* subject matter should be taught in the native language, that even reading must be taught first in the native language, and that the skills will later be easily transferred to English. There is no reliable evidence to support any of these ideas.

Linguists, too, have tended to take an abstract idea and overemphasize it. We have been made aware that languages and dialects, as well as cultures, are to be equally valued. Linguist and anthropologist Rudolph Troike made the familiar observation: "No dialect is inherently better or more adequate or more logical than another, just as no language is inherently superior to another."[7] Similarly, Einar Haugen, a Harvard University professor of linguistics, stated, "The first step to applying our best scientific knowledge to language problems is to realize that no man's speech is inferior, only different."[8] Proclaiming these truths helps combat the old prejudices in our society against the linguistically and culturally different. To be looked down upon as less intelligent or less civilized because of dialectal differences is a painful experience many of us have gone through in this ethnically diverse country. My own studies in dialectology, in fact, gave me a feeling of liberation and pride, a psychic lift. To know finally, and to have it proclaimed by experts, that the Neapolitan dialect I spoke during my childhood was equal in structural logic and expressive capacity not only to standard Italian but also to English was a marvelous discovery!

But when this single revelation of linguistic equality—attractive and logical in the ábstract—is applied to public education policy, it may actually run counter to the best interests of the children for whom it is invoked. Noel Epstein, national education writer, has said that while all languages or dialects are equal in the scholarly sense, "they certainly are not equal in the political, economic or social sense, whether one is referring to English dialects among English speakers, Spanish vernaculars among Spanish speakers, or minority languages in the general society."[9] Standard English is not lovelier or grander—but it is the most useful dialect to master in this country.

Extreme positions are the rule rather than the exception in the bilingual debate. The polarization of positions follows political lines from the push by the conservative right for adopting English as the official language of the United States to the left's demand that First Amendment protection be extended to every family to preserve its language and values and that these family possessions must be specifically embraced by school instruction as a student's entitlement. On the other hand, after twenty years of public discussion, there are still many people who naively ask, "Why the need for these bilingual programs? When my grandfather came to America, he didn't get any special help. He had to learn by himself." Fortunately, this uninformed attitude is diminishing. The general public has come to understand the need for special help for non-English-speaking children, who are often from economically disadvantaged families. Still, many citizens fear the increasing expansion of bilingual services, such as the printing of voting ballots in other languages, as leading toward a fragmentation of the national identity to a degree that has not happened before.

Promoters of bilingual programs since the 1960s have questioned the necessity and even the desirability of a common identity. That tumultuous decade that began with the dream of integration ended up with scorn for assimilation and an idealization of cultural pluralism. Presenting a defensive posture at all times, the more doctrinaire members of the bilingual establishment routinely accuse anyone who proposes a moderate, integrationist approach of being biased against foreigners—a hater of other languages and probably a racist.

Extreme positions do not serve the crucial needs of the

children who are hostages to the political battle. Between the right-wing notion that these children should be left to sink or swim as earlier generations did and the left-wing notion of preserving each group's language and culture in perpetuity, there is a moderate, pragmatic view that proposes a range of alternatives in education, giving different communities the right to choose the most effective approach for their own children and the public funding to support their choice. That pragmatic, liberating view is the focus of this book. People need to be well informed about the effectiveness of different programs in order to make intelligent decisions that are not controlled by the political rhetoric.

A Spanish bilingual program director said to me recently, with great bitterness, "If learning English is all that kids need to get ahead in life, then American children shouldn't have to go to school at all." No, learning English is not all that is needed—not by a long shot; but it is obviously one of the crucial elements leading to equal opportunities in schooling, jobs, and public life in the multicultural American society.

How did we right-thinking, social justice advocates in the education field originally become so convinced that TBE was the one true answer to the problems of educating language minorities? And, having become disillusioned when the reality in the classroom no longer matched the absolutist rhetoric, what new possibilities did we open up to help us achieve our goals? That is the story in this book—a story of my seventeen years of personal involvement, a period that covers the whole development of this field whose aim is the education and integration of language minority children.

Chapters 1 and 2 highlight the crucial problems in teaching limited-English children, the growing awareness of the ineffectiveness of bilingual education, and the way in which the search for more productive and democratic alternatives brought on harsh political retribution by the bilingual bureaucracy. Chapters 3, 4, and 5 debunk the basic assumptions about the relationship of second-language learning to native-language development; provide what I hope is a crisp and intelligible insight into major advances in language teaching, including new programs in other multilingual societies; and explore a selection of successful alternative programs in U.S. cities.

Chapters 6, 7, and 8 confront the momentous questions posed for our country: What is the proper role of our public schools in delaying or promoting assimilation? How can we strike a balance between the fear of losing cultural group identity and the danger of drastically fragmenting our dynamic, multicultural society? Out of this debate comes a redefinition of societal goals for the next two decades to help language minority children become full participants in American life.

1
Firsthand Experience in Educating Language Minorities

———————— ◇◇◇ ————————

My introduction to the American school system began when I entered a first-grade classroom not long after arriving in the United States at the age of six. Feelings of fearfulness at being separated from my family were heightened when I lost my way home on the first day of school. I wandered for what seemed miles in central Newark, New Jersey, crying, until I was brought home by a policeman who lived in our neighborhood.

During those first few months, the hours I spent in the classroom were a haze of incomprehensible sounds. I copied what the other children seemed to be doing, scribbling on paper as though I were writing; otherwise, I silently watched the behavior of teachers and students. Although I cannot recall the process of learning English and beginning to participate in the verbal life of the classroom, I know it was painful. I can remember, however, that within two years I felt completely comfortable with English and with the school community—how it happened I do not know. I suspect that a combination of factors worked in my favor: a close-knit family, personal motivation, good health, sympathetic teachers, peer acceptance, and who knows what other intangibles of time and place. When it finally began to happen, I remember the intense joy of understanding and being understood, even at a simple level, by those around me.

Reading Richard Rodriguez's moving account of his experience as an underprivileged Mexican-American child, I am surprised that it affects me so deeply now. He said,

One day in school I raised my hand to volunteer an answer. I spoke out in a loud voice. And I did not think it remarkable when the entire class understood. That day, I moved very far from the disadvantaged child I had been only days earlier. The belief, the calming assurance that I belonged in public, had at last taken hold. . . . It would have pleased me to have my teachers speak to me in Spanish but I would have delayed having to learn the language of public society. I would have evaded learning the great lesson of school, that I had a public identity. . . . Only later when I was able to think of myself as an American, no longer an alien in gringo society, could I seek the rights and opportunities necessary for full public individuality. . . . Those middle class ethnics who scorn assimilation romanticize public separateness and they trivialize the dilemma of the socially disadvantaged.[1]

Changing Educational Expectations

In my generation, many immigrant children did not succeed either in learning English or in mastering academic subjects. It was this common immigrant experience of failure, the widespread dropping out of school, that gave rise in the 1960s to the demand for effective, humane language programs. The expectation among educators of those earlier times was that immigrant children would either "sink or swim." This cruel experience forced many to leave school early, prepared only for unskilled labor. This aborted schooling was not as serious a drawback then, however, be-

training opportunities for Toñita when her youngest child reached school age. Clearly, I went beyond what was expected in a tutorial sponsored by the university. Because I was a mature woman with a family who had lived the experience of being in an alien culture, I found an easy rapport with the Santiago family, and they visited occasionally with my family before returning to Puerto Rico a few years ago.

—————————— ◇◇◇ ——————————

New Experiences and New Lessons

In 1974, with a bachelor's degree and a view of myself, at age forty-three, as the oldest "new" teacher in the world, I began teaching in Springfield, Massachusetts. Here began, first, my excitement in being part of a new experiment in education and, later, the evolution of my thinking on the impractical aspects of bilingual education in the classroom. The Armory Street School had just been desegregated in a citywide master plan that reassigned fifth- and sixth-grade students to different schools to achieve racial balance. Among the 500 students at Armory 49 percent were blacks, 10 percent were Spanish-speakers, and the rest were white students from predominantly low-income families of Irish background in the "Hungry Hill" neighborhood. Kindergarten children living in the vicinity, more than half of whom were from Puerto Rican families, also attended the school.

My prescribed teaching duties were dauntingly varied. First, I was to teach the kindergarten children *in Spanish* for about an hour daily, developing the basic concepts of size, shape, colors, numbers, and letters—in short, those things typically taught to American kindergarteners. I also was to provide twenty to thirty minutes of English for these children, usually through stories, songs, and games. The rest of the day I was to teach fifth- and sixth-grade students their subject matter—mathematics, science, and social studies—in Spanish and give them intensive lessons in English as a Second Language (ESL), the generic label for the teaching of English speaking, reading, and writing skills to speakers of other languages.

After the first year of groping for teaching materials and searching for good ways of getting ideas and facts across to the students, I began to feel somewhat less shaky about what we were accomplishing together in the classroom. As the only bilingual teacher in the school, I was also called on to be the interpreter for families arriving with new students to be enrolled, to make emergency telephone calls to non-English-speaking parents, to act as interpreter for parent–teacher conferences in various classrooms, and occasionally to visit the home of one of our students with the principal when some unusual situation arose.

I learned invaluable lessons from Jim Moriarty, the principal at the Armory Street School. By example he disproved the notion that children can only be inspired if taught or supervised by someone from their own racial group or ethnic culture. Jim's first concern was for the students—their physical safety and their opportunity for real *learning*. How did he communicate this to the students and to everyone on his staff? Not by his words, since he is not a particularly expressive or articulate person, but by his daily actions. He got to know each child and something about each family in his district early in the school year, and he certainly knew his school staff. There was no mistaking his priorities when he said to us one day when we were complaining about some onerous duty at school, "This school is not being run for the convenience of the teachers but for the benefit of the students—let's always remember that." Although he was paternalistic and authoritarian to some degree, we respected Jim for his fairness and his consistent advocacy for *all* students. In the years since desegregation, Armory, under his leadership, has established a reputation in Springfield for high student achievement. The school often ranks in first place or close to it on citywide test scores in reading and mathematics.

Such contacts, coupled with the generalized euphoria of starting a new career in a new field that was being created daily, carried me through the first year or two of teaching. Idealism, the sense of mission, and the satisfying knowledge that I was helping students in ways that I had never been helped kept me from analyzing too closely what was going on in my classes. But the time for reflection arrived, and the questioning of my early assumptions about the value of bilingual education became a preoccupation.

––––––––––––– ◊◊◊ –––––––––––––

Awakening to the Realities of Bilingualism

As I began to know my students and their families, I saw that very few were new to the United States and totally non-English-speaking. The small number who were came predominantly from Italy, Greece, or Central America. The large majority were Puerto Rican children who either were born on the mainland or had arrived as very young children. The languages of their homes were Spanish and English. Older brothers and sisters spoke mostly English; parents spoke mostly Spanish. Years of shuttling between San Juan and New York or Holyoke and Springfield, and perhaps moving three times in one year within the city of Springfield, produced the expected outcome of languages in transition: Spanish became stronger when the family spent some time in Puerto Rico; English became stronger when the family returned to the mainland. And there was the mixing of the two, with the words or expressions in so-called Spanglish creating a neighborhood argot for informal communication.

I soon realized that teaching in Spanish to the kindergarten children required much preliminary work in vocabulary enrichment in standard Spanish. These children, like other children in our society from disadvantaged homes, need more language development, no matter what the language, just to help them begin academic learning. Often I found that as I spoke Spanish, they answered in English. *"Juan, que color es este?"* I would ask, as I pointed to a green box. "Green" (pronounced "grin") would be Juan's reply. So, I would correct him, *"Verde,"* and he would again say, "Green." In the early years I followed the curriculum and taught all subjects in Spanish, but I came to feel that I was going about things the wrong way around, as if I were deliberately holding back the learning of English.

When I gave the required thirty minutes of English-language lessons in the kindergarten, scrupulously separate from the Spanish teaching and of much shorter duration, the students responded with equal enthusiasm. They sang the songs in English, shouted the rhymes and number games, and play-acted with me "Three Billy Goats Gruff" and "Jack and the Beanstalk." I do not know how they felt about the patchwork use of two languages in the classroom, but I know how I felt: odd at first, and then very doubtful about the efficacy of what I was doing.

Today, fourteen years later, I open my hometown newspaper in Amherst, Massachusetts, and read a regrettably comparable story about the new bilingual classroom established in one of our elementary schools. The reporter quotes this bit of dialogue between a nine-year-old girl from Spain and her teacher: "Pointing to a picture illustrating the text, the child asks, 'Is this a *fuego?*' and the teacher replies, *'Si, por favor hable en Español.'* The teacher explains to the reporter, 'It's very simple. We learn easiest in the language we know best. Most of these children can speak English but their academic skills are very weak. The goal is to build up a foundation of skills in their native language and then transfer those skills to a second language.' "[3] But that child from Spain is obviously ready and eager to continue her learning in English! She is capable of thinking and speaking in grammatical English and only needs the one word *fire* in English. Why is the teacher not following the obvious course of teaching academic subjects in English since her students can already speak the language?

Refocusing on English-Language Skills

At the Armory Street School I also was teaching fifth- and sixth-grade students, who spent three hours or more with me daily. These students came to my room from their various homerooms for special instruction because the school did not have a large enough group of limited-English students to organize an entire bilingual classroom of fifth graders or sixth graders. Those whose English was sufficient to the tasks studied their subjects in their homeroom and came to me for English-language reading and writing; those whose English was very limited spent more time in my class, receiving instruction in the fifth- and sixth-grade math, science, and social studies curriculum in Spanish, in addition to an intensive English program.

We bilingual teachers were told by the citywide director of the program to teach spoken English but not to teach reading in English until the students could read *at grade level* in Spanish. Supposedly, the reading skills in Spanish would easily be transferred to English. This is, indeed, the common practice in bilingual programs across the country. Working with students who were ten to fourteen years old and who were not reading above the first- or second-grade level in Spanish, I doubted that this magic transfer of reading skills from Spanish to English would happen before they finished high school—if they stayed in school that long.

Instead, I decided, quite on my own, and based on this firsthand experience, to devote most of the teaching time to intensive work on English-language skills—speaking, reading, and writing. I reasoned that my students needed a rapid infusion of English if they were to cope with their junior high school classes and succeed. Two hours a day we moved from one activity to another to broaden their English vocabulary and focus on specific concepts related to the curriculum of the school. We did science experiments to understand the water cycle, grew plants, and demonstrated simple machines by rolling toy cars down inclined planes. We set up a classroom "grocery store" to learn hands-on about nutrition, money, and classification of objects. We wrote our own dramatic version of a children's classic, "Clever Gretel," in the students' own English and performed it for other classrooms. We had a weekly cooking lesson, and the students produced a recipe book in English with artwork, binding, and all. Everything we did in some way advanced the use of the English language for academic, as well as social, situations. I did, of course, continue to provide some native-language help to the students who needed it, relying on my judgment of their abilities. But out of this highly representative classroom experience came my determination to create the most direct means for my students to reach English proficiency and academic achievement.

We did not, however, neglect the cultural background of the students! We read folktales and learned songs of their island, looked at Caribbean art, and studied the history of Puerto Rico and the mainland United States. I made the culture of my students familiar to the other students in the school through various activities. An annual event at Christ-

mas time was the serenading of each classroom by the bilingual group. We presented typical Puerto Rican songs, ac-
companied by maracas and bongos—sounds and rhythms
unfamiliar in English Christmas carols but joyful and ap-
preciated by the students! We gave weekly mini-lessons in
Spanish for interested classes, with the bilingual students
acting as expert assistants.

The Clear-cut Need for Change

Where did all this lead me in my anxieties over the best
ways to help these students after a third and fourth year
went by? My conviction was strengthened that both at the
youngest school age and in the higher grades in the elementary school we were not following the most natural
course of concentrating on the English language and on
helping students learn their subjects in English—and these
are, indeed, the two stated goals of the bilingual education
law and of all bilingual programs. As I visited other schools
and talked with teachers at professional meetings about
their experiences, I began to believe, along with many of
my colleagues, that the underlying rationale of native-language-based programs was wrong-headed. How else could I
account for the fact that so many of my fifth- and sixth-
grade students—who had never been out of the mainland
United States, and had, indeed, grown up right in Springfield—had not yet learned enough English to be taught their
subjects in English? How could I account for the ability of
students from other countries who arrived in the fifth and
sixth grade and responded quickly to English-language instruction without bilingual support? Looking at the structure of the program in grades one through four revealed at
least part of the answer.

Impediments to English-Language Learning

In Springfield, as in hundreds of other school districts across the country, the TBE program, as noted previously, is based on early and extended native-language instruction. One of its central concerns is the preservation, through language, of the child's native "culture." In first grade, limited-English students are placed in a classroom where a bilingual teacher provides all instruction in their home language (typically, Spanish)—reading, language arts, spelling, mathematics, science, and social studies. For a small portion of the day—perhaps thirty minutes daily, three times a week—an ESL teacher, that is, one skilled in intensive English-language instruction, gives oral English lessons. These language minority students may be "integrated" with English-speaking children a few times a week for art, music, or physical education. This same schedule continues in grade two, with the possibility of mathematics being taught in English. Reading in English is not introduced until third grade, and only if the bilingual teacher considers the students ready. (See figure 1.1.) The transition from native-language instruction to English is so gradual, and the increase in use of English and in opportunities for these students to be integrated with their English-speaking peers is so minimal, that the process is like a meandering, slow-motion dance.

Another factor contributing to the slow transition is often the composition of the teaching staff. As an example, during my entire time in Springfield the bilingual program director made annual trips to Puerto Rico to recruit teachers, asserting that we needed bilingual teachers with native skills in Spanish and a knowledge of the children's culture. Because the enrollment of limited-English students at Armory Street School was increasing and I could no longer teach all of them, first one and then another teacher from Puerto

Figure 1.1   Transitional Bilingual Education Model
Instruction in Native Language and in English

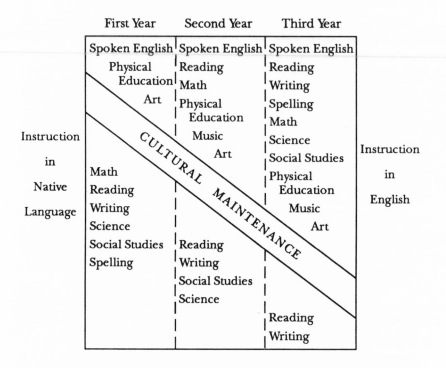

Rico was added to the staff, specifically to work with the kindergarten children. Competent as these teachers were, however, many of them knew little or no English and, therefore, could hardly be called "bilingual."

Clearly, the cultural identity of the teachers became a criterion for hiring, and the bias became evident in other ways, as well. On three occasions I trained college students in my classroom as part of their practical experience before they received their college degree and state credentials for teaching. When Springfield had openings for bilingual teachers, I recommended two of these students for the jobs because they showed great promise. They were turned down, although they had good Spanish-speaking skills and were well prepared for elementary-level teaching. They were told that the bilingual teachers had to be from the same cultural group as the students in order to be effective. In Springfield at that time we lost some excellent candidates because of this narrowly cultural view. I believe it was a deliberate policy of the administrators in our school district to build an establishment whose primary language skills would be in Spanish, with only marginal concern for their English-language ability.

The higher education establishment supported and promoted such an approach. In order to implement the new TBE law in Massachusetts in 1971, the first to be passed in the nation, the state needed hundreds of bilingual teachers, yet very few were trained. We early candidates were subjected to examinations in Spanish and English in order to establish our oral and written competency in both. As bilingual education came under the control of a more determined element of latino activists, however, the testing procedure changed. For a number of years thereafter, testing of bilingual teacher candidates at our state university was done *only in Spanish*—prospective teachers were not even tested in English! One nonhispanic woman who had lived and taught in Mexico for several years and had completed a master's degree in languages told me of her great disappointment when she failed the examination. She was told that her Spanish-language ability was fine but that she did not have enough knowledge of Puerto Rican history and culture. She could not, for instance, name three small rivers in the interior of the island.

Another example of this exclusionary bias occurred in 1980 when, at the first meeting of a graduate course at the University of Massachusetts at Amherst, the instructor lectured for a while in Spanish and then in English. He proclaimed passionately that bilingual education meant that he could use his native language now. One of the students, a

Portuguese bilingual teacher, raised her hand and asked if she could use Portuguese in class also. He replied, "No, Anna, bilingual means Spanish around here," and added, "there was a Chinese student who wanted to take this class, and I told her she could but she'd have to have a Spanish interpreter come with her." These attitudes and actions did nothing to promote the recognition that in the 1970s eight languages were used in bilingual programs in the state. Nor was there any attempt to initiate training courses for bilingual teachers of other languages to staff any of these other programs.

These stories illustrate the history of politics surrounding bilingual education in Massachusetts and at least partially explain how the programs evolved with such a heavy emphasis on native-language development and such limited concern for the stated goal of teaching English. However, these instances are not unique to Massachusetts. In my travels during the past dozen years to lecture in different states and to participate in the work of the National Advisory Council on Bilingual Education of the U.S. Department of Education, I have learned how widespread such practices are in other states with large numbers of limited-English students, principally California, Texas, and Florida. They demonstrate the zealousness with which the search for Spanish-speaking personnel has been pursued. However, no one seems to have been asking, Who should teach English to these children, and how can this best be done?

The Travesty of Teacher Selection and Preparation

Administrators in Springfield ignored the crucial questions about teaching English. I observed the haphazard assignment of ill-prepared teachers to teach ESL. In most cases, they had little idea at all of how to teach a foreign language—which is what English was to their students. My experience, once again, is representative. In the minds of school administrators, anyone who can speak English can teach English. In Springfield, they press-ganged all sorts of people into teaching limited-English students: high school English teachers and foreign language teachers, elementary classroom teachers, speech pathologists, remedial reading teachers, and teachers of the hearing impaired. Some teachers with good skills and high motivation really did a creditable job, even though it was a seat-of-the-pants effort with no curriculum, no books or materials, and some pretty odd places to work. It was not unusual for small-group English lessons to be given in hallways, broom closets, cafeterias, and boiler rooms. After two years of teaching in a coat closet at Armory School, I felt elated when a classroom was finally assigned to me.

More destructive was the practice of assigning ineffective teachers to ESL classes or to some of the remedial programs serving students with serious learning problems. Teachers who could not maintain discipline, who were not competent in teaching their subjects, or who, for various reasons, were functioning at a low level were sometimes given the job of working with students whose needs were greater than those of average children, whose situations cried out for the most able teachers to work with them. While a student teacher, I was an observer for a month in the classroom of a teacher who was close to retirement and in poor health yet had been given the ESL assignment. That experience was so heartbreaking it almost dissuaded me from entering the field. The teacher had given up on these students—six- and seven-year-olds—and had no expectations for their achievement. She merely served out her time, giving them dull, repetitive exercises to copy from the board. It was a painful experience for everyone in that classroom.

Years later I added to my file a similar complaint concerning the assignment of untrained language teachers made by linguist Christina Bratt Paulston. She writes about the situation in Sweden, where immigrant students were not receiving instruction in Swedish from trained teachers:

I find the neglect of Swedish as a foreign language (Sfs) quite unaccountable. . . . Swedish is necessary for the possibility of upward social mobility, for school success, for access to good jobs, yet Sfs is neglected in funding, in teacher training, in general attention. For successful adjustment in Sweden, it is the most important subject for the immigrant students, yet they get saddled with castoff teachers who lack training and inclination. I would urge National Board of Education and appropriate officials to make a major effort on behalf of improvement in teaching Sfs.[4]

Teacher-training workshops sometimes did not encourage rigorous instruction either. In the graduate courses I began to take, we were exhorted, in the jargon of the day, to teach students "where they're at" and to know "where they're coming from." I translated this to mean that we should be conscious of our students' current level of school knowledge and of their language ability so that we would not plan lessons that would be far beyond them. However, helping students feel comfortable with their own language and culture in a strange, new school setting promoted the development of some unusual, if not bizarre, strategies that the lunatic fringe in this field still promotes.

Fads and Fantasies

I once attended a workshop at Brown University in Providence, Rhode Island on teaching reading skills to Cape Verdean children, whose language is a dialect of Portuguese. The speakers described a three-year federally funded project to develop a written form of the Cape Verdean dialect and then to write storybooks in that dialect. The proposal, which was very enthusiastically presented, was to teach the children to read in Cape Verdean, then to read in Portuguese so they could participate in the Portuguese bilingual program, and sometime in the future to transfer their skills to reading in English. I thought that I, like Alice in Wonderland, had fallen down the rabbit hole. Could anyone really believe that this circuitous route through a nonexistent island dialect script would lead to *faster* learning of English and a better ability to learn subject matter taught in English? It seemed much more likely that the project leaders were high on the idea of Cape Verdean identity and "where the children were at" rather than on the practical outcome of such a program.

Another example of this kind of convoluted logic was described to me by a teacher from Laredo, Texas, where, in the 1970s, Rodolfo Jacobson of the University of Texas, in studying the spoken language in the community, noted that people switched from English to Spanish, back and forth, sometimes within the same sentence. Professor Jacobson decided it would help students make a closer match between home and school by having teachers use the same language-switching pattern found in the community. Laredo school administrators were persuaded to train teachers to switch from one language to another in their sentences, giving equal time to each language as they taught school subjects. This method, though it has not gained many supporters, is still included in a review of teaching strategies as "the concurrent approach."[5]

Even if one ignores the obvious core of confusion in such a manner of teaching, is it not one of the primary functions of education—bilingual or not—to expand every student's repertoire of language and thought? Surely, it is

velous opportunity to put into practice what I believed would be a better way of educating language minority children. It was to be in Newton that my ideas would be tested, and it was here that the full force of the political pressure for TBE would come down on me.

Setting out for Newton, I had no misgivings. My five years of classroom teaching experience revealed the problems, the complexity, and the shortcomings of bilingual education as the purported solution to the education of language minority children. I was ready to make changes. I had just completed a master's degree and a year as a visiting scholar at the University of London. I was full of language-learning theory, socio- and psycholinguistics, multicultural awareness, and just enough naive confidence to think that I could successfully apply it all in some real-life situation. Like the Splendid Castle that sat waiting for the Perfect Knight, Newton and I were destined for each other.

2
Confronting the Political Power of the Bilingual Bureaucracy

The economic wealth of Newton, Massachusetts, was not what initially attracted me to its public school system, for I was only vaguely aware of this before I went to be interviewed. Three other factors were of greater importance. First, Newton's limited-English students represented many different languages, rather than predominantly one, and a variety of socioeconomic backgrounds. Second, Newton had a national reputation for excellence and for innovation in educational programs. I found that this reputation was not a myth but a solid reality. Third, Newton had a long-standing commitment to improving the education of minority students—a crucial factor to me. Norm Colb, the assistant superintendent at that time, summed up the Newton approach: "If the state says we don't have to spend one nickel on these kids, Newton will still spend the nickel." The factors that first drew me to the Newton public school system remain among its greatest strengths.

My Introduction to the Newton Program

In Newton, I found an atmosphere that not only tolerated but encouraged experimentation in the pursuit of effective teaching methods, the search for ways of providing the best learning situation for all students. The district's support for individual teacher initiatives was impressive. Classroom teachers worked cooperatively with curriculum specialists in developing not only materials to be taught but also innovative ways of teaching students from different backgrounds. In this fertile setting, the possibilities for developing a good program were almost limitless.

I was hired to head the bilingual program and, specifically, to organize and regulate an ad hoc set of practices. In 1974 a bilingual program had been started for the large number of Italian immigrant children of limited English who lived in the district. Soon thereafter a few dozen Chinese children were identified as needing special instruction, and services were then expanded for the growing population of Spanish-speaking children from Central and South America.

By 1980, when I arrived, the limited-English children represented thirty different language groups and a variety of social and economic backgrounds—amazing diversity in a city that had (and continues to have) one of the highest per capita incomes in the United States. These 400 children, in a total school population of 8,000, could generally be divided into three main groups: (1) refugees from Southeast Asia, Iran, Afghanistan, Russia, and Central America, some with very good academic preparation and some with little or no formal schooling; (2) a sizable working-class immigrant population of Italians and Chinese; and (3) upper-middle-class children of visiting scholars and professionals from Israel, Japan, Scandinavia, and other areas, generally planning to be in Newton for one or two years only.

The specifics of the program we organized to provide an effective education for all of these students is the story for a later chapter. I write "we" because I had the enthusiastic cooperation of the teaching staff as well as the strong support of the administration, the School Committee, and the parents in restructuring the program. At this point, it is important to note that, despite abundant evidence that the program was effective for all of its participants, unanticipated reactions to the program's success occurred.

The political fallout for the Newton Public Schools and for me, personally, has been severe. The Newton experience is representative of the defensiveness of the bilingual education establishment and the damaging power of the reigning ideology in this field. The establishment, entrenched in state-level bureaus, freely wields its power in two key ways: (1) suppressing the spread of information on successful alternatives to bilingual education, and (2) threatening to withhold state funds from a school district with an innovative program and to deny the program the annual approval required by law. The Newton case illustrates these destructive practices, which are also common in California, Texas, and other states with large language minority populations.

Alternatives as Anathema: The First Bitter Lesson

In March 1982, two years after taking charge of the Newton program, I gave a public lecture in Boston at the state conference of the Massachusetts Association of Bilingual Education—an action that was to have harmful consequences for me. In the excitement of finishing my doctoral dissertation, I was eager to present a paper at the state conference describing the kind of successful alternative program that Newton was developing. A large audience attended my lecture, including a number of administrators from the State Department of Education Bureau of Transitional Bilingual Education, who sat up front, concentrating on the presentation. I was flattered by their attention; as it turned out, I should have been apprehensive.

In describing the innovative elements of the Newton program, I announced, clearly and carefully, that I did not necessarily prescribe the same practices for other cities but that some elements of our program could certainly be duplicated elsewhere, especially in cities with similar populations. I tactfully avoided any pejorative statements about Transitional Bilingual Education and merely asserted that there are other types of programs that can work well for language minority children. Some audience members viewed this moderate appeal for a flexible approach to the education of limited-English children, this acknowledgment that there are many different groups with different attitudes and different goals, as a threat to the hegemony of bilingual education. I was marked as a dangerous upstart.

The Foundations for a Backlash

The reasons for such a reaction should have been clear to me. Throughout my graduate studies at the University of Massachusetts at Amherst, I had seen—and experienced—corrupt, discriminatory practices that were used in service of a political ideology in this field. For example, I had seen both undergraduate and graduate programs admit unqualified latino students, who then received credit for courses they never attended after the first day of class. On one occasion I had been told in a private meeting that, despite my qualifications, I need not apply for a fellowship to support my master's degree work because none of these fellowships would be given to "gringos."

I realized, too, that such biases existed on a larger scale. Massachusetts was the first state in the nation to pass legislation requiring TBE programs in all school districts with twenty or more children of the same language whose English is limited. The people who fought for the passage of the law became some of the first program administrators and state education department specialists. They were necessarily aggressive about their demands for bilingual education on behalf of children for whom little or nothing had been done in the past. As the field developed, though, two things became obvious: (1) it was not going to be a totally hispanic preserve as more and more new language groups arrived, and (2) there was no valid evidence that TBE was indeed the best, or only, program appropriate for these children. These developments would, ordinarily, dictate the need to look for new ways to educate language minority children, to experiment and modify existing programs in search of different solutions for different situations. But the bilingual establishment in Massachusetts had an entrenched power base to maintain. The last thing to be gladly received was the notion of change or innovation, and it was into this political mine field that I walked, idealistically expecting to open up a public dialogue among professionals on bilingual education.

Politics and Academic Pressuring

In May 1982, I sat for my dissertation defense, the oral examination that would be the last formal step in fulfilling the requirements for the Doctor of Education degree at the University of Massachusetts in Amherst. My graduate studies had been in the area of bilingual education, with a major focus on second-language acquisition and the teaching of English as a Second Language (ESL). My advisor throughout was Dr. Gloria de Guevara Figueroa, who came to the University of Massachusetts from the University of Puerto Rico. After the defense had been completed and I was informed by the entire dissertation committee that my work was approved, the faculty gave the customary congratulations, and we all prepared to leave. My advisor asked me to stay for a private conversation. What she revealed in that talk deprived me of the joy I had anticipated on reaching such a milestone, an academic accomplishment never dreamed of in my family.

I well remember her message:

Rosalie, I must tell you of something very unusual that has happened. Now that you have successfully defended your dissertation and there is nothing to get in the way of your receiving the doctorate you have worked for, I can tell this to you. A week ago, a high official from the Bilingual Bureau of the State Department of Education called here to talk with the head of the bilingual teacher training program in this university, Dr. Luis Fuentes. This person told Dr. Fuentes that you had spoken in public and that the dissertation you were preparing to submit would be damaging to the field of bilingual education and that he should not let you go ahead with it.

Dr. Fuentes then called me and threatened to come to your dissertation defense and make trouble for you. I asked him if he had read your dissertation and had any specific questions about it. He said he had not read it but urged me not to approve it. I told him that your work was well documented and well written and that although I might not agree with all your conclusions, it deserved to be approved. I also suggested that he was welcome to attend the dissertation defense, as these events are open to the university community, but that it would be ill advised to come and make a scene.

I am glad to see that he thought better of it and did not try to make trouble for you today, but I thought you ought to know about this for your own sake. You should also know that I tell you this in private because, given the political nature of this field, I cannot involve myself publicly in this situation.[1]

Just writing these words brings back vividly the terrible feeling of injustice I experienced at that moment. A few

weeks later when I met with Dean Mario Fantini of the College of Education for the routine interview scheduled with
all doctoral candidates before graduation day, I decided to
be candid with him about this incident. We first discussed
my experiences in the graduate program, its strengths and
weaknesses, and my suggestions for changes or improvements. I then related a few of the difficulties I had experienced as a result of bias against nonhispanic students: the
double standard in grading, and differing expectations for
hispanic and nonhispanic students. I also deplored the lack
of content or academic rigor in some of the courses. Finally, I told him the story of my truly incredible experience
with the dissertation. The dean professed to be absolutely
shocked, and he condemned outright not only the attempt
by a state official to violate the academic freedom of the institution but the threat by a member of the faculty to pressure my advisor to suppress scholarly investigation and reporting. He said that this struck at the very foundations of
what a university stands for—the publication of new research for public consideration—and that these were signs
of the worst corruption. When I offered to go to the dean
of graduate studies to report this situation, he counseled
against it, saying that it would be better if he handled this
personally within the College of Education without having
the "dirty laundry" aired in public. He thanked me warmly
for confiding in him about this unsavory incident and
wished me well.

How did the dean "handle" this sordid episode? The following year, the dean granted Dr. Luis Fuentes tenure in
the College of Education. Dr. Gloria de Guevara Figueroa
was not reappointed to her academic position but transferred, instead, into an administrative post, out of the College of Education.

Why did I silently tolerate this outrage, the final insult
from a university department where I had been discrimi-

nated against and where I had seen any number of corrupt practices in the service of a political ideology? At that time, I rationalized and did not protest publicly because, due to family considerations, I could continue my studies only at that university. Further, I would need references from the college in the future, and a reputation as a trouble maker would only hurt my own chances for employment. I also rationalized that I had to put up with unfair practices until I completed my doctorate and then I would not in any way be constrained from speaking out. I knew the uneasy feeling that we ought not complain about biased actions that benefit "minorities," because such unfair measures are only temporary and are necessary to redress historical wrongs in our society.

The constraints persisted, however. When I confided the details of the attempted denial of my doctoral work to my supervisor in Newton, he offered to talk with the state commissioner of education about this abominable offense, but I advised against it. I reasoned that Newton, like all other cities, is expected to file a program plan every year for its bilingual program and that the plan is subject to approval by the Bilingual Bureau. If we lodged a complaint, it might put Newton in an awkward position with the bureau. After considerable discussion, he reluctantly agreed not to take any action. In the best interests of Newton, I put this matter aside. My decision and its consequences eventually caused anguish and upheaval for many Newtonians.

Newton's Struggle against Bureaucratic Vindictiveness

In 1983 the Bilingual Bureau notified Newton that its bilingual program would be formally audited. A state audit is a formidable undertaking and requires preparations by the whole school system for months in advance. Although for the sake of accountability, all bilingual education programs should be audited every few years, the Bilingual Bureau has never had enough staff to monitor all of the Massachusetts cities with bilingual programs (30 in 1980, 51 in 1989). Generally, the bureau attends to the most pressing situations, that is, large urban programs that are having serious problems, school districts that are either not providing services at all or are doing far too little, or places where legal complaints have been filed by bilingual parents.

None of these conditions applied in the Newton situation. No one had complained; in fact, the Newton parents had clearly and consistently expressed satisfaction with the program. Funding for the program had been increased every year, and no cutback in services for bilingual students was anticipated. There was public support for bilingual students from the School Committee, from the mayor and the city at large, and from administrators, who described our program in a *Newton Tribune* interview in January 1982 as "a source of pride for Newton."[2] And, most important of all, Newton's limited-English students were making solid progress academically, with less than 1 percent dropping out before high school graduation and 60 percent going on to higher education.

We asked the bureau staff if there was any special reason for this audit; they said it was just routine, Newton's turn had come up. However, the timing of the Newton audit seemed odd. The Bilingual Bureau had decided to give its careful attention to a program that was working well and to the satisfaction of everyone concerned, instead of addressing some of the problem areas in the state where language minority children were being so poorly served that a class action suit had been brought against six school districts. The political attack on Newton had begun.

It was my task to mobilize the school system to prepare for the actual on-site visit by the audit team, a burdensome job of assembling vast amounts of records that took many hours of extra effort by teachers, principals, the superintendent, and others. The audit team had twelve members who spent five days in Newton, reviewing documents and interviewing teachers, administrators, support staff, students, and parents. The director of the state Bilingual Bureau, who had earlier pressured the university to reject my doctoral dissertation, personally supervised the writing of the final report. Such a heavy weight of bureaucratic scrutiny of a relatively small program that had enjoyed annual approval from the state for ten years was hard to fathom. We were mostly intent on getting through the audit and getting on with the real business of educating children. We actually thought we would come out of it with some minor suggestions for improvements. We even thought we might receive some commendations for the special program features that went far beyond what was required by law, such as our multicultural preschool for three- and four-year-olds, and our after-school Italian-language and -culture classes.

Addressing Trumped-up Charges

When the audit report finally arrived, we discovered the extent of the Bilingual Bureau's animosity toward Newton. We were told that the report would be delivered to our superintendent late Friday afternoon to give us at least the weekend to study the document before it was made available to the press. The document we received catalogued some thirty or more areas in which Newton was found to be in noncompliance with the Transitional Bilingual Education law, a severe judgment and a very difficult one for us to accept as just. Far more damaging was the memorandum attached to the audit report, an internal communication from the Bilingual Bureau to the assistant commissioner of education, taking Newton to task for denying the civil rights of its limited-English students. This memorandum used harsh and judgmental language in attacking the school system. We did not even have a grace period in which to study these documents for, somehow, the local press had obtained them before we did and published the first in a series of very critical articles.[3]

Newton immediately protested to the State Department of Education over the unprofessional nature of the memorandum attached to the audit and got the astounding reply that the memo was not meant to be seen by us and had been passed on to the press by mistake. Of course, the damage was already done. The local reporter did not bother to study the long audit report but mainly quoted from the private memo. For a city and a school system that have openly and strongly supported civil rights and equal opportunity and have a dedicated and honorable history in these areas, it was a damaging blow. As the substance of the complaint by the state became known, there was deep anger among teachers, parents, and school officials.

Documenting Newton's Successes.   What was the real nature of our "noncompliance"? To be sure, there were a number of small infractions of the law cited in the report, mostly paperwork issues, such as the inappropriate wording of a form letter to parents or our failure to translate school report cards into all the home languages of the students (since each of the fifteen elementary schools had its own reporting system through parent–teacher conferences, we provided an interpreter for the conference instead). Also, the report noted, we did not provide a written handbook for bilingual parents in their home languages (our practice was to interview each new family and give them, face to face, an orientation to the school system and the bilingual program). These and other similar failings, which could be either explained or quickly corrected, were presented as damning evidence.

When the thick, bureaucratic layers in this sixty-five-page document were peeled away, however, what remained was one central accusation: Newton was not providing full native-language instruction, that is, we were not teaching the children enough hours of the school day in Chinese, Italian, or Spanish. That single complaint was raised repeatedly in the audit.

Our defense was based on the actual wording of the Transitional Bilingual Education law, chapter 71–A: there is no mention of any specified number of hours that the native language must be used for teaching, and innovation in bilingual programs is encouraged. We prepared a careful response emphasizing Newton's desire to be in compliance with the law and to correct any problems. We reminded the Bilingual Bureau that Newton had been one of the first cities in Massachusetts to start a bilingual program and that our program plan, submitted annually to the Bilingual Bureau, had been approved every year. How could they find us in serious noncompliance when they had approved our program every year without challenging anything we were doing? We noted that Newton had more well-trained, experienced teachers—all of whom had the appropriate degrees and certification—than did most other Massachusetts cities. All the elements for a successful program were in place. The proof, we argued, was in the success of the bilingual students, who were learning English, earning good grades, and participating in school activities—all of which made the bilingual parents feel very well served by our program and supportive of its goals.

Program success—that is, demonstrably good results for the students—meant nothing. We carefully explained that Newton's program design was different from that of most other bilingual programs in Massachusetts in degree, but not in kind. Rather than providing a large dose of native-language instruction (up to 80 percent of the school day) to limited-English students and a small amount of English-language instruction (thirty to forty-five minutes), we provided a larger proportion of intensive English-language instruction (up to three hours daily) and a smaller proportion of native-language use, based on the needs of individual students and on their ages and academic backgrounds. All bilingual students were placed in regular classrooms with English-speaking children for part of the day to prevent their being segregated by language, as in conventional bilingual programs, for most of the day or for several years. We did this deliberately to expose them to more English and to help them feel "connected" and included in the life of the school.

We argued for the continued use of these modifications of the conventional Transitional Bilingual Education program, given the needs of Newton's children and the broad-based, wholehearted public support for the goals and design of our program. As we pressed on with the work of addressing the politically aimed audit findings, we felt a guarded optimism in light of our convictions and our proven success.

There is a wonderful irony in the juxtaposition of two events in May 1985, when the audit report was released. In the same week that the State Department of Education issued a severe judgment against Newton's program, the associate commissioner of education, James Case, gave an encouraging, liberating speech at the opening of the New England Bilingual Education Conference. Here is the core of his remarks, which I recorded: "The discipline [bilingual education] needs critics within and without, or it is dead. There is a great deal of ferment within the discipline, and it is healthy. . . . Bilingual education has decided it cannot become doctrinaire."[4]

Confronting Bureaucratic Hurdles and Entrenched Biases. In Newton we were led up and down a few blind alleys by the State Department of Education. There is a provision in the law for requesting a waiver if the school system faces unusual difficulties in complying with some part of the law, for example, if it cannot find teachers with certain language skills. We asked for some assistance in filing a waiver request that would allow a modified bilingual program. It was almost impossible to find any guidelines or advice, since this had never been done before. We persisted and, with the help of a Bilingual Bureau specialist, drew up lengthy documents supporting this request.

While the waiver request was before the bureau for review, before being passed on to the State Board of Education as an appeal, we were advised by the bureau to survey all the parents of our bilingual students, asking them to state their preference either for the modified Newton program or for the traditional "doctrinaire" type of bilingual program. We were told this would illustrate the measure of parental support, since the bilingual law requires that parents review and approve the local program every year. We succeeded in surveying all of the parents of our bilingual students, and they unanimously supported continuation of the Newton program.

When we turned these results over to the Bilingual Bureau staff, their response was incredible. Because the parents had all, according to the bureau, "rejected bilingual education and chosen a program that does not have state approval,"[5] Newton was no longer legally required to provide a program! The parents had been tricked into forfeiting their rights. The bureau denied us the right to go before the State Department of Education with our waiver request. State funding for Newton's bilingual students was summarily terminated.

After a whole year of extraordinary efforts, we were totally stymied. The effect on the school system, and especially on the Newton teachers, was demoralizing. The sense of an implacable and spiteful vendetta against Newton had, by June 1986, become obvious to anyone even slightly familiar with the case. The comment I heard most often from townspeople was, "Why are they giving Newton such a hard time when the kids are learning English and doing well in school?" One of the parents from mainland China confronted a State Department of Education official at a public meeting and asked, "So what's the problem? Our kids are doing good; Newton is giving a good program—so what's your problem with us?" That question was not answered.

The Newton Public Schools faced two options: (1) appeal to the State Board of Education and pursue the case through the courts, or (2) live with the problem, continue to provide the best program possible, and wait for a change in the state law to provide relief for Newton—a very long term solution. I advised the former; the school administration decided on the latter.

Responses to Bureaucratic Censure

Cases such as this, no matter what their merits, are drawn-out, costly pursuits. However, I believe Newton had the chance to stand up for a principle—the right of a town to choose an alternative form of education that is rational, well planned, and supported by the community. The case is representative of the limited choices available. The Berkeley, California, Unified School District, for example, when faced with a similar situation, fought it out in court and won a landmark decision for local choice in programs for language minority children (*Teresa P. et al.* v. *Berkeley Unified School District*). This case, in which I participated as an expert witness, is described in more detail in chapter 7, as it has important implications for the future course of bilingual education in the United States.

The federal courts have established three criteria to determine whether school districts are meeting their responsibility to help students overcome the language barriers to an equal educational opportunity:

1. The educational theory or principles on which the instruction is based must be sound.
2. The proper resources must be provided to operate the instructional program.
3. After a reasonable period of time, the application of the theory must actually overcome the English-language barriers confronting the students and must not leave them with a substantive academic deficit.

In practice, when a state-mandated program such as Special Education or Vocational Education is audited, there is a period of negotiation between the school district and the state agency doing the auditing. Some complaints are proven to be unfounded and are rejected, some recommendations are adopted and improvements are begun, some corrections can be made at once, and some complaints are treated as long-term problems. At some point, there is a reconciliation of objectives, the audit is completed, and everyone gets on with normal operations. This negotiation process never took place between Newton and the state authorities. As of 1989—four years after the audit began—the program was still in limbo and had not received the state approval it had routinely been granted for a dozen years. Knowledgeable Massachusetts educators consider the bureau's withheld action disgraceful, the worst example of bureaucratic oppression.

Newton continues to provide a fine program for all limited-English children in its schools, in spite of all the provocations and frustrations and in spite of the loss of state funding for the program. Teachers continue to teach, and parents continue to be very pleased with the achievements of their children. Efforts continue to be made to return to a normal situation with the Bilingual Bureau, to have the stamp of approval publicly restored. For the school administration, such approval is part of operating procedures; but for the teaching staff and for bilingual parents, it is a necessary symbol of approval.

Reverberations from the Newton Experience

The unrelenting attack on the Newton program clearly sprang from the political expedience of the dominant ideology and had nothing to do with good education for children. The Bilingual Bureau was not merely fulfilling its professional obligation to review a program and help the school system correct any problems. Instead, it was openly pursuing two major objectives: (1) to discredit the Newton program and keep it from being recognized as a reasonable alternative, and (2) to discredit me personally, since I was the only vocal advocate for a flexible education policy in the state. The bureau heads sought thereby to discourage other school districts from even *thinking* of copying any part of the Newton program and to frighten anyone else who supported flexibility and community choice from joining me in the public discussion.

The Squelching of Legislative Change

Newton has been made a scapegoat, and education leaders in Massachusetts have carefully observed and remembered the lesson. In 1986 and 1987 new legislation was filed at the State House proposing changes in the TBE law, Massachusetts chapter 71–A. On both occasions the clearly stated intent of the bills was *not* to limit or dispense with programs for language minority children but rather to improve and expand these services for all limited-English students in the state. The purpose of these legal changes was to allow local choice of programs for limited-English students and to correct the inequitable state funding formula. Chapter 71–A only provides funding for cities that have groups of twenty or more children speaking the same native language and for bilingual education programs that teach students in their native language. Over 5,000 Massachusetts students receive little or no special help because their communities are not given state funding for these children.

These legislative bills also proposed, among other improvements, state support for communities that want their children to maintain their home-language skills, after they have learned English. Under the current law, state funds are not available for "maintenance" language programs. Although some of the proposed changes had general support, the crucial element of the bills that made them anathema to the bilingual establishment was the provision for local choice in the type of program to be offered for limited-English children. Through this revision of the law, every community with limited-English students would continue to be legally required to provide a special program, no matter what the size of the group or the languages they speak, but each school district could choose to provide TBE, ESL, or Structured Immersion, a program using all-English instruction deriving from a successful Canadian experiment de-scribed fully in chapter 4. Although this flexibility would al-low different communities to provide the kind of program most suited to their needs, it would not absolve any com-munity from its mandated responsibility to give special help to these children. The Bilingual Bureau would, of course, continue to have the duty of monitoring these language programs.

Bilingual Bureau staff were involved in fund-raising ac-tivities to defeat this legislation, although it is illegal for state employees to lobby for or against pending legislation. The Massachusetts Association for Bilingual Education mounted a well-organized campaign, complete with dem-onstrations in front of the State House, emotional appeals not to destroy bilingual education, and scare tactics to nourish the fear that any degree of choice would end all bilingual programs. The shrewd political maneuvering had the desired effect: it whipped everybody into line on the side of righteousness. What politician or public official would carefully study the bills and make a thoughtful de-cision for or against them when there was an obvious, "right" stance against change that required no thought or courage? As for the educational leadership, a few school ad-ministrators went on record as supporting the bills; several others told me privately that they agreed with the bills but could not get involved in the debate publicly for fear that their schools would suffer retribution from the state, as mine had.

The Battle Against Choice

The attitude fostered in Massachusetts by the bilingual establishment—that there must be only one type of pro-gram—is extremely rigid and ignores current trends in other states. In California, New York, and Texas, which have

the largest state-funded programs for language minority
student populations, programs may be either TBE or an alternative design, and they are equally acceptable, depending on local circumstances. That is not to say that pressure
is not employed there, also, to maintain the bilingual education orthodoxy, but there is at least the legal foundation
for choice. The overwhelming number of programs are of
the TBE type, *even when there is local choice.*

The defensiveness and paranoia of the bilingual education establishment are exaggerated and self-serving. Bilingual programs are increasing, not declining, in number, but
they are changing in character. There is a growing acceptance, in many states, of diversity in educational approach
to accommodate the tremendous variety of language groups.
A careful scrutiny of a number of successful alternatives
in the United States and abroad is provided in chapters 4
and 5.

The Impossibility of Open Public Debate

Before I leave this account of political retribution for not
following the party line—by no means limited to Massachusetts—I must describe an incident at the National Conference on Latino Economic Development held at the Boston
College Law School, March 14–15, 1986. This two-day conference organized by the Minority Law Students Organization focused mainly on different areas of economic growth
and progress in latino communities and on possible strategies for attacking problems. There were several panel discussions among latino bankers, economists, lawyers, and en-
trepreneurs. A debate was scheduled on the question of
"Bilingual Education—Does It Meet the Needs of Latino
Children or Does It Need to Change?" in connection with

the effort at that time to change the Massachusetts bilingual education law. Adriana de Kanter, a researcher from the U.S. Department of Education, and I spoke for change; two lawyers who are hispanic legal advocates in Boston spoke against legislative change.

Speaking first, I gave a brief history of bilingual education and what I, as an educator, saw as the pressing needs for improving the education of language minority students. The first of the two lawyers on the other side, Camilo Perez-Bustillo, surprised us all by launching into a fierce personal attack on Ms. de Kanter and on me, ignoring the topic of the debate, accusing us of being "Reaganites" and of trying to destroy the language and culture of hispanic children. What was equally surprising was that the moderator, Professor Houghteling of the Boston College law school faculty, did nothing to curb this intemperate attack but rather shook his head a few times and muttered "Tsk, tsk."

Adriana spoke next and, before presenting her views on the topic of the debate, took an extra minute to refute the most flagrant lies that had been directed against her. To the chagrin of the audience, she also mentioned that she is a Mexican-American and a Democrat and that her mother is a bilingual teacher. The second lawyer, Alan Rom, gave his arguments, which were opposed to ours but civilly delivered. I thought we were going to finish with a few questions from the audience and call it a draw. As soon as the first question was asked, Mr. Perez-Bustillo rose to launch another fierce attack against us and to ignore the question. The accusations were so biased and uninformed that there was obviously no profit in giving reasonable answers, and the moderator proved ineffectual in curbing this second tirade. Adriana and I decided to walk out, expressing our disappointment that there could be no debate under such circumstances.

It was a grueling experience. Both Adriana and I have

delivered numerous public speeches and have sometimes faced sharp arguments, but this occasion was ugly. It was not a debate but a political harangue with sexist overtones designed to destroy publicly the credibility of two women. The audience thought it quite a circus, which says something regrettable about the ethical values of some of our nascent legal professionals. The second lawyer, Alan Rom, was sensitive to the unseemly performance of Perez-Bustillo and wrote each of us a note of apology. We also received long, apologetic letters from the dean of the law school and the president of the college. The encounter has left scars that others in the language wars across the United States have also suffered.

Unfortunately, public discussions in this highly politicized field too often lack civility and respect for different opinions. Instead, an atmosphere of distrust, a siege mentality, and the inability of some bilingual advocates to accept and respect others' views hinder efforts to better the situation for language minority children. Beneath the defensiveness that characterizes this passionately partisan field lie two wellsprings: (1) the beliefs that led to the establishment of special language programs, and (2) the experiences during the past twenty years. The time for public scrutiny of those has arrived.

3

Reassessing the Assumptions Underlying Twenty Years of Bilingual Education

One basic assumption and two subsets of that form the original foundation for bilingual education. Twenty years ago educators and legislators enthusiastically accepted these premises when the federal government first became involved in the promotion of special programs for limited-English students. Once we recognize what these assumptions were and why they were so readily accepted, we can then understand why they are now seriously questioned and what policy changes need to be made at both the community and national levels.

The Vernacular Advantage Theory

Among the basic assumptions the primary one is what people in the field call the vernacular advantage theory, the umbrella concept under which other bilingual education ideas took form. According to this theory, there are good reasons for children who do not know the language of the school to be instructed in their native language for an extended period of time while they are learning a second language. The terms *home language*, *native language*, and *mother tongue* are used interchangeably and mean the first language a child learns. Bilingual educators have assumed that use of the familiar language in the classroom not only eases the child into an unfamiliar situation but has the following educational benefits.

- For young children, developing their first language well can help them learn a second language more successfully.
- Students who are taught all their school subjects in their native language, while they are learning a second language, will not fall behind in learning school subjects.
- Delaying the start of a second language until age eight or nine will avoid the confusion of "semilingualism," or the imperfect learning of two languages.

Early proponents of bilingual education strongly supported these views and cited the theories of Canadian linguist Jim Cummins[1] and the research of Finnish sociologists Tove Skutnabb-Kangas and Pertti Toukomaa to lend legitimacy to the bilingual education method.[2] The studies of the latter authors focused on the population of Finnish immigrant children living in Sweden and have been most often cited as proof for the vernacular advantage and the justification for establishing native language teaching programs in the United States.

Tenuous Support for the Vernacular Advantage Concept

When I lectured at Finnish universities in Helsinki, Tampere, and Jyvaskyla in 1981, I discussed the Toukomaa and Skutnabb-Kangas findings with several linguists. From them I heard repeatedly that the research had been discredited for the unreliability of the data and for the apparent chauvinistic bias in the reporting. My Finnish colleagues expressed surprise that the unsubstantiated theory about the advantage of teaching children in their native language was still widely accepted in the United States and seemed to be the basis for a national education policy.

The Finns were not the only ones to find fault with the research reported. A report by Baker and deKanter, commissioned by the U.S. Department of Education under the Carter administration, analyzed the Toukomaa and Skutnabb-Kangas studies. The authors concluded that there was no evidence that a relationship exists between the ability to learn successfully in a second language and the development of the home language—a thorough rebuttal of the original claims. Baker and deKanter also cited the absence of data in the Skutnabb-Kangas and Toukomaa studies as a serious flaw in the validity of the work.[3]

Christina Bratt Paulston, a Swedish-born sociolinguist who heads the linguistics department at the University of Pittsburgh, recently completed a critical review of the original studies for the Swedish National Board of Education on the bilingual education debate in that country.[4] I paraphrase some of her conclusions to make clear why we in the United States should not have become overreliant on the Scandinavian research:

1. According to Paulston, Toukomaa and Skutnabb-Kangas used biased, selective primary data and presented very opinionated conclusions, often with the express purpose of promoting policy recommendations.
2. She denounced semilingualism as a popularized notion completely unsupported by empirical evidence. She suggested that the myth of semilingualism has persisted because Finnish groups have used it in their demands for Finnish-language schooling in Sweden.
3. In direct contradiction of the Toukomaa results, Paulston found solid evidence that children's proficiency in Swedish (their second language) was *not* a direct result of their proficiency in Finnish (their first language); that

school achievement in subject matter areas was independent of home language. There were no differences in motivation or school adjustment between students in Finnish-language classes and those in Swedish-language classes.

The Paulston conclusions concisely indicate how the most widely accepted argument for bilingual education, the vernacular advantage concept, can be skewed for political and nationalistic reasons. Paulston concurs with one of the Swedish officials whom she interviewed, who said, "In the beginning the officials were duped into a mother tongue policy—then the bureaucracy took over." And, Paulston adds, "The press helped in this duping with the best of liberal intentions."[5] We shall see that in the United States the education establishment and the public have been similarly misled.

Unfounded Conclusions as a Basis for Decisions

Paulston's research suggests some of the reasons why the current body of research on bilingual education has such a uniformly poor reputation among supporters and critics alike. Much of it consists of local evaluations with inadequate research designs. The most serious flaw in bilingual education studies is that they report on what a group of children in a particular school accomplished, not on a comparison of two groups of children who are provided different programs. The other problem is that even when two groups of students in different programs are being compared, there is no pretesting to see if the students are all starting with the same level of knowledge or language ability. These evaluations should not be used to draw conclusions on the effectiveness of bilingual education, because they do not prove that what students have accomplished can be attributed to the bilingual education program alone. Unfortunately, many reviewers compound the error by citing these and other flawed studies as support for the vernacular advantage concept and thus for bilingual education.

A further problem is that the evaluators and reviewers often are also passionate advocates of bilingual education for political or ideological reasons. Given this bias, the proponents all too often interpret flawed studies as support for bilingual education and ignore or denounce any studies with conflicting findings. There are several reasons, to be sure, for teaching children in their home language instead of the language of the majority community, such as promoting language loyalty, community closeness, political hegemony, and control by ethnic leaders. However, such reasons exist quite apart from reasons of equal educational opportunity or effective second-language learning or social integration. Nothing in my fifteen years in this field—from firsthand classroom experience to concentrated research—has begun to convince me that delaying instruction in English for several years will lead to *better* learning of English and to a greater ability to study subject matter taught in English. When all the rhetoric is stripped away, the vernacular argument is still a hypothesis in search of legitimacy, and not a documented, empirically proven, successful method of second-language learning.

My personal experience and professional investigations together impel me to conclude that the two overriding conditions that promote the best learning of a second language are (1) starting at an early age, say at five, and (2) having as much exposure and carefully planned instruction in that language as possible. Effective time on task—the amount of time spent learning—is, as educators know, the single greatest predictor of educational achievement; this is at least as true, if not more so, for low-socioeconomic-level, limited-English students. Children learn what they are taught, and if they are taught mainly in Spanish for several years, their Spanish-language skills will be far better than their English-language ones.[6]

——————— ◇◇◇ ———————

The Concept of Mother-Tongue Literacy First

The second basic assumption, according to bilingual education advocates, is that children will learn to read best in a language they know well and that they can later transfer these skills easily to reading in a second language. This concept, a subset of the notion of vernacular advantage, has had a far-reaching influence on the education of language minority children. The demand for schools to teach reading first in the native language was particularly pressed on behalf of Spanish-speakers.

The Lack of Empirical Support.   Proponents have argued that learning to read in Spanish is easy because of the phonetic regularity of the five vowel sounds, unlike English with its more complex pattern of pronunciation based on twelve vowel sounds and its irregular spellings. No reliable evidence exists for this assumption—not for Spanish-speakers or for anyone else. Even Kenji Hakuta, an educational psychologist and bilingual education advocate whose research I evaluate in chapter 7, has noted that "what is remarkable about the issue of transfer of skills is that despite its fundamental importance, almost no empirical studies have been conducted to understand the characteristics or even to demonstrate the existence of transfer of skills."[7]

One of the few reported studies on the development of reading and language skills that compares students who read first in Spanish to those who read first in English was recently completed by the Southwest Educational Development Laboratory.[8] Researchers conducted a six-year study of 250 Spanish-speaking, limited-English children in six Texas schools, tracing their progress from kindergarten through third grade. This study, titled *Teaching Reading to Bilingual Children Study,* covers extensive data, but I will cite only a few of the most pertinent findings.

1. Children who started school with well-developed oral-language skills in either Spanish or English had an advantage in learning to read.
2. Enrollment in the Spanish reading program generally had a negative correlation with learning to read in English.
3. Knowledge of the English alphabet on entering kindergarten was strongly related to successful reading performance in grades one to three.
4. By the age of five, most children had gained control of their first language (Spanish) for all practical purposes.
5. Students who learned to read first in English transferred their reading skills to Spanish more easily than those who started reading in Spanish and tried to effect the opposite transfer.

These findings indicate little evidence for teaching reading in the home language first. This research does, however, establish the need for better language development for language minority children, either at home or through preschool language enrichment in nursery schools or Head Start-type programs.

Even if there were a demonstrable advantage for Spanish-speakers learning to read first in their home language, it does not follow that the same holds true for speakers of languages that do not use the Roman alphabet. Consider for a moment the grab-bag logic of applying this principle to all of the 145 languages in which bilingual education is currently provided. To read in some of these languages first—Arabic, Chinese, Farsi, Khmer, Korean, or Japanese—children would have to spend several years mastering an extensive system of symbols before going on to read in English. Some of the languages do not at present even have a written symbol system—Hmong, Inuit, and various native American languages, for example. Should written forms be created for these languages so that children can be taught, first, to read in an artificial script for which there are no existing texts and, then, to transfer those skills to reading in English?

Misdefining Students' Needs

There is yet another dimension to the reading controversy that bears on the policies toward which our nation must move. It focuses once again on Spanish-speaking, limited-English children. The majority of these children are not immigrants with no knowledge of English but rather residents of the mainland United States, largely from Cuban, Mexican, or Puerto Rican backgrounds. Even children whose parents speak only Spanish generally have older siblings who know English and use it in the home. For anyone living on the U.S. mainland or in Puerto Rico, to have had no exposure to the English language would be almost impossible. In fact, federal statistics show that up to 60 percent of the children in bilingual education programs are English dominant, that is, their English-language skills are stronger than their Spanish-language ones.[9] Teaching these children to read in English does not mean teaching them in a totally alien language.

Not surprisingly, information gathered by the U.S. Department of Education shows the widespread misclassification of such students as "limited-English proficient." As part of the monitoring of school systems receiving federal funds for bilingual programs, researchers found that in many Texas districts students were classified "limited-English" even if the home-language survey showed that the child spoke only English and the parents spoke Spanish only occasionally.[10] Another survey, conducted at the request of the Cherokee Nation to determine whether bilingual education was needed in their community, revealed that 82 percent of the students knew only English. However, the test administered to these children classified 48 percent of them as limited-English, presumably in need of instruction in Cherokee to improve their English.[11] In California, in a sample of school districts, only half of the hispanic students identified as limited-English were actually more fluent in Spanish than in English, and in one school district 40 percent of the hispanic students categorized as bilingual spoke no Spanish at all.[12]

The Clear Need for a New Approach. It is an unsound educational practice to teach hispanic students reading first in Spanish in the belief that this will improve general school achievement. What is abundantly clear, instead, is the need for both special language enrichment programs and other forms of early, intense special help to compensate for the lack of overall school skills, especially for economically deprived hispanic students.

I am convinced by recent, sound research that the kindergarten year is an excellent time for second-language development and for activities that prepare children for learning to read. When I was teaching, my experiences led me to conclude that it was not sensible to spend the entire kindergarten year teaching reading skills in Spanish when the students were so obviously ready to learn a new language, building on what they already knew from participating in their community, watching television, and playing in school with English-speaking children.

Very little has been reported yet on the special programs where language minority children are taught reading in English first, but new research is beginning to appear. One such study is the El Paso, Texas, Bilingual Immersion Pilot Project's interim report, published after three years of work with 2,500 limited-English students in grades one through three.[13] All are from Spanish-speaking homes and from comparable economic backgrounds. Half the students are enrolled in a traditional bilingual education program where reading, mathematics, and other subjects are taught in Spanish. The other students are provided an alternative, experimental program called the Bilingual Immersion program, which is distinguished by these features: (1) English is used in the classroom as the language of instruction from the first day of school; (2) all subjects are taught in English, although Spanish is used occasionally to reinforce a new concept; and (3) English is not taught as a separate subject but is the medium for learning subject matter.

Results from standardized tests in reading and language reveal that the Bilingual Immersion students outscored students in the TBE program at every grade level. The immersion students scored as high on the mathematics tests as the other group, and they scored above average on state tests in science and social studies, *without* a substantial amount of native language use in the classroom. An extra bonus was reported: 90 percent of the immersion students in grade three, who had received minimal instruction in Spanish, had reading and writing skills in Spanish comparable to those of the TBE students.[14] One limitation, however, renders these results tentative: the students were not pretested to make certain that their initial language abilities were comparable.

The researchers also interviewed teachers in both groups, all of whom were Spanish-English bilinguals. They reported the following:

1. The immersion teachers were much more optimistic about the effectiveness of their program in motivating their students to learn English.
2. Only one-third of the TBE program teachers believed that their students would successfully transfer to reading in English.
3. All the school principals who had experience with both programs expressed the opinion that the immersion program is a better approach to educating language minority students.

All this does not suggest that language minority students should be dropped into regular classrooms and neglected without special help. Because reading is so basic to most academic learning, and literacy in English is the goal of all bilingual programs, it is necessary to look at what success language minority students are achieving and to compare different teaching approaches. Until very recently, neither federal bilingual funds nor the support of the bilingual education field has been available for essential experimentation because of the strong political and ideological commitment to an unproven principle.

The Linguistic Interdependence Hypothesis

The third underpinning of doctrinaire bilingual education is the linguistic interdependence hypothesis, another subset of the vernacular advantage concept. Advocates of bilingual education have long argued that limited-English students could only learn new concepts in the various academic subject areas if they were taught in their home language. Using the native language to teach mathematics, science, and social studies until the student learned enough English to

participate in classes taught in that language seemed humane and less frustrating. Canadian linguist Jim Cummins
and others hypothesized that children can learn English for
social uses quickly, but that it takes from five to seven years
before they develop the conceptual depth in English to
learn academic subjects taught in that language. Cummins
has argued that language minority children must be taught
new concepts in their native language until the age of abstract reasoning (about eight years of age), because they will
not be able to learn these concepts in a second language.[15]

There is no evidence yet, however, to support the linguistic interdependence hypothesis, and the argument
seems fallacious. It may take a child several years to become as fluent in another language as a native speaker, but
long before that time he or she will be capable of learning
subject matter taught in that language. Increasingly, educators and linguists have concluded that teaching English
and subject matter at the same time is the most effective
way to develop English-language skills for academic purposes. In some alternative programs, limited-English students are demonstrating the capacity for learning new subject matter and are performing academic work at grade
level in English within one to three years.[16] This approach
is even more practical given the hundreds of different languages now present in bilingual programs across the country and the mammoth task it would be to produce native-
language textbooks in all these languages in all the school
subjects. Because most school districts with language minority children now enroll speakers of anywhere from two
to thirty different languages, providing native-language
teachers, as well as textbooks, is both impossible and unnecessary.

Application Unsupported by Reliable Research

Cummins's linguistic interdependence hypothesis has
been highly influential and widely cited in support of TBE.

For example, Toukomaa and Skutnabb-Kangas cited this hypothesis in a UNESCO report in which they concluded that "the migrant children whose mother tongue stopped developing before the abstract thinking phase was achieved thus easily remain on a lower level of educational capacity *than they would originally have been able to achieve.*" [emphasis mine][17] This conclusion rests not on proven results but on an idea of what might have been and on a political attitude in favor of extended native-language instruction.

In the United States, the teaching of all subjects in the native language of the child for the first few years of schooling has become a non-negotiable condition of the TBE framework. We saw in chapter 1 a diagram of the TBE model (Figure 1.1) depicting the proportions of native-language and English-language usage in teaching school subjects over a three-year period. There is as yet no reliable body of research persuasively supporting the claim that subject matter is better learned in the native language while a student is learning a second language. Most of the reported studies look only at what is happening in a bilingual program and fail to control for pretreatment differences— two major shortcomings of bilingual education research, as noted earlier.

In Massachusetts, for instance, after an almost total lack of reported research on bilingual education programs for fifteen years, a study prepared by Eduardo Carballo and Catherine Walsh was published in 1986 titled *Transitional Bilingual Education in Massachusetts: A Preliminary Study of Its Effectiveness.* The study's authors concluded that TBE was, indeed, effective in Massachusetts for the students of the six school districts surveyed.[18] They compared the success of these students to that of a disproportionately small number of limited-English students who, for whatever reasons, were not in any special programs, were given no extra help, and were having difficulty with English and with their schoolwork. The authors concluded that bilingual education works better than no help at all. Practicing researchers have severely criticized the study for its poor professional quality, and one of the critics, Dr. Christine Rossell of Boston University, recently published a review of the work's flaws.[19] I cannot omit the fact that Mr. Carballo, one of the study's coauthors, is a long-time employee of the Massachusetts Bilingual Bureau, since this certainly compromises the objectivity of the work.

The Walsh-Carballo Study is the only published report of research on bilingual education programs yet produced in Massachusetts—hardly sufficient validation of the extensive eighteen-year investment in this educational initiative. In contrast, Dade County, Florida, with one of the highest concentrations of Spanish-speakers in the country, has published the report of a three-year experiment, entitled *The Dade County Bilingual Curriculum Content Pilot Project.*[20] This report describes a study of 508 limited-English students in twelve schools in kindergarten through second grade, matched for age and socioeconomic background. Students were randomly assigned either to one of six schools providing mathematics, science, and social studies teaching in Spanish or to one of six schools where the subjects were taught only in English, using a curriculum especially designed for limited-English students. The study's basic question was, Will first- and second-grade students who are limited in English at the beginning of kindergarten achieve a higher degree of academic progress in school subjects if they are taught in the native language or in English? A nationally recognized test (the Comprehensive Test of Basic Skills) was used to measure mathematics, science, and social studies performance in English for one group, and locally developed tests in Spanish in those subjects were given to students in the other group.

The three-year experiment ended in 1988, and the researchers reported the following results. First and foremost, there was no difference in the pattern of achievement for students who were taught in Spanish and those who were taught only in English. Students who were limited-English when they started school achieved comparable degrees of academic success in subject matter learning in grades one and two, with or without native-language instruction. Two other findings also run counter to the assumption that native-language instruction for school subjects is superior. Students who were in the classes receiving native-language instruction for only one year scored higher on the tests than students who were in native-language classes for two or three years. The teachers, all of whom are bilingual, rated student attitudes toward learning and toward school in general to be comparable for the two groups. In other words, the children who were being taught in English from the first day of school were apparently not suffering emotional distress or anomie, and those who were taught in Spanish did not have a noticeably higher level of self-pride. Thus, from an educational and an emotional standpoint, instruction in the native language added no benefits.

Dade County duly noted that the results of their comparison study indicated no discernible advantage in teaching limited-English students the school subjects in their native language. Yet, rather than conclude, as logic would suggest, that no good reason existed for continuing native-tongue teaching in the subject areas, the Dade County report recommended *increasing* native-tongue instruction in the bilingual program! Educators are so wedded to the idea of bilingual education that even in the face of empirical evidence to the contrary, they seem compelled to continue. We discern, in fact, the impulse for preserving jobs and budgets for the bilingual establishment, whether they are necessary for effective education or not. This illustrates again what I referred to earlier in the problems Newton experienced with the state bilingual agency. There was less concern for the students' achievement than for the doctrine that school subjects be taught in the native language.

———————— ◇◇◇ ————————

Rethinking the Early Assumptions

The most promising occurrence at present is that the challenging of early hypotheses in the education of limited-English language minority children has led researchers to study new approaches that produce successful learning for children with varied backgrounds, resources, and needs. Serious educators are not proposing that we do *less* for language minority children but, rather, that we look at better ways of teaching, unfettered by bureaucratic insistence that all efforts must initially include native-language teaching. Different programs are not to be seen merely as a way of saving money for the school district. All of the three major models for special language programs—English Immersion, TBE, and ESL—require investments in teacher training, the hiring of qualified staff, and the purchase of texts and materials. The proper role, then, of state bilingual bureaus is to monitor the local programs to see that the highest-quality, most appropriate special services are provided for limited-English students. The bureaucratic mission should not be narrowly to dictate one educational program for all communities and to make everyone fit into that mold.

The recent studies described thus far in this chapter suggest a trend in bilingual education at the school level that is not yet widely acknowledged. New approaches are being tried in some districts in Texas, Florida, New Jersey, and

California because the old ways are not working. Schools are beginning to change practices, choosing pragmatic methods and quietly rejecting the unsubstantiated theories despite the unchanging stance of the establishment—the National Association of Bilingual Education, La Raza, LU-LAC (League of United Latin American Citizens), and others. A strong advocate for bilingual education, Carlos Yorio of Lehman College in New York, reflected this growing awareness when he said in an unusually candid statement at the Massachusetts Association of Bilingual Education conference in November 1986, "Our detractors are not lying—our children are not learning English well."[21]

Transitional Bilingual Education as a Failed Panacea

In the early 1970s an influential, but also unwarranted, fear reinforced the establishment's stance. Some sociolinguists argued that TBE would actually *accelerate* the loss of the native language because it promoted the rapid learning of English. Dr. Rudolph Troike remarked in 1977, "I have long said that Transitional Bilingual programs would more efficiently lead to the extinction of native languages in this country than any amount of repression has succeeded in doing in the past."[22] As a consequence of this belief, the bilingual establishment began insisting on *maintenance* bilingual programs of longer duration than the three-year TBE. But the fear that children in TBE programs would quickly lose their native language has not, however, been realized—in fact, the opposite has occurred.

A study of the Boston Public Schools bilingual program, completed in 1986 and quietly shelved, is a good example.[23] It revealed that several hundred hispanic middle school students who had been in the city's bilingual program for six or seven years, many since kindergarten, had not yet mastered English sufficiently to be able to take classes taught in

English. These students certainly had not lost their native language, and on that count it might be deemed a success.

The TBE students could claim no victory, however, regarding English-language learning or overall academic success. Although designers and supporters of the Boston program have not acknowledged that the program itself may be flawed, they have proposed that more training sessions for bilingual teachers be offered. The Boston situation is not an isolated case but is representative of many other cities where years of practical experience with bilingual education are not producing the anticipated results in English-language learning.

Exposure to English: A Decisive Factor

Recent research has highlighted the important link between the type of language program offered, the role teachers play, and students' use of English. In a 1987 study by SRA Technologies and the U.S. Department of Education the investigators compared language use in three types of programs: (1) an English Immersion program in which all instruction was in English; (2) a TBE program in which Spanish is used for classroom instruction one hour a day and students are mainstreamed in three years; and (3) a Maintenance Bilingual program in which Spanish is used most of the day for all subjects and students are mainstreamed in five to six years.[24] After observing and tape recording 3,500 children in kindergarten through fourth grade, the researchers reported two findings that had been largely anticipated:

1. Teachers used English most extensively in the immersion programs; the use of English dropped to 52 percent of the day in the transitional programs and only 21 percent of the day in the maintenance programs.

2. Students' use of English in all three programs mirrored that of their teachers. Students in immersion classrooms spoke English among themselves the most, and maintenance program students spoke English the least. These differences carried over to out-of-school settings as well.

To the extent that learning a second language is affected by exposure to and use of that language, then, the frequency of English use in the classroom has a decided effect on the students' rate of progress in learning and using English. The reliable evidence from this study clearly shows that teachers' and students' behaviors and attitudes toward the use of Spanish and English are influenced by the type of program offered.

Once and for all, it must be proclaimed forcefully that we are being deluded if we continue to believe that programs where the native languages are used most of the time for classroom teaching will result in the highest level of English-language learning for students. The extensive research just described confirmed the conclusion that experience and reason had already suggested, and such information has helped unmask the weakness of the most basic assumption of bilingual education.

Advances in Language-Teaching Practices

The past two decades of implementation of TBE in the United States have coincided with a time of unprecedented activity worldwide in the study of language acquisition, language teaching, and language learning. The high level of immigration since the end of World War II has led to a concern for providing an equal education to language minority children in other multilingual societies such as Australia, Israel, Germany, Sweden, England, and Canada. It has also spurred the search for new teaching methods and new policies to solve the problem of equal opportunity.

Attention to the need for special measures in educating young children with a limited knowledge of the language of the country in which they live is, therefore, a recent phenomenon. Second-language or foreign language teaching was once concerned with adolescent and adult learners, and it was assumed that young children would "acquire" a second language with almost no special help. Educators no longer believe this. Today, in the face of massive population shifts, new methods are being developed to help young students learn a second language more effectively, to help them achieve academic success, to give them access to jobs and higher education, and to help them become productive citizens of their own countries.

The Shift in Approaches

The two approaches to the teaching of ESL that were most widely used until recently have declined in practice. The grammar/translation method, which teaches the grammatical rules and reading knowledge of another language for translation purposes, does little to promote the ability to use the language for ordinary communication. The method may suit scholars preparing to read texts in a foreign language, but it does not help the child who needs to speak, understand, read, and write a new language formally in school and informally in family, neighborhood, and play settings. The audiolingual method, developed during World War II and popular in the fifties and sixties, relied on a behaviorist theory of drilling sentence patterns over and over until they could be produced automatically. This method seems to have failed, too. Critics have pointed to the boring lessons and to students' inability to transfer the skills learned in the language lab to actual communication out-side the classroom. Many of us suffered through "I have a hat . . . he has a hat . . . she has a hat . . . do you have a hat?" but could not respond to a simple request for direc-tions from a native speaker of the language, or understand the answer when we asked where the toilet was.

New Techniques for Language Teaching

The focus of language teaching has shifted to the student and his or her ability to communicate and *use* the language appropriately in real-life situations of every kind—emo-tional, social, formal, and academic—that is, for total expression. Similarly, teachers have become increasingly sensitive to the variety of language minority children and their various needs, and aware of the importance of train-ing in the language learning process in all its scope and complexity. Language teaching is inevitably, then, a theo-retical as well as a practical occupation. Both the tech-niques and the materials used must rest on sound under-lying linguistic principles that the teachers understand. The major techniques that have been developed in recent years reflect this awareness.

The Natural Language Approach. The natural language approach proposes that second-language learning in the classroom should duplicate the stages of the child's first lan-guage acquisition in infancy by exposing students to the language in a natural manner without drills. Furthermore, students should be allowed a prolonged period of listening before they are expected to speak or read, giving them time to become comfortable with the new language and ready to risk using it. The approach also promotes the use of com-prehensible language in both oral and written lessons at a level that enhances understanding while challenging the student. It stresses the inevitability of errors in the language-learning process and suggests that teachers need to avoid overcorrection in the first few months while students develop a degree of confidence and fluency.

The Integrated Approach.   Another recent language-teaching method, the integrated approach, has been used widely in recent years. It proposes that all the language skills should be taught simultaneously—listening comprehension, speaking, reading, and writing—rather than delaying the literacy skills in the second language until the oral skills are well developed. It was the conventional wisdom when I began teaching in a bilingual classroom that "you cannot read or write what you cannot say," and we were ordered not to teach reading or writing in English for at least six months to a year. Linguists now emphasize the importance of *not* dividing up the skills, because, they believe, these reinforce each other; that is, language is learned more effectively if it is seen and written, as well as heard.

Content-Based Language Teaching.   Content-based language teaching combines the teaching of second-language skills with the teaching of subject matter, that is, science, mathematics, social studies. Language lessons focus on both the vocabulary and concepts particular to certain subjects. By careful structuring of the lessons, content-based instruction allows children of different language backgrounds to be grouped together for lessons that convey both English language and subject matter. This kind of teaching incorporates information from the learner's own experiences, for the learner has acquired many kinds of knowledge, which he or she need not be retaught. What the learner needs are the labels for this knowledge in a new language.

New Understandings from Linguistics Research

The practical application of recent linguistics research has led to new understanding by teachers of the language-learning process and to ways of improving classroom teaching. The research has slowly been changing teacher attitudes and has led to the realization that second-language learning is a lifelong process, not something completed in a year or two. An analysis of different languages helps us determine what problems are likely to occur in going from one particular language to another. For instance, English pronunciation, word order, and spelling will present different problems for students whose native language is Spanish, Mandarin, or Farsi, and different teaching methods will be needed for each group. Analyzing the kinds of errors made by students at different stages in the learning of a second language also helps teachers plan appropriately staged lessons so that students learn to recognize and correct their own errors.

What has evolved is a view of language as consisting of whole blocks of discourse, of verbal and nonverbal clues, of a wide repertoire of behaviors that allows thoughts and feelings to be communicated. Thus, we no longer teach children to "speak in complete sentences," because that is not natural in conversation, as it is in writing. Here is an example of a conversation between two speakers in which much of what is conveyed is not said in words, and certainly not in sentences:

A: Telephone.
B: I'm in the bath.
A: Okay.

To understand the piecemeal conversation as a completed discourse, we effortlessly supply the missing pieces implied in the brief phrases:

A: (That's the) telephone. (Can you answer it, please?)

B: (No, I can't answer it because) I'm in the bath.

A: Okay. (Stay put. I'll answer it.)[25]

Emphasizing Effectiveness in Language Education

The search for better ways to teach language and school subjects for language minority children is urgent because their survival and achievement in a majority language environment depend on it—unlike American high school students studying a language as an elective, for whom foreign language classes are desirable but not crucial. This is the basic distinction between second-language learning and foreign language learning. Furthermore, language minority students deserve top-quality language instruction because language itself is an infinitely creative system, and they should be helped to express themselves as creatively in their second language as their individual capacities allow.

Although the approaches I have described, together with the theories on which they are based, show promise, there is at present no decisive evidence for the superiority of one teaching method over all others. In fact, the approaches overlap to a certain degree, and teachers should always be free to incorporate into their teaching what is most effective for their particular style and situation, developing their own eclectic approach. Much more training in new theory and applications needs to be provided to all professionals who work with language minority students, and it is most effective if the training is provided after the teachers have had some classroom experience.

My own observations of the most effective teaching of limited-English students in these recent, challenging years have led me to the following conclusions, which the best language teachers I know also endorse:

1. Providing as much time as possible for limited-English students to use and practice the English language in thoughtfully planned, real-life situations, both social and academic, produces the greatest success in English-language learning.
2. Providing appropriate English subject matter for classroom work, both comprehensible and challenging at the students' age level, enhances both language learning and academic achievement in all subject areas. Mathematics is generally the first subject to be taught easily in the second language because of the controlled vocabulary.
3. Promoting rapid language learning and early integration of limited-English students with their English-speaking classmates creates the best conditions for school achievement.
4. Enhancing the ability of limited-English students to "think" in English can be accomplished by reducing the amount of native-language use in bilingual programs and discarding the practice of "instruction by translation," which generally is confusing and ineffective.
5. Making the students feel both challenged *and* self-confident, as good teachers know, works for all students.

My conclusion has been inherent in my survey of the best new methods: Perpetuating the course prescribed by the earnest, original advocates of bilingual education, who now constitute an entrenched bureaucracy, places politics, ideology, and self-interest ahead of effective education. The advocates' fear, unfounded as it is, that language minority children will not maintain their native language outweighs the concern for the children's acquisition of English and access to an integrated, equal academic opportunity with their classmates. The Supreme Court, the federal government, and the Office of Civil Rights have firmly established the goal of equal educational opportunity for these children.

The bilingual education establishment, almost exclusively hispanic, places retention of the native language in the way of that goal by promoting linguistic isolation and substantially separáte schooling for these children. I believe it is cruelly demeaning to the large populations of indigenous and immigrant Spanish-speakers in the United States to proclaim by policy and practice that, despite all the special help available to them that was not given to earlier immigrant groups, they are the only group that cannot be educated in English. That view is patronizing and unworthy of educators and citizens alike.

Although we in the United States have come far in recognizing the extraordinary needs of our language minority students, we have much to learn, particularly from other countries that have committed energetic efforts to these same problems.

4

Learning from Other Multilingual Societies

By the year 2,000 one-third of the young population—those under thirty-five—in urban Europe will have an immigrant background. . . . The future Europe largely depends on how these groups—which today we call minorities—are treated socially and educationally by the indigenous populations.

—Arturo Tosi, *Immigration and Bilingual Education*

The United States is not unique in its multilingual, multicultural composition. Other countries in North America, Europe, and the Middle East are also making strenuous efforts to meet the educational needs of growing populations of immigrant and migrant children who do not speak their national language. Critical lessons can be learned from the language policies and practices of these nations.

The rights of children, in particular, have received global attention in this century of massive population movement, marked by the highest levels of immigration and dislocation in human history. UNESCO initiated a resolution adopted by the UN regarding the basic right of every child to maintain his or her language and culture in whichever new society that child is living.[1] Schooling is only one among the many social, familial, and economic factors that affect children's ability to adapt and succeed in an unfamiliar environment, but for immigrant children it plays a disproportionately important role. Problems in a nation's

85

educational system, we know, reflect the problems of the society at large. Neither parents, educators, nor policymakers are now willing, however, to accept this fact as an excuse for not attempting to improve school programs that serve the needs of minority children. Virtually everyone now recognizes that, even given the persistence of discrimination, a sound education is important for all citizens.

The following sections focus on recent educational efforts on behalf of language minority immigrants, migrants, refugees, and indigenous peoples in West Germany, the Soviet Union, and Sweden because these countries and the United States share many common concerns, despite substantial differences in their governments and educational structures. Each country has established national policies, developed education programs, and expended major resources in the promotion of a pair of basic and worthy goals: (1) teaching the official or majority language so as to bring minorities into the mainstream of national life and (2) supporting retention of the mother tongues or native languages of these people for ethnic self-pride and the maintenance of minority cultures. I later single out Canada for its innovative language-education approach that has allowed hundreds of thousands of children to become functional bilinguals, with fluency in two languages for both social and academic purposes.

Concerted attention to the unique education needs of language minority children in these and many other countries, as well as in the United States, is a recent phenomenon. In the United States it was long assumed that children would either absorb the new language and adapt to the schools or wait out their time until the legal school-leaving age of twelve to fourteen and go to work. Their parents, however, often could take adult English-language classes offered by various agencies. Other countries have taken similar approaches.

A major advance in the consciousness of educators and legislators in both industrial and developing countries occurs when they acknowledge the need for special efforts on behalf of language minorities to give them equal access to educational and employment opportunities. These desired outcomes are more likely to occur if the following principles are given high priority:

1. Learning the national language—the language of public discourse, power, and control—cannot be left to chance but must be approached through early and intensive instruction in the classroom.
2. Language minority children should not be separated from speakers of the majority language if they are to have the greatest opportunity for second-language learning and for integration into the life of the school and community.
3. Beyond compensating for linguistic handicaps, schooling must promote pride in the home language and culture.
4. All schoolchildren should be taught to value the contributions of different groups in their society.

Who are the language minority groups in the countries I have selected, how are they being treated, what educational policies are in place, and how successfully are the schools meeting the particular needs of the different groups of children? A concentrated tour of four countries gives us an opportunity to compare their experiences with ours in the United States and to draw the most useful conclusions as we move to develop the best policies for the United States.

———————— ◇◇◇ ————————

West Germany

Following the huge industrial expansion in the 1960s, West Germany invited large numbers of workers from other European countries to fulfill its labor needs. These workers with their families came principally from Mediterranean countries suffering from high unemployment among unskilled laborers. The community of "guestworkers," as they are called, now numbers five million out of a total population of sixty-one million. The worker group is growing at a faster rate than the rest of the country, even without any increase in immigration. Thirty-five percent are from Turkey, and the rest are mainly from Yugoslavia, Italy, Greece, Spain, and Portugal.[2]

From the beginning, these workers have been viewed as temporary residents who would return to their native lands in a few years. They are not allowed to apply for citizenship for ten years; and even if their children are born in West Germany, they also must apply for citizenship. With time, the assumption that there would be a "back migration" proved unfounded. Guestworkers remained, united their families in West Germany, began to improve their standard of living, and, according to government records, gradually reduced their remittances to their relatives in the native country. Currently, 50 percent of these workers have been in the country ten years or longer.

I witnessed firsthand something of the nature of their lives in 1982 when I spent three days on a Turkish ship sailing from Ancona, Italy, to Istanbul, Turkey. All but a few of the passengers were Turkish. I learned, during the course of some pleasant conversations, that many of the passengers were residents of West Germany who were going to spend their annual holidays in their homeland (my knowledge of rudimentary Turkish was acquired when I spent the first two years of my married life in Turkey). The group contained a wide social mixture of working-class and professional people. I noted with interest that long summer vacation trips were within the means of factory workers, but it amazed me even more that almost everyone—and certainly all the children and young adults—was speaking *German!* A couple with three young children confided to me that with each trip the children found it harder to adjust to speaking only Turkish in the summer and then to readjust to German-language schools on their return. The strong impression remains with me that they considered West Germany their home, so the language shift was a central factor in their family life.

What the West German government attempted to do in the education of its language minority children mirrors this problem of language shift and runs the gamut from integrationist to segregationist programs. Basic to the early efforts was the stated goal of educating children so that they could complete their studies in West German schools or in the schools of their native land, with good enough skills in both languages to accomplish either course of study. But in West Germany, as in the United States, education policy is not centrally dictated, so various approaches have been developed in different parts of the country. All, initially, looked promising, but the best solution has not been found. The three major instructional models that have been implemented represent polar extremes as well as a compromise among them, and it is from their trials and errors that we in the United States can learn much.[3]

The Bavarian Model

The Bavarian system of national language schools is one of the extremes, designed to provide all classroom subject teaching in the native language of the children, with only five to six hours of German-language lessons per week. All subjects are taught in the native language through grade five, teachers are recruited from the homeland of the children, and textbooks and materials are imported. From grade five on, all subject matter is then taught in German.

Ideally, this model should provide students with a strong preparation for upper-level West German schools and with an equally strong preparation in the home language and culture for possible return to the country of origin. In practice, this kind of program has proved far from effective for the students. The minority children are, in effect, cut off from their West German classmates for several years. Moreover, the program does not adequately prepare students to transfer into all-German schools at the sixth-grade level, since their German-language skills have not developed sufficiently. Rather than enhancing their learning, it deprives them of equal educational opportunity and is not considered a success in West Germany. In fact, it has been said that these national language schools principally promote the caste of assembly-line workers, denying opportunities for higher education and better jobs in West Germany.

The Berlin Model

The Berlin program is the direct antithesis of the national language schools. Its goal is to integrate the foreign students with their West German classmates by helping them adjust to the school and language as quickly as possible. The immigrant children are placed in regular classrooms from the first day of school and given no special treatment except a few hours a week of German as a Second Language. Their native language is not used at all during the regular school day, but after-school classes in the native language and culture are available. According to published data, only a small percentage of Turkish children attend the voluntary after-school lessons, but almost all the Greek children participate.[4]

Immigrant children have not achieved great success in these schools either, although the results are not thought to be as negative as in the Bavarian national language schools. Problems stem from several factors. There are not nearly enough trained language teachers, and the children are not given enough special help to achieve full proficiency in German for the highly competitive school curriculum. Since the subject matter studied is rigidly structured, immigrant children miss valuable academic lessons when they are taken away for German-language classes, as necessary as these few hours of German are. With all its good integrationist intentions and in spite of its serious shortcomings, this program is still the most widely used in the country.

The Krefeld Model

Since neither the Bavarian nor Berlin extreme has proven successful, a "combined" approach somewhat similar to the TBE programs in the United States is gaining popularity. Both immigrant children and West German children are taught together part of the day for mathematics and the arts; they are then separated for instruction in reading and other subjects in their home language. The goal of this program is to integrate immigrant children but at the same time help them retain their bilingual/bicultural identity by providing classes in the language, culture, and religion of their group during the school day.

This comprehensive approach has not been in use long enough to assess the results, but it is already apparent to observers that the time devoted to bicultural activities during the school day reduces the crucial instruction in school subjects. I expect that this model, in spite of its good, humane intentions, will prove to be as ineffective as the American bilingual programs and for the same basic reason: the second language is not learned well enough for the children ever to catch up with their classmates and compete at their own full individual capacity.

Challenges within the West German Education System

Some of the difficulties that hamper language minority children in West Germany are particular to that country and its education system, whereas others appear to be present in all the countries surveyed. West German schools, above the primary level, are especially competitive and selective. Nationwide, only 20 percent of West German children qualify for the academic high schools, and of that number only half go on to a university. Of resident immigrant children, only 5 percent enter the academic high schools, and an even smaller number attend a university.[5]

These odds are formidable and entail, to be sure, other cultural and socioeconomic differences that affect school achievement. West German parents, for example, expect to offer their children several hours of help daily in the early years of school. For the children of immigrant parents, who may be illiterate, this help often is not available. Also, immigrant parents frequently expect girls to attain only minimal literacy, so girls receive little encouragement for academic efforts.

West German students are expected to study English as their first foreign language in high school, since this is required for university entrance. The new programs supporting native-language maintenance for immigrant children now offer these children the opportunity to study their own language (Turkish, Italian, Spanish, Portuguese, Greek, or Serbo-Croatian) as their first foreign language in high school instead of English. The crucial question, then, is, Will these students fare better by developing literacy in their native language or by studying English and competing for university entrance, since an increasing number of their families are now settled permanently in West Germany? Language choice at this stage, then, bears directly on the acquisition of advanced skills and future achievement.

The West German education system has attempted different strategies to effect the maximum development of two languages and the maintenance of two cultures for its guestworkers' children. The fact is, whether the school program is integrationist or segregationist or somewhere in the middle, these children still bear a heavier burden in keeping up with two languages and cultures, whether it is during or after school. It puts them at a disadvantage academically, and it may not be what the children most desire. At least one scholar of the West German education system predicts that the language maintenance programs "will increase in Germany as it becomes clear that many 'foreign' children intend to remain in Germany and, at the same time, wish to retain their bicultural identity."[6] The question arises, then, Is it the 'foreign' students themselves or their parents, with different roots and aspirations, who want this bicultural identity? What cost will be borne by one or the other of these generations?

Lessons from the West German Experience

It appears to me that an important lesson for the United States in the West German experience is the conclusive evidence that providing native-language instruction for language minority children is not the cure-all. Where the greatest effort was made, in the Bavarian approach, the highest degree of segregation of immigrant children was the outcome. Nor has the other extreme—simply putting immigrant children in regular German-language classrooms with little or no help by special teachers—turned out well. The compromise between these two extremes looks a lot like the American TBE program, and I am not optimistic about its future success. West Germany's efforts reveal the complex nature of the problem of attempting, with the best intentions, to provide good education for minority groups. The West German experience also helps us understand better that the acceptable solutions are neither simple nor easily applied.

In West Germany, as in the United States, competing tensions exist between the impulse toward maintaining cultural pluralism and the efforts to hasten assimilation. These are intergenerational tensions: the immigrant parents value a bicultural identity, whereas the younger generation yearns to be part of the mainstream of West German life. As discussed later, these same stresses have caused deep concern in the United States.

———————— ◇◇◇ ————————

Soviet Union

The Soviet Union is unique in the world in the scale and complexity of its linguistic and ethnic composition. In the larger culture 150 languages are spoken, with Russian used by only 50 percent of the people. Surprisingly, twenty different languages are spoken by a million or more people each, as shown in table 4.1.

Even so, the Soviet Union has, until recently, been a relatively stable society of fifteen republics, with a different "national" language concentrated in each region and a host of "minority" languages scattered throughout. There is very little immigration and a limited amount of movement of peoples within the country. Russian is the official language of the Soviet Union, but it has been the policy since the

Table 4.1   Major Languages of the Soviet Union

Nationality	Number of Speakers (1980)
Russian	137,397,000
Ukrainian	42,347,000
Uzbek	12,456,000
Byelorussian	9,463,000
Kazakh	6,556,000
Tatar	6,317,000
Azerbaijan	5,477,000
Armenian	4,151,000
Georgian	3,571,000
Moldavian	2,968,000
Tadzhik	2,898,000
Lithuanian	2,851,000
Turkmen	2,028,000
Kirgiz	1,906,000
Yiddish	1,811,000
Chuvash	1,751,000
Latvian	1,439,000
Bashkir	1,271,000
Moksha-Mordvinian	1,192,000
Estonian	1,020,000

SOURCE: Barry McLaughlin, *Second-Language Acquisition in Child-hood*, vol. 2 (Hillsdale, NJ: Lawrence Erlbaum, 1985), 51.

founding of the state that the fifteen national languages are to be maintained for promoting universal literacy. All children must, however, learn Russian, and they are to be educated in Russian from the sixth grade on.

After 1917, the czarist doctrine of the Russian language as "the cement of the empire" was denounced forcefully. Stalin and Lenin proclaimed the equal value of all national languages. Almost certainly the enormous task of rapidly developing a literate citizenry could not have been accomplished without relying on the national languages for instruction. With time, though, the predominance of Russian has grown steadily as it has become the language of higher education, scientific communication, advancement in the Communist party, and international status. Stalin himself, from the 1930s on, emphasized ever more strongly the need for linguistic homogeneity, with Russian as the national language. He is said to have regarded the regional languages as "the opiate of the nations."[7] This assimilationist trend continues, although it is still official policy to promote large-scale bilingualism in the national languages and Russian as "the linguistic model appropriate for this stage of developed socialism."[8]

A centralized government such as the Soviet Union's, unlike the U.S. government, can effect social engineering to a high degree. Teaching methods, materials, and texts are, therefore, highly standardized in order to achieve the educational goals within a short time and with limited resources. The three major types of schools[9] demonstrate most dramatically for us the profound impact of centralized policy on regional cohesion as well as regional isolation.

National Language Schools

In national language schools, the most common type in the Russian educational system, all primary classroom teaching is conducted in the language of the particular republic for the first five years. Very short Russian-language lessons are given during this time, mostly in speaking, but the reading and writing skills in Russian start in the upper-level schools. In areas where people desire to preserve their literature, customs, and religion and to maintain a cohesive culture, as in Central Asia, these schools are strongly supported. There are substantial concerns, however, about the effectiveness of these schools in teaching Russian well enough for children's broader educational and career needs.

Minority Language Schools

Within any of the republics where there are groups of people who speak a language other than the indigenous language of that republic, such as Ukrainian-speakers living in Moscow, schools have been organized to give children their primary education in their home language. These schools are, in fact, dying out in spite of the official policy to maintain them as a civil right. The simple fact is that in these schools the children spend almost all their time studying languages and, consequently, fall behind in school subjects. They must first be taught in their home language, then they must learn the national language of the republic, and then they must also master Russian language for the upper schools. It is a trilingual, rather than a bilingual, process—not unlike the roundabout proposition described in chapter 2 for teaching children in Cape Verdean, then in Portuguese, and then in English. Minority language schools require an additional year of schooling for their students to allow them to have equal educational opportunity. These schools have proven not to be the first choice of parents if there is a Russian-language school available to them.

Russian-Language Schools

The Russian-language schools were originally established for the instruction of Russian-speaking children living in regions where a different language is spoken, but over the years, they have increasingly replaced the two types of schools just described. There are several important reasons why the Russian-language schools have become more prevalent. In many regions, especially in the large urban centers, there are dozens of language groups represented in one school—even in one classroom—making it not only uneconomical but unfeasible to educate every single child in his or her home language. Since the 1960s and 1970s there has been a some-what higher level of internal migration, making for much greater linguistic diversity in different parts of the country and leading to a much greater use of Russian for communication. And the last and most powerful reason is parents' belief that Russian-medium schools will give their children the best life opportunities.

Challenges within the Soviet Education System

As noted earlier, the Soviet Union is, perhaps, the most linguistically and ethnically diverse country in the world. M. N. Guboglo describes his country thus: "National literatures are written in 78 languages, plays are performed in 42, journals are published in 46, school textbooks are printed in 56, and radio programmes are broadcast in 67 languages."[10]

Despite the government's well-established efforts to promote literacy and bilingualism and to teach Russian widely, the Russian language is not learned well in the non-Russian-speaking republics. The government acknowledges that there are more people in those republics with a high school or higher degree than there are people with a solid knowledge of Russian.[11]

Other problems have less bearing on policy decisions for the United States. A severe shortage of Russian-language teachers exists, and it is one of the high priorities of the 1980s to train a sufficient number for the needs of the country. Another problem has been the difficulty of recruiting teachers to work in the more remote regions. A further problem is the rigid approach to language teaching, a practice I also observed when visiting schools in the Peoples' Republic of China. A national curriculum is in place, with standardized tests to measure achievement, and it allows no deviation and no opportunity for individual teachers to develop innovative strategies. This is what we call a "teacher-proof" curriculum in the United States, a system that is so carefully planned and detailed that no teacher, for better or for worse, can affect its outcome. The approach was popular in American schools briefly during the 1960s but was discarded when it became apparent that greater benefits lay in promoting creative teaching than in requiring uniform lessons.

Strict adherence to use of only the native language in the first five or six years of school and the serious teaching of Russian only in the upper schools delay the development of high-level proficiency in Russian. The Soviet education system has been organized in this manner for two main reasons: (1) an emphasis on maintaining widespread literacy by teaching in the national languages and (2) their linguists' belief that a single language competence, or "set," underlies all languages we learn. According to this theory, competence in one's first language is the basis for second-language learning. This theory is similar to the ideas of linguists in the West such as Cummins, whom I cited in chapter 3, but it is still a hypothesis that lacks clear supportive evidence, either in the United States or the Soviet Union.

In the Soviet Union, as in the United States, the 1960s saw a growth of interest in the search for "roots," an increase in nostalgic ethnicity in some regions, and a resistance to the dominant national language. Nevertheless, the majority of the Soviet population has over time favored Russian-language education for pragmatic reasons. We should note for our own purposes that the government, for all its public respect and support for the various languages and cultures, is quietly pursuing an assimilationist policy. A 1983 statement by then general secretary of the Communist party, K. U. Chernenko, typifies the thinking:

There are still several instances when a weak knowledge of the Russian language limits a person's access to the riches of international culture, narrows his circle of activity and communication. The Central Committee of the CPSU and the Council of Ministers of the USSR recently adopted a resolution on creating conditions facilitating instruction in the Russian language for the population of the national republics. It must be actively implemented.[12]

Given the size and complexity of Soviet society, it will probably always be necessary for bilingualism to be supported. The increasing emphasis, however, on universal Russian-language proficiency is not only a state goal but an advantage clearly recognized by the parents of schoolchildren. It is difficult, of course, to know exactly what the future course of language priorities will be in the Soviet Union. It may be possible for all Soviet citizens to continue to enjoy the best of both worlds—to acquire a common language to a high level of fluency and to maintain their various national and minority languages and ethnic cultures. The Soviet Union is an increasingly industrial country, and their ethnolinguistic policies bear watching, particularly given the recent opening of relations with the United States and, indeed, the growing similarity to the United States as a technological and entrepreneurial society.

Lessons from the Soviet Experience

What we in the United States must note especially, however, are the conditions that made it possible for indigenous languages and cultures to be maintained over a period of seventy years: the diversity was due not only to government language policies but to the traditionally restrictive nature of Soviet society. Compared to the United States, the Soviet Union has had little mobility within the country and very few immigrants from other countries. Therefore, different national languages and ethnic cultures could be maintained in spite of the impulse toward Russian-language education. Soviet education policies could not be similarly applied in the United States, however, not only because of the still fundamentally different dynamic of our society but because of the decentralized character of our educational system. The expectation of cultural pluralists that we may nurture concentrations of different cultures and languages and maintain them successfully in the United States is unrealistic and could only be accomplished either by government policies that most Americans would find offensive or by self-segregation of communities, as has been done by certain religious groups. Neither course seems to have wide appeal. The Soviet situation up to the present serves, therefore, as an example of the extreme measures required for maintaining distinct cultures in a pluralistic society—measures that are probably impossible in an open democracy and, in fact, are growing less possible in the Soviet Union.

Sweden

Sweden has distinguished itself among multicultural societies for its unswerving commitment to human rights issues, particularly to the goal of preserving the language and culture of each minority group in the country. The National Swedish Board of Education, the central planning authority, stated in 1973 that the goal of bilingual education was to ensure "a parallel command of both languages for all children."[13] Within four years it became a legal requirement that all language minority children receive instruction in their home language and that they be entitled to receive even day-care and preschool classes in their home language.

In a population of eight million people, approximately one million are immigrants. Of these, 45 percent are from Finland, and other large groups are from Yugoslavia, Denmark, Norway, Greece, Turkey, and West Germany, with several dozen other groups in small numbers.[14] The schooling of these children has been organized along four basic instructional models, similar to those developed in West Germany. They range from the most integrationist to the most segregationist, based on the amount of time students are separated from Swedish children and taught in their home languages. They can be characterized as follows:[15]

1. In mainstream only schooling, immigrant children are simply grouped with Swedish children in regular classrooms and given no special help in learning Swedish.
2. In mainstream plus home language schooling, all instruction is in regular Swedish classrooms, with four to five hours per week of teaching in the home language. No special help is provided in learning the Swedish language.
3. In composite schooling, like the West German "combined" program and the TBE model in the United States, language minority students are taught separately, in their home language, for 60 percent of the school day, and the rest of the time in Swedish. This proportion slowly changes, and by the end of sixth grade the children are taught in Swedish all but 15 percent of the time.
4. In mother tongue, or language shelter, schooling, all teaching is done in the home language for the first three years of school. Instruction in Swedish begins in the fourth grade and occupies 20 percent of the time, and it increases to 70 percent by grade six.[16]

Immigrant parents in Sweden have the right to choose the type of program they wish to have their children enrolled in, and this right is taken seriously. As in other multilingual countries, some parents (about 40 percent) want rapid assimilation for their children, and they reject any instruction in the home language; others do not want their children to lose the family and community closeness, and they choose one of the home-language programs. These decisions are sometimes made because of pressure from the educational establishment.

Semilingualism and the Finnish-Language Struggle

The notion of *semilingualism,* a term I used earlier, became popular in Sweden in the late 1960s and promoted the fear that immigrant children would grow up with poor skills in *two* languages. The only cure for this condition was proclaimed to be the teaching of children in their home language. Greek parents who had, like a majority of immigrant families, decided on Swedish-language school for their children opted instead for home-language classes because they feared the "danger of semilingualism."[17] Swedish linguists Löfgren and Ouvinen-Birgerstam protested in the strongest terms: "We wish to dissociate ourselves from those arguments for teaching in the mother tongue which attempt to frighten parents into choosing mother-tongue teaching by threatening emotional and intellectual underdevelopment in those children who do not receive mother-tongue teaching."[18] These reasons for pressuring parents into enrolling children in native-language programs are the same ones that are used in support of bilingual education in the United States, as I pointed out earlier—that children will not learn very well and will suffer emotional problems if denied their native language in school. It is not a fact in Sweden or in the United States.

According to linguist Christina Bratt Paulston, an authority on Swedish bilingualism, the term *semilingualism* had
its roots in the Finnish-language struggle, that is, the demand by the Finns in Sweden for schooling in their own
language. She and other linguists have criticized the use of
this term because there are no studies or empirical data to
prove the concept's existence. It may be a myth, but as a
political scare term it has had profound effects on the
schooling of children not only in Sweden but also the
United States, where it also has been accepted without a
particle of evidence.

Politicization versus Sound Research

The mythology of semilingualism succinctly illustrates the
politicization of the controversy over bilingual education
and why Sweden's experience has been used by proponents
in the development of the field in the United States. It
shows how effectively an unproven notion with no supporting evidence can be promoted for ideological reasons
and then become accepted as fact, even by the academic establishment. The same has occurred with the politicized research on the effectiveness of bilingual teaching in Sweden.
To support the chauvinistic political goals of Finnish immigrants living in Sweden, Finnish sociologists Toukomaa
and Skutnabb-Kangas, as I indicated earlier, have made exaggerated claims for the benefits of mother-tongue teaching
for language minority children. Their research studies have
been severely criticized, but one continues to read in scholarly journals that Finnish children who are taught in their
home language for five or six years learn Swedish better
and faster and are more successful in academic subjects
than children who begin to learn Swedish in kindergarten
or first grade. In fact, there are no hard data to support this
rationale.

Paulston, a Swedish native, was comissioned by the National Swedish Board of Education to examine the Swedish research on bilingualism and the debate surrounding bilingual education in that country. Her carefully reasoned conclusions can be summarized as follows:

1. Children learn the language they hear meaningfully spoken around them, no matter what language their parents spoke in another country. *If the children don't hear the language, they don't learn it.* Early and intensive second-language teaching and as much contact as possible between immigrant children and native speakers are crucial.[19]

2. There are no research results that indicate whether the establishment of national mother-tongue schools supports or hinders language minority children's long-range possibilities for finding jobs or enjoying social conditions equal to those of native-language children.[20]

3. Many—perhaps most—proponents of mother-tongue teaching have a vested interest in holding back the assimilation of migrant children, and their advice on educational language policy needs to be considered *cum grano salis* (with a grain of salt).[21]

4. Demands for mother-tongue classes almost invariably come from parents, parents' groups, and immigrant organizations *but not from the children.* Such classes are a mechanism for segregation.

5. Much more training of teachers of Swedish language needs to be done, and immigrant children need to be given more and better instruction in this language. It is the most important subject for immigrant students, but it is too often taught by untrained or ineffective teachers.

6. Mother-tongue instruction is appealing and makes possible a recognition of the values of the old country. It is a handsome gesture of the Swedish government but a very expensive policy.[22]

Much of what Paulston concluded about Sweden's bilingual programs mirrors the situation in the United States. We have borrowed the forms and theories from the Swedes without carefully considering where these practices will take us and without examining carefully what results are actually being achieved in Sweden.

———————— ◊◊◊ ————————

Canada

Close to the United States in language and culture, Canada has officially been a bilingual country for over a hundred years. Of Canada's population, 67 percent speak English, 27 percent French, and 6 percent other European, Asian, Canadian Indian, or Eskimo languages.[23] French-language usage is now a divisive political issue, and Americans can learn tough lessons from the Canadian experience.

The Quebec Francophone Efforts

In spite of the legal status of the French language granted by the British North American Act of 1867, the general tendency has been toward an increasingly wider use of English. In the 1960s, the province of Quebec, home of the largest concentration of French-speakers in the country, became the arena for a separatist movement—"Québec Libre," an effort that sought to revive French-language pride and to separate Francophone Canada from the rest of the country not only linguistically but politically and economically. This movement sought autonomy and the reestablishment of the "French fact," which was characterized in a 1970 government white paper this way:

The renaissance of the French fact in Canada, so striking during the past decade, has had profound effects within Canada and upon its foreign relations. Canadians of French expression no longer see themselves as a small disadvantaged minority in an English-speaking continent but rather as an essential element in the great international French culture, the most significant group of *francophones* outside metropolitan France.[24]

Since the late 1960s, government policy in Quebec has actively promoted French as the language of public education. The 1977 Chartre de la Langue Française not only promotes French as *the* official language of the province; it declares that Quebec must be a solely French-speaking province, different from the rest of the country. The new charter imposes exclusively French-language education on all children in the province, no matter what language their families speak at home. New immigrant families do not have a choice between English or French schools. The only exception made for education in English is for children whose parents can *prove* that they attended English-language schools *in Quebec*. English-speaking families that move to Quebec from other parts of Canada are not allowed to enroll their children in English-language schools. Thorough research on the social and economic effects of this policy is not available, but there has been a measurable shift of business firms from Montreal to Toronto and of families out of Quebec and to other provinces where they can obtain English-language schooling for their children.

Canada's legislature has been debating a constitutional amendment that would recognize Quebec as a "distinct society" within Canada. This change is opposed by former Prime Minister Pierre Elliot Trudeau and by Liberal party leader Donald Johnston.[25] Johnston says such a move would foster a "two nation vision" of Canada and make it easier for French-Canadian nationalists to push for the imposition of French as the only official language of Quebec. He believes that this could eventually provide the basis for Quebec's separation from the rest of the country, an option Quebec voters actually rejected by a three-to-two margin in 1980.[26]

The French-Canadian fear of a loss of identity and of becoming part of the majority culture—the reason for their opposition to bilingualism—is poignantly expressed:

The more bilingual our children become, the more they use English; the more they use English, the less they find French useful; the less they find French useful, the more they use English. The paradox of French-Canadian life is the following: the more we become bilingual, the less it is necessary to be bilingual.[27]

The intention of the Quebec Chartre is clearly to support and expand the use of French, not to promote bilingualism. It is a calculated attempt to advance the interests of the French-speaking population and is basically related to power, jobs, and political control. The goals are clear and understandable and must necessarily be pursued in this forceful manner if the province is to reverse the long history of drift toward English. Preserving a language that is, at a given time, perceived as less prestigious requires two types of heroic measures: (1) keeping out any taint of other languages as much as possible, linguistically sealing the community, and (2) ensuring that successive waves of adults will be prepared to use that language in commerce, the arts, and all areas of public and private life by requiring the use of the language in all schooling from the earliest years. That approach to language learning should rivet our attention.

The French Immersion Experiment

In the 1970s the Canadian Ministry of Education generously supported the establishment of various experimental programs for English-speaking children to learn French and become thoroughly bilingual and literate in both languages. What emerged as the principal model is the now famous French Language Immersion Program. Not only has this type of education been widely implemented—over 100,000 children have participated over the past seventeen years—but it has also been carefully studied. The effects of the immersion program on children's ability to learn a second language and to do schoolwork in that language have been thoroughly and precisely researched and reported. The programs have been exceptionally successful.

The idea of immersion in another language is a familiar one—many of us have taken the opportunity, as young adults, to study in another country for a period of time, perhaps living with a local family, to be completely "immersed" in the language and forced to learn it sufficiently not only for daily communication but for understanding and expressing ideas and subtle feelings. This informal and nonprogrammatic kind of experience can be successful, depending on one's personal motivation and on any number of chance factors. The objective in the careful planning of the Canadian language immersion experiment for large numbers of schoolchildren was to create, in the classroom, a situation that would approximate living and studying in another country but with a controlled environment, leaving as little as possible to chance. Canadians were dissatisfied with the quality of foreign language programs in the high schools, because students studied a language for several years and generally emerged with little ability to use the language for real communication. Therefore, skepticism had to be overcome (as in the United States at present).

Background of the French Immersion Experiment. The French Immersion experiment started in 1965 with Wallace Lambert's pioneer program in the Montreal suburb of St.

Lambert (no relation to Wallace). He developed his program with the cooperation of a group of Anglo-Canadian
parents who were seriously interested in having their children learn French and willing to enroll them in this experiment. It is to the credit of psychologist Wallace Lambert
and linguist G. Richard Tucker that they set in place the
evaluation mechanisms to monitor and analyze the results
of language immersion education so that other researchers
have been able to study and compare the effects of the different types of immersion programs.[28]

The possible variations on the basic immersion idea involve just two factors: (1) the age of the child on entering
the program and (2) the amount of time that classroom instruction is given in the new language.

• Early Immersion: child begins at age five or six
• Late Immersion: child begins at age ten to twelve
• Total Immersion: all classroom instruction is given in
  French
• Partial Immersion: only part of the instruction is in
  French

Acknowledging that real-world educational programs can
never be as stringently controlled as laboratory experiments, one can still categorize the immersion programs that
are operating in the schools of Quebec according to those
two-factor definitions. The Early Total Immersion program
is the classic model from which all the variations derive,
and this is the program I want to describe in detail.

Before considering what immersion education is, however, one must understand what it is not. It is not a random, unstructured, casual plunking down of children in a
classroom full of students who are all speaking an unfamiliar language, in the hope that the children will somehow
pick up the new language and someday catch up with

everybody else in their schoolwork. Not at all! It is systematic and carefully planned, and it requires well-trained bilingual teachers.

Over the years all the research has focused on three considerations: (1) What are the effects of these programs in developing children's ability in French? (2) What are the effects of these programs on the children's academic achievement in subjects such as science, mathematics, and history? (3) What are the effects of these programs on the children's home-language (English) skills? Achievement of the immersion students was compared with the performance of two other groups—(1) English-speaking children in regular English-language schools and (2) native French-speaking children in regular French schools. These served as the control groups for determining the success of the immersion programs, as measured against the three research questions just mentioned. All groups were matched for social and economic status, with a range of students from middle- and working-class families.

It has been the intent of the French Immersion programs that the new language be learned to the highest level possible but that literacy skills in the home language (English) be developed as well. In other words, parents have wanted their children to learn French but not at the expense of English and not to the detriment of their ability to do schoolwork competently.

The Early Total Immersion Program. The Early Total Immersion program, originally called the "home–school language switch program," begins in kindergarten. All instruction, from that first day and for three years, is given in French, a language that is totally unknown to the children. The teacher, who is required to be fluent in French and English, speaks to the children only in French. The children are encouraged to use the new language for all communication with the teacher and among themselves through storytelling, vocabulary building, songs, games, and group projects. The focus is on natural language learning for real-life uses, and grammar is neither taught nor emphasized in the first year. Language learning is deliberately involved with subject matter learning, and that is the key to successful immersion programs—students learn by doing.

For example, while doing a simple science experiment and talking about it in the new language, the students are simultaneously learning the science concept and the vocabulary and grammar needed to describe it. In the evolution of my own early efforts, as I have described, I came around by common sense to plan lessons of this sort when I taught fifth and sixth graders. Whether instruction involved planting seeds and measuring growth under different conditions, growing mold on different substances, or tracking constellations over a period of time, the students were actively involved in learning scientific methods, basic science facts, and the English language to express them.

Children in immersion programs are not subjected to language "drills" or mechanical grammar exercises. They learn to speak, read, write, and think in the new language. Using only the new language for all classroom work for three years, these students acquire a very solid and lasting knowledge base in their new language. That second language becomes as natural as the first language they learned at home. In fact, it is reported that within the first half year most children become sufficiently comfortable in the new language to begin using it in informal social settings such as the school playground.[29]

But what happens to the child's home language, English, in this situation? Does it atrophy and die from lack of use in the school? By the end of second grade the students have already mastered reading and writing in French. Beginning in the latter part of the second grade (the child's third year in French immersion), language arts are taught in English, and reading and writing skills in English are developed as well. From fifth grade on, equal time is given to instruction in each of the two languages. For instance, mathematics and history may be taught in French, while science and literature are taught in English, or vice versa. Over the years, both languages develop, and students are capable of learning new subject matter in either language with equal facility.

The other types of immersion programs can be briefly described. The Early Partial Immersion program gives students only 50 percent or less of their instruction in French in kindergarten and throughout their primary grades. In the Late Immersion program French instruction in the school subjects typically begins in grade seven or eight and continues until high school graduation.

Results from Immersion Programs.   A comparison of the results achieved in these immersion programs highlights, by contrast, the dramatic advantages for Early Total Immersion, as I have described it. Among the reported studies I have surveyed over the past dozen years, the key findings are generally as follows.

1. French-Language Learning.   Children in the Early Total Immersion programs generally achieve the highest level of French-language skills in speaking, reading, and writing, reaching near-native proficiency. Fluency in conversational French for informal situations is extremely high for these students and is not related to IQ. They are far more creative and uninhibited in their use of French than English-speaking children in regular foreign language programs. In reading and writing skills, students' ability in French is more closely related to their IQ scores. Above-average students score higher than do average or below-average students. This relationship between literacy and IQ is acknowl-

edged by educators and apparently exists no matter what language the child uses.

Late or partial immersion students also demonstrate better ability in French than their English-speaking peers who received only thirty to sixty minutes of daily French lessons. In fact, the late immersion students' performance on tests of spoken French generally averages in the high three-to-four range of a five-point scale, with five representing excellent or nativelike competence.[30]

2. Academic Achievement. Extensive testing in the primary schools has demonstrated that the immersion students usually learn concepts and computational skills in all aspects of mathematics as well as their English-taught peers, despite the fact that they receive all instruction in French. As with the achievement in reading, content learning is more closely related to IQ than to language of instruction. French Immersion students usually learn content material as well as the English control students. Above-average students will score high whether taught in French or English, and students of lower skills will perform accordingly. This is also true for late immersion students in grades seven and above who scored as well as their peers in the English control group on tests of mastery of physics, chemistry, and history.

3. English-Language Skills. These results involving English-language skills are perhaps the most remarkable of all. The early total immersion students, in spite of hearing no English spoken by their teachers for the first three years of school, measured up to their English control group peers in understanding, speaking, and oral vocabulary. This is decisive testimony to the strength of the influence of the home language. These students scored lower than normal on tests requiring reading and writing in English, which is natural, because they had had no schooling in English. But the sig-

nificant fact is that they were already reading in English before any formal English literacy training took place in
school. Even more impressive is the fact that by the end of
the third grade, after only one year of English-language lessons, the immersion students had achieved parity with the
English group in all literacy skills except spelling—and that
happened in another year.

These results have been reported by all the principal researchers who have evaluated immersion programs. There
is conclusive evidence, then, that being taught initially in a
second language does not necessarily destroy a child's
knowledge of his or her native tongue. Children can successfully be taught completely in French for the first three
years of schooling with only a temporary delay in their ability to read and write in English when English begins to be
used in the classroom.

Other Canadian Initiatives

French Immersion programs have been used almost entirely with English-speaking children, but other types of education programs for new immigrants and for indigenous
language minority children such as Canadian Indians and
Eskimos are being developed and tested. Nevertheless, the
pedagogical limitations and political distortions have
emerged in Canada, just as they have with the native-language-based approach in the United States. The official policy of the Canadian government since 1971 to promote
"multiculturalism within a bilingual framework" has given
a strong impetus to these programs.[31] There is a continuing
effort to promote a multilingual/multicultural Canadian
identity and to reduce the dominance of Anglo-Canadian
culture.

Heritage-language or mother-tongue maintenance programs, as a consequence, are in operation throughout the

country, mainly at the elementary schools. They range from a thirty-minute daily lesson in Italian, Greek, or Portuguese, for example, to more comprehensive programs such as those in the province of Alberta, where the students may be taught in Hebrew, Ukrainian, or German for 50 percent of the school day. These programs are based on the same rationale as bilingual education in the United States—that children who do not know the majority language of their country should be taught in their home language to avoid emotional and academic problems. The objective is also the reviving or maintaining of a language that is in danger of disappearing, as in the case of some of the indigenous Canadian languages.

Advocates for heritage-language programs claim that they successfully promote the development of home language while not impeding the development of second-language English skills.[32] My reading of the reports is far less optimistic. These programs have not been studied as long or as carefully as the immersion programs, and the conclusions are tentative. Although there is not yet a reliable body of evidence, either in Canada or the United States, available evidence from Canada strongly suggests that teaching in the native language for three to six years and delaying the use of the second language in the classroom actually make children less proficient in the second language.

Limitations of the Canadian Efforts

Successful as the French immersion experiment program has been, no comparable attempt has been made to provide English immersion programs for language minority children in Canada. Like the TBE experiment in the United States, immersion programs, let us be clear, were conceived for political purposes, to promote not only educational but societal goals perceived to be of present and future benefit.

The crucial difference between the Canadian and U.S. educational initiatives, which are quite opposite in their approaches, is that the Canadian experiment has met with consistent success and the U.S. experiment has not. Yet Canada, with its high influx of immigrants and refugees, does not offer English immersion programs to its new arrivals. Why not?

Immersion Programs and Social Class Bias.   The linguists, educators, and researchers whose career advancement is linked to the success of immersion education argue protectively that this program is only appropriate for middle-class children who, secure in their majority language and status, are learning a less-valued language. They have clung to this bias despite the fact that the large percentage of children in the Canadian immersion programs are from low-income working-class families. Denying the use of immersion programs because they supposedly are good only for middle-class children reinforces a stereotype—that language minority children are inferior, emotionally weaker, and intellectually less capable. This essentially pejorative view has had a very detrimental effect on the development of programs for language minority children in the United States.

The contention is—without any proof—that language minority children, such as Greek or Italian or Vietnamese children, would not do well in immersion programs because they would lose their cultural identity, fail to keep their native language, and generally be ill-served. One must ask why, with French Immersion education so successful in the province where French *is* the majority language, should not English Immersion programs be used in other parts of the country where English is the majority language? Regrettably, a double standard seems to be operating. For the ideologues, it is clearly desirable to develop showcase programs and allocate abundant resources for these projects in the service of Quebec's majority language—French. Unfortunately, however, it is evidently not in their interests to make these same benefits available to children needing to learn a second language, if that language is English.

Such a view ignores important recent research. A Canadian expert in the field of psychology and education who has researched and written on Canadian immersion programs for fifteen years, Fred Genesee, has concluded that "the most effective program [for second-language learning] is one in which the use of the child's native language is postponed until the third or fourth grade. . . . The early use of the student's first language interferes with second-language learning, perhaps because it promotes a reliance on the first language."[33] Genesee's statement echoes Paulston's view, as cited earlier in this chapter. The idea is as bold as it is simple: If you want children to learn another language really well, start them at an early age and give them a lot of concentrated professional attention. But this makes sense only if you are more concerned with a child's civil right to the opportunity for self-fulfillment than with the self-interested, and thus segregative, agenda of political activists. One of the damaging ironies in the public debate is that while many educators agree with Genesee that immersion is the best language-teaching approach, they will still skew that agreement by saying, "Yes, of course, that's true, but only for middle-class majority children."

Lessons from the Canadian Experience

Canada has pointed the way to effective second-language learning on a large scale, for children of different backgrounds and of different ability levels. The results are highly successful and reliably reported. However, the pro-French-language government policy in Quebec is being forcefully advanced there for political ends while comparable programs are not being provided for language minority groups elsewhere in the nation.

Although the immersion programs require a large number of trained professionals, especially in the early total immersion schools, the consistently positive outcomes favor this model, or some variation of it, for wider use in other countries. The important conclusions to be drawn from the Canadian experience are straightforward, and the evidence is reliable.

1. Starting second-language learning early, at age five or six, with a total classroom immersion in that language, promises the best results in learning that language.
2. Beginning in their first year of schooling, children are capable of learning subject matter content taught in a second language.
3. Children are capable of becoming literate in their home language quickly if it is used in the classroom in later years.

Early total immersion students, in short, become the most competent in their knowledge and use of a second language. The evidence of direct correlation between early, intensive second-language learning and high level of competence in the second language is inescapable, as is the time-on-task principle—that is, the more time spent learning a language, the better you do in it, all other factors being equal.

The Canadian results should have an important bearing on the development of programs for language minority students in the United States. They have not yet been sufficiently reported or usefully discussed, however, in our national debate over fundamental language issues. My proposals for adapting Canada's immersion model for language minority children in the United States are presented in chapter 8.

Having surveyed the experiences of other multilingual societies and pondered the lessons they offer the United States, we can better assess some of the new alternative American programs to see how well they are working and why. A close examination of other countries' experiences leads us to a reassessment of American bilingual education in particular and compels us to ask whether this twenty-year-old experiment is advancing or blocking the opportunities for students and the minority communities of which they are members.

5

The Fresh Breeze of Innovation in U.S. Alternative Programs

Our experience by now should convince us that there are really only two distinct approaches to the education of language minority children: (1) use their native language for classroom teaching or (2) provide a special program that does *not* use their native language. The main division in program types, then, is the question of whether to use the native language at all and, if so, to what extent. This is the fundamental issue that divides educators of language minority children not only in the United States and the countries reviewed in chapter 4 but in several other countries with a substantial population who do not speak the national language. This issue bears on educational policy, civil rights, and allocation of community resources.

Twenty years of research intended to show the success of programs using the native language have not, either in the United States or in other countries, established that outcome. What we have learned from other countries with similar situations and challenges is that there are no unilateral solutions that can be applied everywhere and that political motives play a more decisive part than considerations of good education in the language field. Bilingual education, for instance, is squarely in the center of the debate in the United States over cultural pluralism or assimilation of ethnic minorities, as we will see in the next chapter.

As the field of bilingual education in the United States develops, however, an increasing number of school districts are modifying their programs to respond more directly to the needs of specific new language groups, like Vietnamese, Khmer, Laotian, Farsi, or Korean, and to incorporate some of the newer teaching strategies that show promising outcomes. Not nearly enough is yet being done in experimenting with different approaches in different speech communities with different educational aspirations.

The Importance of Flexible Options

There are three compelling reasons why this flexibility has not yet been employed on a larger scale.

1. Until May 1988, 96 percent of all federal funding for limited-English students was restricted to bilingual programs using the native language.[1]
2. Legal strictures at the state level have prohibited such approaches. As in Massachusetts, state funding has also been denied for such experimentation.
3. The counterpressure of the state bilingual education bureaus has been strong. California is a representative example. Although that state has had a bilingual education law that permits and funds alternatives to bilingual education—what they call Planned Variation programs— only *six* of these programs existed in the entire state as of 1988. Even since the bilingual education law in California expired in June 1987, strong pressure from the state education authority for native language programs continues.

Over a decade ago the noted sociolinguist Bernard Spolsky stressed the need for flexible options:

Basic to establishing a sound policy is, I am convinced, an understanding of the speech community in which the school exists. While there may be good political and administrative reasons for setting national and regional goals, each school should be able to modify these goals and interpret them according to the needs of the local community. To speak of a single model for a whole nation, or even for a specific sector within the nation (all minority speakers, for instance) is most unwise.[2]

In similar terms, the assistant superintendent of the Brookline, Massachusetts, Public Schools, in testimony before the Massachusetts legislative committee on education, asked that the state law be revised to "give us an intelligent skeleton, and let each district flesh it out according to its own community's needs."[3]

Parents, too, have differing attitudes regarding the kind of schooling they want for their children. The national Parent Preference Study, completed in 1988 by the Educational Testing Service, surveyed parents of Puerto Rican, Cuban, Mexican-American, and Asian children.[4] The report on that study contains two major conclusions that have important implications for public education policy: (1) parents agreed that special language programs should be provided to language minority children, but (2) opinions varied widely both within and among ethnic groups as to what the most desirable language programs are. Other important findings from that study are the following:

- All parents wanted their children to achieve in school and to learn English. Asians were the most likely to declare learning English as one of the three most important objectives of schooling and gave a much lower priority to the teaching of the home language in school than the other three groups.
- A large majority of parents said it is the family's respon-

sibility to teach children about the history and traditions of their ancestors. Among ethnic groupings, Puerto Rican and Mexican-American parents were more likely than Cuban and Asian parents to want to assign that task to the schools.

- All hispanic groups were more in favor of using the home language for teaching English reading and writing skills than were Asians, and the same held true for teaching school subjects in the home language.
- As for the desirability of either transitional or maintenance bilingual programs, Puerto Rican and Mexican-American parents were more likely than Asian or Cuban parents to desire such programs.

These results held true despite such variables as educational level of parents and family income. The association of ethnicity and parental preference for the use of the home language in instruction remained stable. The concluding statement in the summary of the report clearly highlights the need for flexibility: "Thus, to the extent that schools attend to parent preferences in their program development, it would appear that this study would call for some options in the types of special services available to language minority children."[5] Information of this sort helps us anticipate different objectives among different speech communities. It is important, accordingly, to determine what local citizens actually want and not to make assumptions based solely on broad external survey conclusions.

The Expansion of Alternatives

Successful alternatives to traditional bilingual programs are already operating in various parts of the country. Despite the meager encouragement in the field, a number of local initiatives indicate a trend in the evolution of bilingual education. As districts become increasingly multilingual, they modify their programs, introducing new approaches that are more intensively or even entirely English language oriented and less reliant on home languages. Another noteworthy trend is under way in large urban school districts such as El Paso, Texas; Elizabeth, New Jersey; and Dade County, Florida, where experimental efforts are being tested that employ the new language-teaching methods discussed thus far—natural language and content-based approaches— and the new structured immersion and two-way experiments that are described later in this chapter. These new methods cannot be fitted into the traditional bilingual education mold because they require freedom outside its prescribed structure. For instance, although early immersion in a second language, as in the Canadian programs (chapter 4), has clearly been proven successful, it cannot be undertaken in bilingual programs that require early and extended teaching in the home language. Similarly, although content-based language teaching is one of the best ways to teach a second language and school subjects simultaneously, it cannot be used in bilingual programs that require subjects to be taught in the native language for several years. Education research, we have seen, makes the compelling case for time on task as the most important single determinant of success in learning *anything*. Students in immersion programs, therefore, succeed in learning a second language quickly and thoroughly because they spend *all* their school time using that language, and not just thirty minutes a day.

Some school districts are vigorously pragmatic and thus open to new thinking in setting their institutional goals. They are less locked in traditional methods and more willing to rely on their own experiences in drawing conclusions about what works. It is to some of the innovative, multifaceted, new programs that we now turn, with an in-depth look at the Newton, Massachusetts, program and an overview of several other productive alternatives. Out of this discussion comes an impressive vision of what can be done for our minority children in the United States.

Innovation in the Newton Public Schools

Newton, Massachusetts, an upper-middle-class community of 90,000 bordering Boston, has a well-established reputation as a lighthouse district in educational innovation. Newton is known for its commitment to promoting academic excellence and to improving the achievement of minority students. For twenty-one years Newton, along with other eastern Massachusetts cities, has participated in a regional busing program, the Metropolitan Council for Educational Opportunity (METCO), that brings black students from Boston to Newton schools for their entire twelve years of schooling.

Faced with a growing number of limited-English-speaking or non-English-speaking children in the early 1970s, Newton began, as I indicated in chapter 2, a bilingual program for its Italian-speakers in 1974 and soon added native-language instruction for its Chinese- and Spanish-speakers, one of the first cities in Massachusetts to do so. Out of a total school population of 9,000 students, this special program serves 300 to 400 children from very different socioeconomic backgrounds: 40 percent are children of Italian and Chinese immigrant families of low income, some below the poverty level; about 35 percent are refugees from Southeast Asia, Iran, Afghanistan, Russia, and Central America, some with very good academic preparation and some with little

Table 5.1   Limited-English Students in Newton Public Schools
(October 1988)

Native (Home) Language	Number of Students	Native (Home) Language	Number of Students
Arabic	5	Jamaican	1
Armenian	1	Japanese	40
Bengali	1	Khmer	5
Cape Verdean	1	Korean	10
Cantonese	38	Mandarin	20
Dari	3	Norwegian	2
English	6	Polish	1
Estonian	2	Portuguese	5
Farsi	22	Pushtu	7
French	8	Russian	11
Greek	17	Spanish	48
Hindi	1	Swedish	2
Hungarian	6	Tagalog	3
Hebrew	45	Vietnamese	13
Italian	16	Total	340

SOURCE: Compiled from data provided by Newton Public Schools, based on annual census of school enrollment, required the first of October of each school year by the Massachusetts State Department of Education.

or no schooling; and about 25 percent are middle-class children of visiting scholars and professionals from Japan, Israel, Europe, and South America, planning to be in Newton for one or two years only. Within a short time the variety of languages represented grew to twenty-nine, as is the case today, a marvelous global assortment in miniature (see table 5.1).

The population changes have necessarily altered the original program, requiring an array of activities that are of most interest, no doubt, to the specialist (other readers may want to turn directly to the conclusion on pages 139–141). Essentially, two overlapping, complementary programs emerged. The original bilingual program still provides some

menting with programs that focus less on native language and more intensively on English use, and they are generally reporting good results for their students.

In the past eight years Newton has developed standard practices throughout the school district that are directed at improving the education of language minority children. It takes some years of focused effort to train teachers, write curriculum, establish contacts with parents, and build good-will for the whole program within the schools themselves and in the community. The reason for my detailed account here is to show how a well-integrated program can, even without teaching each child in his or her native language, provide a strong and effective education for these students leading to their success in schoolwork as well as in English-language learning. The Newton program is thus representative of the new ideas being tried in a number of other school districts. Some or all features of this program could be put into effect in other school districts, even those with limited resources.

Central Screening of New Students.   The first crucial contact between new limited-English students and the school system occurs in a central location, the ESL/Bilingual Office. The family and the student are interviewed in their home language, through an interpreter if necessary; the student's ability in English is tested; and information is gathered on the student's previous school experience. Parents are given both an orientation to the school system and a "Handbook for Parents of Bilingual Students," available in six languages. Providing parents with the full, accurate information they need in the initial interview allows them to make an informed decision, since they have the legal right to accept or reject this special program.

At the junior and senior high schools, students are tested in reading and mathematics—in English, if possible; otherwise, in their native language. The testing results and previous school records are important in determining how many hours of ESL the student needs and in selecting appropriate courses.

Grouping for Instruction. Since the percentage of limited-English students in Newton is relatively small—5 percent of the students in the district—the ESL program is offered in five of the fifteen elementary schools, two junior high schools, and two senior high schools. Clustering the students in fewer elementary schools allows the assignment of full-time ESL/bilingual teachers to these schools. The plan has benefits that outweigh the inconvenience of taking children out of their neighborhood school. Newton has found this grouping arrangement superior for both students and teachers and preferable to the earlier practice of having the limited-English students scattered throughout the city, with ESL teachers in the role of itinerants, traveling from school to school to give brief lessons.

Plan of Instruction. Limited-English students are scheduled for time in the special program according to their individual needs—that is, those who know no English are given the most hours, whereas those who are advanced but still need help are given the fewest hours (see table 5.2). This flexibility in scheduling takes into account the fact that not all children, when they arrive, are the same age or possess the same language or academic background. Not all students enter school in September and stay until June, either. This is a highly mobile population with a 30 to 40 percent student turnover rate annually. Students arrive and leave at any time during the school year, creating a demanding challenge for teachers. Regular monitoring of student progress allows students to leave the program during the year as they are ready, rather than on a rigid timetable.

Table 5.2   Newton Learning Plan
for Limited-English Students

Grade	Time per Day in ESL[1] Class	Time per Day in Regular Classes[2]
Kindergarten[3]	30–45 minutes	2 hours
1–3	1–2 hours	4–5 hours
4–6	1–3 hours	3–5 hours
7–12	1–3 hours	3–5 hours

[1]ESL—English as a Second Language
[2]Regular classes include ones in art, music, physical education, mathematics, science, and social studies, as students are ready.
[3]Preschool children are in school three hours daily.
SOURCE: Compiled from data provided by Newton Public Schools.

The time spent in the ESL classroom is a planned immersion in English for academic and real-life situations. English, in simplified form at first but gradually more sophisticated, is combined with subject matter in mathematics, science, and social studies that links directly with the main school curriculum. Teachers use drama, songs, objects, and audiovisual materials and involve the students actively in the lessons to help convey meaning and content. Reading and writing are taught in English, using reading techniques that are currently considered to be most effective with second-language learners.

One key to the success of this program in the elementary schools is close communication between ESL/bilingual teachers and mainstream classroom teachers. They confer regularly on the progress of each student, determining together when a student is ready to take part in additional regular classroom work, and they jointly plan how to coordinate their instruction. Thus, ESL teachers can reinforce the regular curriculum to some extent in their English teaching lessons, for example, in discussions of the water cycle, geometric shapes, natural resources of Venezuela, or stories about Pippi Longstocking. ESL teachers do not try to teach every element of the curriculum of each grade level—an impossibility for a teacher who has students from kindergarten to sixth grade—but they select as topics for their English classes certain items that are clearly connected to the curriculum the students will be involved in as they become fluent in English.

At the junior and senior high school levels, limited-English-speaking students may be enrolled during their first semester in as much as three hours of ESL daily, plus a few other courses such as math, physical education, and art or music. The focus of the ESL lessons is on basic social and academic language, orientation to the U.S. schools and culture, and connecting of vocabulary in English to concepts already learned in the native language. For instance, a Russian student who has studied chemistry does not need to be taught the subject again, but he or she does need the relevant terms in English to use this learning.

U.S. and world histories, geography, literature, and real-life skills—filling out applications for employment or college, taking different types of tests, understanding the rules of driving, writing a report—play a significant part in the English-language lessons. Each half year, ESL groups may be formed anew as new students arrive and other students reduce their time in the ESL classroom. This flexibility acknowledges the established fact that second-language learning happens at a different pace for each student and relates less to intelligence than to factors such as motivation, age, personality, family background, and culture.

Staff Qualifications and Staff Development. If we are in agreement about anything in education, it is the primary importance of well-trained teachers to the success of any program. In the Newton program and all of the others I am highlighting, ESL teachers are required to hold a bachelor's and/or master's degree in an appropriate area such as elementary education, high school English, mathematics, history, or science. They are also required to have completed some coursework in linguistics—applied, psycho- or sociolinguistics, phonetics, structure of the English language—together with language-teaching theory and methodology, educational testing, and the teaching of reading. Fluency in another language is an important and desirable asset, but this is not a requirement.

Newton provides generous support for staff development activities. Twice a month, workshops or meetings are held for all ESL/bilingual teachers and teacher aides for training, writing curriculum, and previewing new textbooks and computer software. Staff are encouraged to attend regional and national conferences and are given paid professional days to do so.

The ESL/bilingual department director supervises staff and writes staff evaluations, with school principals contributing to the evaluation. This allows the department head to make frequent visits to the classroom, working closely with new and experienced teachers in developing their skills. It is far more effective than having teachers evaluated by administrators who have only a limited knowledge of what constitutes good language teaching. A chart of the complete staffing of the department is provided in table 5.3.

Special Features.   Over the years a variety of initiatives have been undertaken in the regular kindergarten through twelfth-grade ESL program to enhance both the social adjustment of limited-English students and their equal access to educational and extracurricular activities.

1. Multicultural Preschool. Three- and four-year-old limited-English children are provided a half-day program for developing fluency in English and preparation for kinder-

Table 5.3   Newton Program Staffing

Grade Level(s)	Number of Students	Number of Staff	Full-Time Equivalents[1]
Multicultural Preschool	47	2 teachers	1.6
		3 aides	1.5
1–6	198	9 teachers	5.9
		4 aides	3.0
7–8	40	2 teachers	1.5
		2 aides	.8
9–12	55	3 teachers	1.6
		2 aides	1.5
Preschool–12	340	1 bilingual/special needs monitor	.5
		1 bilingual psychologist	.2
		1 program administrator	1.0
		1 secretary	1.0

[1] 1.0 = a full-time employee; for part-time employees, .2 = one full day per week. For example, one multicultural preschool teacher is 1.0 FTE, and one, part time, three days per week, is .6 FTE.
SOURCE: Compiled from data supplied by Newton Public Schools.

garten. Parents are enlisted as volunteers to help with special activities such as ethnic celebrations and field trips. Parent workshops are planned each year, with interpreters when needed, addressing such topics as creative play, toy making using household items, discipline, and other pertinent areas.

The Multicultural Preschool program, started in 1975, makes a valuable contribution to the early education of limited-English children. A three-year follow-up study completed in 1983 on children who had spent one or two years in the program revealed the following: (1) no confusion existed between home language and English, (2) the two languages remained distinctly separate and were used appropriately in different situations, (3) these children were better prepared for kindergarten than limited-English students without preschool experience, and (4) reading performance in first and second grade is better for these students than for limited-English students without preschool experience. One extra benefit of the program that is not a part of the formal evaluation is the early establishment of a strong home–school relationship, which is especially important for language minority families.

2. Summer ESL Program. S.P.A.C.E., the Summer Program for Academic and Creative Experience, for Newton Public Schools children includes ESL for limited-English students entering grades kindergarten through nine. This five-week program offers students two hours of English and two hours of art, music, science, literature, drama, dance, or computers, according to each student's choice. Students who might have very little practice with the language during the summer gain an additional month of English-language lessons, and new students just arriving from other countries get an early introduction to a new language and culture.

3. After-School High School Tutorial. Four afternoons a week from November to May, high school ESL students may be tutored by their classmates or by a teacher aide in any of their school subjects on such things as homework or writing of a research paper. Tutors are recruited from the high school service clubs and are paid out of work-study funds. Tutees are required to attend at least twice a week for a semester.

4. In-School High School Buddy Program. At another high school the ESL teacher recruits tutors who are willing to give help during free periods, twice a week. The teacher trains these tutors, and they are required to give a progress report twice a month. Tutors receive course credit for this work.

5. International Club. Both high schools have a club that

brings together limited-English students and their English-speaking classmates. Monthly social activities—ice skating, a Halloween Party, an apple picking—and trips to places of historical and cultural interest, such as Plymouth, Boston's North End, or the Boston Science Museum, are valuable both in themselves and for bringing language majority and minority students together.

6. Programs Supporting Native Languages. Support for these native languages and cultures is provided through an Italian Language and Culture After-School program for children in grades one through six, twice weekly; a Chinese Language and Culture minicourse for all third graders in the school through the Chinese Bilingual program, with three classes a week for one month; a Spanish Language and Culture program for first graders, three times a week for six weeks, in the school with the Spanish Bilingual program. These efforts meet parent requests and, in some cases, reflect the initiatives of Newton teachers.

7. Bilingual/Special Needs Monitor. Limited-English students sometimes have learning problems, emotional or psychological problems, or handicaps that require special education not related to their English-language learning. A specialist trained in both the bilingual and special needs fields monitors the testing of all students in this category and determines the most appropriate services needed. A current list of available services and specialists in the area—for example, the Urdu-speaking social worker or the Spanish-speaking psychologist—is maintained. In all cases, information is provided to parents in their own language.

8. Bilingual/Vocational/Chapter I Liaisons. Other special learning assistance is available to bilingual students. There is, however, the risk that students may be assigned to too many special services or not enough, so teachers have to remain vigilant to ensure that bilingual students be neither excessively programmed with overlapping services that frag-

ment the school day nor underserved through a lack of necessary assistance. Building partnerships with other programs has minimized these errors and allowed a number of good collaborations. One example is the Bilingual/Vocational Education Exploratory program, an after-school activity for limited-English students to investigate different vocational programs, to receive English lessons related to these training areas, and to visit some employment sites. Limited-English students are included in the federally funded Chapter I classes for students who are not working at grade level in reading and mathematics.

Newton's Mini-bilingual Effort.   All limited-English students in the Newton schools are involved in the ESL program just described, but about one-third of these children are also taught in their native language. Massachusetts law requires that native-language instruction be provided in a TBE program whenever there are twenty or more children of the same minority language in the school district.

Newton currently provides a bilingual teacher and some instruction by teacher aides in Spanish, Japanese, Hebrew, and Chinese. The bilingual teachers have credentials in bilingual education as well as ESL. They do part of the teaching in the native language when new, non-English-speaking students arrive, especially in the subject matter areas and for orientation to the school. They use English for instruction from the first day, and use of the native language is decreased rapidly during the first year, serving mainly to promote a comfortable school adjustment.

Bilingual staff also serve as minority models for the rest of the school community, and they promote respect for multicultural diversity as well as contribute their talents to various special activities. Their primary goal, however, is to help students develop high-level skills in English and become successful participants in regular classrooms once the students leave the program.

Newton's use of the native language for some children, while in compliance with state law, is really minimal and more symbolic than practical. Our proportions, however, may, in fact, be the right balance for promoting school achievement for language minority children: heavy doses of ESL, frequent contact between language minority and majority children, and a small amount of native-language use in the early months. Does this approach begin to address the issue of maintaining and developing the native language? It does not. Does it properly address the problem of acquiring the language of the majority society for equal educational opportunity and for employment? It does, thereby meeting the stated goal of all federal and state legislation for language minority limited-English children in the United States.

Results of the Newton Program

All of the students who participate in the Newton program become bilingual, with full ability to use English, their second language, effectively in the regular classroom after a few years. Student achievement is monitored on a continuing basis by staff and parents, and these specific accomplishments have been documented:

1. Students acquire a high level of English-language skills for both social and academic purposes within one to three years, according to test scores, grades, and statistics on program participation.
2. Student achievement in the regular classrooms and on district tests after leaving the program is commensurate with students' ages. Evidence for this is the fact that bilingual students are not retained in a grade or referred

for special education services at a higher rate than English-speaking students. No differences have been noted between students in ESL and students who received native-language help for one to three years—no better school attitude, behavior, or academic achievement for either group.

3. Students have a low truancy rate in all grades; a low dropout rate (less than 1 percent); and 60 percent of formerly limited-English high school graduates go on to some form of higher education.

4. Students generally have a positive self-image, are well integrated with their classmates, and participate in many extracurricular activities, such as clubs, sports, arts, and music, according to reports of teachers and parents.

5. Parents of bilingual students consistently express satisfaction with the achievement of their children and with the design of the program.

Newton has developed a model program that rejects a single-track approach, incorporating instead the strongest elements of the immersion, ESL, and bilingual approaches. Careful planning, the flexibility to adapt to changing demographics, and the continual search for innovative teaching strategies and materials are the keys that have resulted in a comprehensive array of effective services. Coherent purpose drives the multifaceted program, and this purpose is understood and agreed on by consensus of teaching staff, parents, and administrators. Most important, because it affects the students who are the beneficiaries of all this activity, is the flexibility of educational services provided. This is a student-centered program, responding to the needs of children from different languages, different cultures, and a very wide range of socioeconomic backgrounds and aspirations.

This model can be implemented in any community that has attitudes and commitment similar to those in Newton.

It is more cost-effective than the programs in three neighboring cities with similar populations—Waltham, Cambridge, and Brookline, Massachusetts. By comparing the number of students enrolled, the number of professional staff, and the annual budget figures for these four cities, it is clear that Newton's program has a lower per-pupil cost. If economy and successful outcomes for students are priority concerns, then Newton's example has relevance for many school districts.

Successful alternative programs in other parts of the United States that share some of the features of the Newton program have, in addition, other strong characteristics that state and national policy should take into account, as I argue in chapter 8.

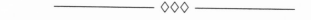

Alternatives Explored in Berkeley, California

Berkeley, the San Francisco Bay city of 103,000 people, home of the University of California at Berkeley and the free speech movement, and one-time counterculture mecca, has one of the most racially, linguistically, and economically varied populations in the United States, even by California standards. Like the state of California, the majority of its population consists of officially recognized minorities, and this is reflected in the school district's racial/ethnic makeup. The school census of fall 1987 reported that of a total of 8,200 students, 39 percent were white, 43 percent black, 7 percent hispanic, 9 percent Asian, and less than 1 percent either American Indian, Pacific Islander, or Filipino.[6] The Berkeley school system distinguished itself in the 1960s by instituting one of the first desegregation plans in the United States, and it made early efforts to give special help to language minority children. Berkeley's school system enjoys a reputation for encouraging creative teaching, valuing cultural diversity, and promoting educational equity through integration.

Berkeley began its special efforts for language minorities in the late 1960s with a bilingual program for Spanish-speakers in kindergarten through grade six. They later started a program for Chinese limited-English students in one elementary school, where the children currently are given about fifteen minutes a day in their native language and two classes a week for language and culture enrichment. This is exactly the way the parents want it.

Berkeley's population of limited-English children has grown in size and diversity and as of 1987 numbered 618 students—a majority from low-income families—representing thirty-six languages. (Such diversity of languages is, in fact, more the rule than the exception. Very few school districts cater to one or two language groups only.) The rich linguistic diversity is described more specifically in table 5.4.

Berkeley developed an ESL program, called the Individual Learning program, for limited-English students in kindergarten through grade twelve. This program strongly emphasizes English-language learning, does not use the native language, and resembles the Newton ESL program in its array of special features (after-school tutorials, peer tutoring, continual training for teachers and aides, and connections with other special services). The Spanish Bilingual program provides the typical reading, writing, and subject matter in Spanish through grade three and an increase of English instruction in grades four through six (actually providing seven years of native-language instruction). Two middle schools (grades six through eight) provide some continued instruction in Spanish. All limited-English high school students are given intensive ESL classes by trained teachers and are helped by teacher aides who speak various languages. These aides are recruited from the bilingual

Table 5.4   Limited-English Students in the Berkeley Unified
School District (March 1987)

Native (Home) Language	Number of Students	Native (Home) Language	Number of Students
Amharic	1	Laotian	31
Arabic	9	Laotung	3
Armenian	2	Malay	4
Cantonese	45	Mandarin	52
Czech	1	Mien	1
Danish	1	Norwegian	2
Farsi	15	Polish	2
Finnish	2	Portuguese	8
French	4	Punjabi	4
German	13	Samoan	3
Greek	2	Spanish	263
Gujarati	1	Tagalog	19
Hebrew	5	Thai	8
Hindi	1	Toishan	1
Italian	2	Tongan	4
Japanese	20	Trieu Chau	3
Khmer	8	Urdu	4
Korean	12	Vietnamese	62
		Total	618

SOURCE: LEP Student Enrollment Report, Berkeley Unified School District, March 1987.

community and from among University of California at Berkeley students to help in the science, mathematics, history, and English literature classes.

Selecting Effective Teaching Techniques

In 1984 a formal review committee of parents, teachers, and administrators studied the two Berkeley programs and concluded that there was an unacceptable dropout rate among hispanic middle and high school students. Too many hispanic bilingual students were reaching the middle and high school level without enough English to make adequate progress and were falling behind, in spite of several years in the elementary school bilingual program. The committee recommended that English instruction be started earlier and given more time in the elementary schools. This change was made in one school, where the amount of Spanish was reduced to 20 percent of the school day; in the other it remained 40 to 50 percent of the school day.

In June 1987 the association of bilingual parents in both Berkeley programs clashed head-on in a debate over the amount of native-language use. A group of hispanic parents asked for the extension of native-language instruction beyond grade six and for the appointment of a full-time bilingual department head; parents of Asian students in the ESL program spoke against the extension of native-language use and in favor of spending additional funds on more teachers, not on increasing the administration of the program. The latter prevailed. Hispanic parents were reassured, however, that the existing native-language program in the elementary grades would be continued.

Assessing Berkeley's Success

Professor Christine Rossell of Boston University recently completed a detailed report on the school achievement of Berkeley's language minority students by analyzing test scores over a three-year period (1986 to 1988) in which she compared students in the ESL program to those in the Spanish Bilingual program.[7] Her results, which can be summarized as follows, clearly show no superior achievement for the students taught in the native language:

- There was no significant difference between Spanish Bilingual program students and ESL program students on a measure of progress in oral English skills from fall 1986 to fall 1987.

- Students tested in reading, language, and math using the Comprehensive Test of Basic Skills (CTBS), a standardized test widely used across the country, showed a comparable rate of progress from spring 1986 to spring 1987, regardless of the program they were in.
- The ESL students showed a significantly greater improvement in CTBS scores from spring 1987 to spring 1988 than did the Spanish Bilingual students.
- Students in both programs were found to be making good progress in terms of grades in regular classroom subjects, which were analyzed up to two years after they stopped receiving special help.
- Using the state California Assessment for Progress tests to compare the academic achievement of Berkeley students with that of students in the Fremont and San Jose districts, which the California State Department of Education characterizes as having "exemplary" bilingual programs, Berkeley limited-English students scored as high as both Fremont and San Jose students in reading and significantly higher than the others in math.

Berkeley has the problems common to other urban districts, but because the personnel are seriously committed to doing a good job for their language minority children, the Berkeley results have been good.

I spent a week in Berkeley observing classes and talking with students, teachers, and administrators. I saw a good deal of highly productive teaching and observed language minority children, interested and attentive to their lessons. The integration of linguistically, ethnically, and racially different students was better than in any other school district I have seen. Berkeley continues to provide two distinctly different programs that directly respond to the wishes of the parents. The attitudes of Berkeley parents closely parallel the results in the report on the Parent Preference Study of Asian and latino parents described earlier in this chapter (pp. 123–24). It is central to Berkeley's success that the school district works cooperatively with parents and gives their wide range of views careful consideration in program planning.

Changes and Controversies in Fairfax, Virginia

The Fairfax County School District, just outside Washington, D.C., is one of the ten largest in the United States, with a total of 133,000 students, 4,200 of whom are limited-English from seventy-five different language backgrounds. The largest language groups are Korean, Spanish, and Vietnamese, representing a total of 2,100 students. Arabic, Chinese, Farsi, and Japanese represent 1,500 students; and sixty-eight other languages are spoken by the remaining 600 students.[8] The population of the county is characterized by a range of income levels and a mixture of ethnic groups. Among the language minority students, 65 percent are from low-income families who qualify for some form of public assistance. The Fairfax ESL program is featured here because it shows that an alternative approach can also work successfully in a large school system with thousands of limited-English students.

Since 1975 Fairfax has had the largest, most visible and controversial ESL program in the country. It achieved notoriety in the education field in 1980 when the U.S. Office of Civil Rights, after a five-year investigation, granted official approval to Fairfax to continue its ESL program. The Office of Civil Rights judged that the Fairfax program was meeting the needs of its students, even though it was not teaching in the native languages—a landmark decision. The declaration that Fairfax was not violating the civil rights of its language minority students rested on the documented evidence that (1) the students were learning both English and subject matter and were performing at grade level in the regular classroom after leaving the ESL program, and that (2) the school district was providing a trained professional staff, a well-developed curriculum, and a high level of funding for the program.

Development of the Fairfax Program

The Fairfax program began in 1969 as a TBE program using native-language teaching in Spanish and Korean. The decision to change to ESL only rested on two reasons, both pragmatic and practical: (1) children in these programs did not seem to be making adequate progress in learning English, and (2) new groups were arriving with such a variety of languages that native-speaking teachers could not easily be found.

Dr. Esther Eisenhower, who developed and still directs the Fairfax program, has documented the fact that 80 percent of the limited-English children have achieved proficiency in English within two years.[9] Bilingual education advocates consistently discount the success of the Fairfax program, claiming that its students are all from upper-middle-class families or are the children of diplomats. This is simply not true. Two-thirds of the Fairfax limited-English students qualify for free or reduced school lunch, an indicator of the low income of their families. What *is* true is that Fairfax allocates a high level of funding for educating limited-English children—up to $1,500 to $3,000 per child above the regular cost of education, as do Berkeley and Newton. This kind of funding, coupled with strong leadership of the program and clearly focused goals, has allowed for the recruitment and training of teachers, the writing of curriculum, and the regular acquisition of textbooks and materials that reflect new ideas in language teaching. Furthermore, it has provided for a range of support services, from summer school and ESL/vocational collaboration to native-language interpreters and translators for home–school communication.

Evaluating the Success of the Fairfax Program

How well students achieve in school after being in a special program is surely an important measure of the program's success. A study prepared by the Fairfax Office of Research and Evaluation answers the question, How are former ESL students performing on standardized tests of reading and the major school subjects two, three, or four years after they have left the program and are working in a regular classroom without special help? The data collected on 150 students in grades four, six, and eight who had left the program between 1980 and 1983 indicate that these students were scoring above the national average on standardized tests of reading, math, language arts, social studies, and science.[10] For the formerly limited-English students to score above the national average on tests designed for English-speaking students is a very good result indeed. One caution: the Fairfax results are reported as indicators of success for these particular students, not necessarily as a scientific evaluation on which to draw general conclusions.

Another important indicator of student achievement is the reported results of the State of Virginia Graduation Competency Test that is given to all high school students. In 1985, 94 percent of Fairfax's former ESL students passed both the reading and math tests given in the tenth grade, compared to a 98 percent passing rate for other students in the Fairfax high schools.[11] These evaluations portray a program that is working well for its students.

The Fairfax County ESL program is highlighted not only for the success of its students but because its example has done much to expand the public policy debate on bilingual education. Dr. Eisenhower has lectured widely at professional conferences and testified before state and federal committees. Her message has been very consistent. She is not concerned with criticizing bilingual programs but with promoting the right of each school district to choose options that may or may not use the native language. She readily explains why the Fairfax program is successful and how it works. She warns, however, that "there is no way in the world that this country will have the teacher power to deliver a bilingual education for an increasingly diverse population—linguistically and culturally."[12] Fairfax County, as a result, has decided to teach all children—no matter what their background—in English.

Benefits of Alternative Programs

I have devoted special attention to Newton, Berkeley, and Fairfax because I see conclusive evidence in the workings of these programs that successful alternatives to traditional bilingual education exist. These are certainly not the only places where new approaches are being tried, but they represent well-organized examples in different settings.

To illustrate a broader range of experimental efforts being made in various parts of the country, I turn to selected programs included in a project I directed in 1987 for the National Advisory Council on Bilingual Education, a group appointed by the secretary of education.[13] This council, of which I was a member from 1985 to 1988, is responsible for collecting data on the state of bilingual education in the nation and submitting this information in an annual report to Congress. Our subcommittee visited schools in California, Massachusetts, New Jersey, Texas, and the District of Columbia. We observed classes, interviewed teachers and administrators, and collected general information to use in describing a representative sample of programs and to document the areas of success and the areas of need as perceived by the practitioners themselves—the teachers and administrators. The school visit report, along with recommendations for legislation and funding, became a part of the annual report to Congress submitted to the U.S. House of Representatives and the Senate in March 1987.

The information collected showed these characteristics to be common to the eight schools visited:

- All had adequate facilities, that is, classroom space, textbooks, and other teaching materials—resources that were lacking in the early days of bilingual education.
- All but one school had a large number of different language groups to serve (from seven to twenty-four languages), in addition to a large group of Spanish-speakers.
- All the schools had an experienced, qualified teaching staff.
- Teachers generally had high expectations for their students' ability to acquire English and to succeed in mastering school subjects.
- Administrative support was given for innovative programs, and funding was available for teacher training and for the writing of new curriculum.
- Communication between bilingual parents and the school was regular, and parents understood and supported the school's goals for their children.

The features just described would be considered beneficial in any school.

———————— ◇◇◇ ————————

Structured Immersion and Two-Way Programs

Two new types of programs that we discovered to be a growing phenomenon in this country have major relevance for the education of language minority children: (1) the straight English Immersion programs, sometimes referred to as Structured Immersion, and (2) the Two-Way, or Dual Language, programs, which offer the opportunity for two groups to learn each other's language.

Structured Immersion

Although still relatively rare in the United States, immersion programs similar to the early immersion efforts in Canada described in chapter 4 are beginning to appear. The appeal of this program—and a presumed advantage— is that students begin to *think* in English fairly quickly. There is a straightforward attempt here to immerse the students in English for maximum success in that language and in school subjects. No attempt is made to teach in the native language, and that is the major difference between the American Structured Immersion idea and the Canadian French/English programs. Here are the first few reports on such programs.

Exemplary Programs. The best-researched and longest-lasting immersion programs for language minority students in the United States are two, one in Texas, the other in California. The Uvalde, Texas, School District has provided a Structured Immersion program for twenty years for a population of Spanish-speaking students from low-income families. San Diego, California, began a similar program for low-income Asian students at about the same time. In both communities, students tested in English reading, writing, and math after three years of immersion were scoring at grade level, an unusual accomplishment for language minority students. Follow-up studies to see whether the three-year program had any enduring effects showed that students tested three years later (in grade six) were still maintaining good grades. Later analysis of the high school data on these students showed that immersion students were more likely to complete a high school diploma, they were less likely to have repeated any grade, and they showed better attendance in the ninth grade.

In Paramount, California, we found an elementary school of 1,000 students, half of whom were limited-English. After fifteen years of offering a Spanish Bilingual program, the school district began an English Immersion program three years ago for 160 students in kindergarten through third grade. This new program is being monitored in a national survey of Early Immersion programs, and reports so far indicate the following:[14]

- These students show a far higher rate of English-language learning than the children in the Spanish Bilingual program.
- Student achievement on state tests in the subject areas is above the state average.
- A higher level of social integration exists between these students and their English-speaking peers than that observed with students in the Spanish Bilingual program.

As of October 1986, the Elizabeth, New Jersey, Public Schools enrolled 1,893 limited-English students, 1,426 of whom were Spanish-speakers, with the rest speaking a dozen different languages.[15] The Structured Immersion Strategies Project started in 1986 as an experiment in total early immersion in English for Spanish-speaking students in three elementary schools. It is unusual not only that this type of program has been welcomed in a hispanic community but that the Puerto Rican community has been actively involved in its development. The city has had a variety of bilingual programs for fifteen years. A full study of student achievement now under way, comparing project participants to students in the regular bilingual program, will provide useful data on the relative effectiveness of the two programs in the same school system and with students from the same linguistic, cultural, and economic background. These results will not be available until 1990, and so far we know only that teaching staff, students, and parents are expressing equally strong approval.

The Potential for Structured Immersion Programs. The examples of straight English Immersion programs just described are representative of a small number of such efforts across the country. The ability to start such programs has been severely restricted either by state laws requiring native-language teaching or by the pressure of bilingual education advocates against the development of English Immersion teaching, which they call "submersion"—the replacement of the native language by English. However, a major study just being completed by the U.S. Department of Education will provide the first published results in this country of a carefully controlled comparison of English Immersion, Transitional Bilingual Education, and Maintenance Bilingual programs. Results of the entire three-year study will tell us with convincing authority how well children learn English and succeed in schoolwork through the different approaches. Concerned policymakers and citizens will welcome reliable evidence of this type because it has been so seriously lacking in bilingual education research.

Two-Way Programs

A radically different, but also promising, recent development in language education is the Two-Way, or Dual Immersion, program in which two groups of native speakers learn each other's language. It is particularly appealing because it not only enhances the prestige of the minority language but also offers a rich opportunity for expanding genuine bilingualism to the majority population. Bilingual programs are generally perceived as compensatory or remedial efforts directed at the speaker of Spanish or whatever other language is considered deficient by the majority speakers in the society. By offering English-speakers the chance to learn another language well at an early age in the same classroom setting with native speakers of that language, the project avoids stigmatizing one group as deficient but instead promises mutual learning, enrichment, and respect. These programs are also considered to be the best possible vehicles for integration of language minority students, since these students are grouped with English-speakers for natural and equal exchange of skills.

Exemplary Two-Way Programs.   Three schools we visited are providing some variation of this type of program, and they are typical of a growing trend in the field of language teaching.

The Oyster School, Washington, D.C., has the best known and one of the oldest Dual Immersion programs in the United States. Its goal is the development of literacy and fluency in two languages, and the school has a fifteen-year record of successful results. Students are totally immersed in the unfamiliar second language from kindergarten through grade two, learning to speak, read, write, and do all schoolwork in that language. Starting in grade three they begin to read in their home language, and all their subjects are then taught in either Spanish or English through grade six.

Oyster School is a model school in the Washington inner-city school system. Students are randomly selected from applicants in the city, not chosen by high scores on an entrance test. The Oyster School has documented success in producing high-quality bilingualism. It has also demonstrated the academic value of this program: students' average reading scores in the third and sixth grades are higher than students' in other city schools and two years above the national average.

Parent support for the bilingual school is exceptional, with parents from different social backgrounds contributing time, skills, and funds to meet student needs. Parent volunteers, for example, walk students home from school, and last year they raised funds to hire an extra art teacher.

Two other schools with Two-Way programs employ variations on the Oyster School model that are of shorter duration but also report student success. The Fallbrook Street Elementary School in Fallbrook, California, has, since 1982, enrolled 300 students in a Spanish/English Dual Immersion program, with the goal of helping students achieve academic success in their first language while learning English or Spanish as a second language. For the past three years the school has reported especially good results: as a group, English-speaking participants are scoring significantly higher in all subject areas than their classmates in English-only classrooms; Spanish-speaking participants are ready for regular classroom work in English by third grade and continue to do well academically in subsequent grades.[16]

A notable Late Immersion program was started six years ago in the Sullivan Middle School, Holyoke, Massachusetts, for 350 students in grades four through six. This program uses a team-teaching approach, with one Spanish- and one English-speaking teacher in each classroom using both languages equally for instruction. In this program students are taught only in their native language until the fourth grade, when they are immersed in the second language. Teachers rate this approach as successful in developing a limited degree of fluency in speaking, reading, and writing skills in two languages, and for both groups it promotes an understanding of each other's cultures.

The Potential for Two-Way Programs.   Two-Way programs are the best opportunity for families that are seriously committed to genuine bilingualism for their children. Such programs are beginning to show a modest degree of success for students of different ability levels—not just the brightest children—and they do not cost any more than the average single-language classes to maintain, although they do require teachers with native-language fluency in the non-English language. There is a strong likelihood that Two-Way programs can strengthen foreign language studies in the United States by linking the development of second-language skills in the early years of schooling to courses in the high schools where students can continue to develop and maintain their bilingualism.

In 1987 the Center for Language Education and Research at UCLA published a Directory of Two-Way Bilingual Immersion Programs, which describes thirty programs in the United States similar to those in the three schools I have reviewed. There are, no doubt, more by now, but the total number of students involved nationwide is not large.

Two-Way instruction is a promising idea that will inevitably be limited to a small percentage of language minority children because it depends on the voluntary participation of English-speaking families to provide half the students. It is not surprising that these programs have to be sold to an American population that is largely indifferent to serious foreign language study. Certainly, there will always be a small, adventurous group of English-speaking parents who see Two-Way programs as a wonderful opportunity, but it will probably not be a sufficient number to create enough places for even 10 percent of the language minority children in the country. We should also not assume that all language minority families want their children in these programs, either.

There are two other problems that must be realistically faced if the growth of Two-Way programs is to be encouraged. Recruiting enough competent teachers who also are native, or even near-native, speakers of another language is difficult, as is the case in recruiting competent teachers for bilingual programs. The other difficulty is the resistance of regular classroom teachers to what they see as a radically different and potentially threatening program that could cause loss of jobs for monolingual teachers. This opposition can be formidable. I personally observed the planning for a Spanish Immersion program effectively halted because of teacher objections. I know that others who have worked on the creation of Two-Way programs have encountered similar attitudes. Time, patience, and persistence, however, can sometimes prevail over these predictably resistant attitudes.

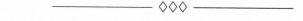

The Importance of Considering Alternatives

It is clear to me after extensive investigation that there are outstanding examples of energetic change and improvement in various parts of the country. I have described real programs serving real students effectively, not theoretical models. These alternatives to the TBE concept are working well and can be duplicated elsewhere. Their existence needs to be known by the general public—citizens, voters, parents, teachers, educational planners, and anyone else interested in the goals of social justice and good education.

My review, selective as it is, represents some of the most enlightened and heartening current trends in the education of language minority children. Public education in the United States has not done nearly enough to embrace and then boost these children to levels of achievement where they can be fully sharing and productive citizens. But the problem of equal access is not with the schools alone. It is surely related to language skills, but it also derives from chronic parental unemployment, poverty, forced mobility, the lack of education of parents for whom schooling is a low priority, and insufficient health care. We need, therefore, to find combinations of educational and legislative measures that help the schools overcome the problems children bring to the classroom with them and to help liberate these children from the permanent underclass.

The language issue, as it intersects with the class issue, inevitably leads us to the most basic considerations of all: what kind of nation we are and wish to be. The education given to our language minority children bears on the most fundamental aspects of our society: Are we expanding or reversing equal access in schooling and jobs? Are we promoting the assimilation of different ethnic and language groups on the one hand or the maintenance of linguistic and cultural pluralism on the other? Are we encouraging racial desegregation while allowing resegregation by language? Are we paying more heed to the demands of the group than to the rights of individuals in the matter of ethnic identification and enforced group loyalty, both elements of intergenerational tensions in immigrant families? Having examined bilingual education and the attempts in the United States and other countries to develop liberating alternatives, we look now, at the wider issues of language and ethnicity as they bear on the overarching matter of nationhood for a multicultural democracy.

6
Beyond Bilingual Education: Language Policy, Cultural Pluralism, and Nationhood

◇◇◇

The renewal of ethnic sensitivity in the 1970s, following on the heels of the civil rights movement of the 1960s, became a celebration of tolerance, an exaltation of all ethnic groups, and a declaration that the "melting pot" had never been. From the 1960s to the 1980s sociologists viewed the melting pot concept—various generations of immigrants merging to form an essentially "American" national character with a core of common values—as a myth, and a repugnant one at that. Various metaphors emerged—a stew; a salad; a mixture with firm, identifiable parts; a nation of nations. In short, the ethnic revival opened up the question of the nature of our nationhood and with it the role of languages in promoting national cohesion or fragmentation.

Assimilation became a dirty word, and the search for one's roots represented a widespread yearning, not only for tribal villages in West Africa but for Jewish shtetlach, Armenian villages in Russia, or Sicilian towns on the slopes of Mount Etna. The slogan "Black is beautiful" was followed by "Kiss me, I'm Italian" and "I'm Polish and proud." The ethnic revival prompted an intensified focus on race, ethnicity, gender, and class in American academic circles, a focus that now permeates all the disciplines in the liberal arts. Demands for Afro-American Studies and Women's Studies resulted in the establishment of those academic departments

159

in many universities, where they are now firmly in place. In different parts of the country, departments of Caribbean Studies, Asian Studies, Judaic Studies, Swedish Studies, and Chicano Studies were established according to the particular ethnic sensitivities of the region.

The Rhetoric of Rights

Bilingual education, for its part, soon appended the word *bicultural* to its program title. The goals of a bilingual/bicultural education program became to help students learn English while being taught in their native language *and* to help students develop pride in their language and culture. The bicultural part of this education program was not only to distinguish between the stereotypical majority culture of white, middle-class America (itself a myth) and the language, customs, and values that the language minority child brings to school but also to promote respect for the culture of the minority child. From the laudable impulse to teach respect for all cultures, languages, and ethnic backgrounds came the new rhetoric of rights. The poster circulated by the National Association of Bilingual Education a few years ago succinctly phrased the demand: "I have a right to my language and my culture." Every child and family, in fact, has this right under the U.S. Constitution; I know of no law that abridges it. Nevertheless, the strong surge of ethnicity brought with it a central question that must be addressed: Is the maintenance of family cultures to be a mandated responsibility of the public schools?

Stephen Arons, a legal studies professor at the University of Massachusetts whose special area of interest is the right of families to teach their children at home, has joined the bicultural rights debate by characterizing home teaching as a First Amendment right. Arons asks whether limited-English students should have to sacrifice their cultural heritage as the price of a public education. He contends that "every family has the constitutional right—without government interference—to inculcate its values in its children so long as those values do not themselves contravene the Constitution."[1] Arons presents an extremely dire picture of the consequences of not supporting the home language and the transmission of the family's cultural values in the schools: the child's self-worth will suffer; the child will be subjected to a humiliation "as deep as any religious persecution, any racism, or any censorship of family beliefs."[2] He calls not only for First Amendment protection for the preservation of language minority family values but an additional First Amendment obligation *that these values must indeed be taught in the schools.* He even contends that we do not have the right to use public schooling to impose an official language, as we do not have the right to try to impose an official religion. His is the most extreme position I have encountered so far in the arena of cultural maintenance, and as such it may serve as a boundary point in the discussion of educational goals and language policies in our pluralist polity. There are, to be sure, some very basic problems with Arons's reasoning and with his absolutist approach. First, English is not an official language, and educators have not been promoting it as such. However, denying children the opportunity to learn the language of the majority society through the public schools would be a gross denial of their civil rights.

In South Africa, we should note, the imposition of mother-tongue instruction, which Arons demands for American children, is used as a way of maintaining the isolation of black South Africans and denying them economic opportunity. The two official languages of the country are English and Afrikaans. The Bantu languages are not used in business, government, or commerce, but the use of Bantu is mandated as the medium of instruction in the primary schools for African children. Many children do not go beyond that point in their schooling. A South African critic of apartheid writes incisively that

Africans feel that mother-tongue instruction has the effect of cramping them intellectually within the narrow bounds of tribal society and diminishing the opportunity of intercommunication between the African groups themselves and the larger world. . . . They need to have access to technological skills, to world literature and, particularly those living in the towns, must have mastery of one of the official languages, preferably English.[3]

Parents in our country who would choose, for whatever reasons, to keep their children away from the majority language may seek some form of alternative private schooling or provide home schooling. That is a matter of family choice that in most places is not denied by public policy.

Rights versus Responsibilities in Public Education

One must question any proposal that the mission, indeed, the responsibility, of the public schools is to teach the values of any one group of families. Such an objective would be counter to the fundamental nature of American education, which Horace Mann called "the great equalizer," as it provides the less privileged members of society with opportunities for social and economic advancement. John Dewey described "the office of the school environment" as the obligation "to see to it that each individual gets an opportunity to escape from the limitations of the social group in which he was born, and to come into living contact with a broader environment."[4]

Surely, one of the noblest goals of education in our plur-alistic society is to open the minds of children to the vari-ety of thoughts and values of the many groups that make up our country, not to teach each group, even if that were possible, only about its own family culture. Furthermore, we know better than to believe, in this rapidly changing, inter-dependent world, that any community's culture remains static. Indeed, in the best of circumstances, what is taught in the classroom may no longer be a reflection of the real-ity that families are actually living. This natural evolution is especially true of groups that have moved from agrarian life to the industrial centers, from hot to cold climates, or from extended, stable family structures to small, dispersed units struggling to adapt.

Finally, one must ask, How is such linguistic and cultural exclusivity compatible with our goal of bringing together minority and majority students in our schools to fulfill the dream some day of an integrated society? How does segre-gation by language and ethnic culture empower the pow-erless and give voice to the voiceless? Antonio Gramsci, the twentieth-century Italian philosopher and cultural critic, analyzed the linguistic diversity of the Italian nation within the framework of class division and political control. He outlined the logical consequences of linguistic provin-cialism:

If it is true that every language contains the elements of a con-ception of the world and of a culture, it could also be true that from anyone's language one can assess the greater and lesser complexity of his conception of the world. Someone who only speaks dialect, *or understands the standard language incompletely,* [author's emphasis] necessarily has an intuition of the world which is more or less limited and provincial, which is fossil-ized and anachronistic in relation to the major currents of thought which dominate world history.[5]

Gramsci elsewhere defended the maintenance of the Italian dialects within the family, but he believed that "without the mastery of the common standard version of the national language, one is inevitably destined to function only at the periphery of national life, and, especially, outside the national and political mainstream."[6] Let me add a pertinent note. This morning, as I write, a summons arrived in the mail for my twenty-two-year-old son to serve on jury duty. Among the conditions that exempt people from jury service are mental or physical incapacity, age (over seventy or under eighteen), felony conviction, or the inability to speak or understand the English language—a telling cluster of handicaps! To be excluded from this important public responsibility, this basic democratic right to sit in judgment of one's peers, seems a fundamental loss to me. Unable to communicate adequately in the language of the society, one is then unable to participate equally and at first hand, without intermediaries, in the communal life of a free society.

Arons's ideas are only the most extreme example of one side of the public dialogue on the role of bilingual/bicultural education in our multilingual, multicultural society. The unresolved issues in public education include integration versus segregation of bilingual students and a redefinition of the responsibilities of families versus the responsibilities of public institutions in the maintenance of native languages and cultures. The unresolved societal issues include the rights of children to cultural freedom versus the rights of families and communities to ethnic solidarity; open access by all citizens to all institutions versus ethnic cohesiveness of neighborhoods, communities, and schools; the role of language in preserving cultural or ethnic group identity; and the tension between the desire of some groups to maintain their culture and the desire for inclusion in the mainstream for economic advancement. These many issues and conflicting claims are summarized by two basic ques-

tions: (1) How can the nation become a more equitable society, providing equal access to opportunities through integration if we harden ethnic boundaries? (2) How, at the
same time, can we promote ethnic mobility and interaction
without, for some, harmfully depleting ethnic identity?

──────────── ◇◇◇ ────────────

Ethnicity and Cultural Pluralism

The issues are emotion-packed. When in 1974 the citizens
of South Boston did not want to have their children assigned to schools in other parts of the city, fearing the dis-
ruption and dissolution of their close-knit ethnic neighborhood, they were condemned as racists, and school
desegregation was imposed by court order. After a decade
of strife in Boston, the community eventually accepted the
loss of neighborhood schools as irreversible. The South
Boston Irish families in particular, resisting the entry of
black students into their neighborhood schools in the 1970s,
are the descendants of an ethnic group that strove mightily
themselves to enter the neighborhoods and the employment ranks once reserved only for whites of English Protestant heritage.

Stephen Steinberg, in his recent study of race, ethnicity,
and class in America, cited earlier in this chapter, observed
that ethnic groups have class reasons for tearing down ethnic barriers ahead of them and class reasons for raising ethnic barriers behind them. It has been argued, convincingly,
that the exclusion of Jews from prestigious clubs whose
membership is mainly white and Protestant is more than
just a matter of ethnic preference; these clubs are places
where business is routinely conducted in a social setting.
But the Jewish residents of Forest Hills, New York, opposed
the construction of a low-rent housing project in their com-

munity in 1971 on the grounds that it would destroy the religious life and culture of the community, presumably by admitting poor, Christian whites and blacks. A similar case occurred in California in that same year when the Chinese community in San Francisco opposed school desegregation on the ground that moving the students out of their neighborhoods would destroy the cultural and educational life of the Chinese community. The resulting legal case was turned down for review by the Supreme Court. Justice William O. Douglas referred to a 1875 Supreme Court decision that prohibited the state of California from denying a license to run a laundry to someone just because he was Chinese. The justice was saying, in effect, that the Chinese could not have it both ways. The same laws that protect them from discrimination on the basis of race or national origin also keep them from discriminating against others.[7]

Desegregation and affirmative action suits in the past twenty years have had a noticeable effect on housing, employment, clubs, schools, and other institutions that were formerly restricted to a single racial, ethnic, or gender group. It is puzzling to me that the same people who are most vocally supportive of the good liberal causes of integration and civil rights are generally the public speakers for cultural pluralism as well. These are two quite opposed social goals.

Reassessing Shifts in Language and Culture

The ethnic revival of the 1970s and the clamor for promoting cultural pluralism raise several questions rarely asked about shifts in language and culture in multicultural societies such as the United States and Canada.

- Do transplanted ethnic groups characteristically maintain their native language longer than two or three generations?
- Can a group's cultural identity be maintained without keeping the language?
- Is it actually possible, for reasons of ethnic pride and community cohesion, to revive or revitalize a language that is dying out?
- How do certain communities successfully maintain their languages by voluntary activities?
- Need the shift to English for upward mobility necessarily be destructive?

These considerations have a direct bearing on how we employ bilingual/bicultural education to be a vehicle for not only English-language learning, as prescribed by law, but for the support of native languages and cultures. The concern extends far beyond the matter of Spanish-language—or, specifically, Puerto Rican and Mexican-American—cultures to a vast number of groups that make up our multilingual, multicultural nation. Bilingualism, as I have noted, is almost always cast in polemics in terms of Spanish/English, so that several hundred thousand children speaking over 100 other languages remain virtually unnoticed. Moreover, it is not just a case of a single Spanish culture that is involved but many ethnic groups using the Spanish language who themselves have an astonishing range of religious beliefs, customs, values, and national origins.

The Process of Language Shifting

Sociologists make an important distinction between the loss of native language by immigrant groups that have voluntarily left their country of origin, seeking economic advantage, religious freedom, or escape from persecution, and people who are annexed as a total colony, with all their values, beliefs, and practices in place, as in the case of Puerto Rico and the Philippines. In these latter instances, where a new language is imposed by the government on a cohesive group, the native language will shift very slowly, if at all. In Puerto Rico the dominant language is still solidly Spanish, even after ninety years of affiliation with the mainland United States and a variety of different language policies that sometimes mandated the teaching of schoolchildren in English, sometimes in Spanish, and sometimes in both languages. Therefore, both the back-and-forth migration between Puerto Rico and the mainland and the steady influx of immigrants from Mexico, Central and South America, and the Caribbean insure that the Spanish language is not in danger of being lost in the continental United States.

In the United States, Canada, and Australia—the three largest immigrant multilingual countries—it has proven difficult to maintain group bilingualism for longer than two or three generations, the exception being French/English in Quebec, as I have noted. The many writers in this field generally agree that language minority groups start by becoming bilingual and eventually, by both practical necessity and benefit, shift to the majority language of the country. In some notable cases it has taken hundreds of years, as in the shift from Gaelic to English in Ireland.

Usually, though, the shift to the majority language happens in just three generations. As so many know firsthand, the first generation of immigrants speak only the native language and begin to learn the new language of the majority; the second generation of the family becomes bilingual, with the parents speaking the native language to the grandparents and to each other, and the new language to their children; and the third generation become speakers of the majority language, with some understanding of the language of their ethnic group but not enough to use it with

their own children. In fact, there is interesting new conjecture, quite informal at present, that the language shift begins with the women of the family, who, being in a subor-
dinate position, are sensitive to issues of power. As a result,
they choose the language in which to bring up their children. I have not found specific studies supporting the thesis, but my own parents bore out this notion. My mother
was eager to learn English, and she used both English and
our native language with us children as we were growing
up. My father strongly resisted learning or using the new
language, stretching the process out to a forty-year, imper-
fectly completed affair.

Religious Practices and Minority Languages. The forces
that support the continued vitality and use of a minority
language are (1) the replenishment of the community by a
steady influx of new speakers of the language, say Puerto
Ricans arriving on the mainland or legal and illegal immigrants from Spanish-speaking countries; (2) religious
boundaries; and (3) back migration, that is, going back to
the place of origin for a period of time and then returning
to the United States.

The influence of religious boundaries can be quite
strong. Paulston, for example, asserts that in the Greek
community in Pittsburgh the Greek language shifts to English over a four-generation span, compared to the three-
generation language shift common in the Italian-speaking
community. She attributes the slower shift in the Greek
community to church-sponsored schools teaching modern
Greek, a standard language of community prestige; strong
pressure to marry within the church and ethnic group; and
the arranged marriages to partners brought directly from
Greece. The Italian community in Pittsburgh, in contrast,
uses a nonstandard, nonwritten dialect of low prestige; does
not receive language support in the Roman Catholic

churches, which now have as many Irish as Italian priests; and does not apply as much pressure for marriage within the ethnic group.[8]

The U.S. Roman Catholic church set up national churches around the turn of the century to preserve the individual cultural religious expressions of new immigrants, staffing them with priests who spoke the language and frequently came from the same country as the immigrants. The Ukrainian churches in Philadelphia, French-Canadian churches in Holyoke, Massachusetts, and Italian churches in Newark flourished when their parishioners came from the same large, homogeneous community. Since the 1960s, however, there has been a movement to "denationalize" the Catholic churches. Today the churches have moved to a broader base to celebrate the various ethnic groups that make up their congregations, and they are reducing the close linguistic ties to any one community. The conflict over maintaining the national character of a Polish church in Bridgeport, Connecticut, reached the proportions of civil disobedience when parishioners demonstrated against the removal of their native Polish-speaking priests. People on both sides of the quarrel have poignantly expressed their views. A lifetime member of the church who feels comfortable with the new ways said in a *New York Times* interview, "I am American first and Polish second. I feel that now that they are here in America, they should go along with our traditions. Otherwise they have every right to go back to Poland." A more recent Polish immigrant who supports the national church disagreed: "We're all going to get Americanized; we can't fight that. Just for now we want the sentimental part. Let us have it, if just for the moment."[9] In such sentiments as these, we see the bearing that traditional religious affiliations have on the reinforcement or diminishment of minority languages.

———————— ◇◇◇ ————————

Maintenance of Cultural Identity

On the question of whether cultural identity or ethnic distinctiveness can be maintained after loss of the native language, there is disagreement. Opinions range from one extreme—the view that the maintenance of culture is impossible without the maintenance of its language and that therefore the presence of a minority language in the schools is essential—to the more generally accepted view that culture does not rely essentially on language for its continued vitality. Groups change, and although they may give up speaking Yiddish or Norwegian or Portuguese, they do not give up all their values, beliefs, or customs. In the United States this is true of native Americans as well as ethnic groups that arrived in the past hundred years. Immigrant and refugee groups seek economic and social assimilation but resist deep-seated cultural assimilation.

In 1953, David Reisman used the term *ethnicity* to refer to group membership, with shared customs and values, and common biological roots, or ancestors. Now, however, *ethnicity* refers to a self-selected designation, a conscious decision to *be* ethnic. Ethnicity, in this view, refers to an individual's choice to be closely related to an ethnic group; it is not inevitable and should not be imposed from the outside. As a specific instance, at Oberlin College last spring I talked with a student of Japanese-American background (American Caucasian mother, Japanese father). The student, Kimi, said she was not comfortable with the pressure from the Asian students' organization to join their activities on campus. Kimi said she does not want to define herself in terms of, or confine her public persona to, a one-dimensional group identification. She is not denying her ethnicity and is, in fact, comfortable with her culture and maintains close ties with her relatives in Japan; however, she resists being labeled. She does not want to be a career ethnic.

Cultural Identity and Political Agendas

Ethnologist W. A. Bennett brusquely characterizes the maneuvers of the new ethnicity as "a set of strategies for acquiring the resources one needs to survive and to consume at the desired level."[10] California Chicanos, who prefer not to be called Mexican-Americans, may have lost the Spanish language in their families, but they have not lost their group characteristics. As the minority population has grown, it has influenced the dominant culture markedly, in music, clothing, foods, and so on. Today a Mexican-American child has options across the scale from complete assimilation to strong pride in Mexican-American culture. There are, however, political and economic reasons for the group loyalty that is reflected in the ethnic-bloc voting in large urban centers. Though group cohesion may suit the ambitions of some Chicanos as they identify themselves with the group in demanding special considerations in schooling and jobs, the identification also becomes a loyalty test for others.

Politics of the Quebec Experience. Language can become a powerful rallying point for ethnic groups in competition for goods and services. There is nothing inherently "natural" about keeping to a group language, but in certain instances the strategy is deliberately used as a means of acquiring advantage. The movement to revive the French language in Quebec has been vigorously pursued for political and economic gain as well as for the self-pride of French-speakers. The language issue became, as I discussed in chapter 4, the symbolic focus of the separatist Parti Quebecois. Reforms then were passed by the national government to head off the disastrous possibility of Quebec's secession from Canada. In the 1980 referendum the Quebec citizens voted three to one against actual political separatism. But the granting of special status to Quebec, as I have shown, has had profound consequences.

It is estimated, for example, that at least 200,000 English-speaking families have left Quebec for the neighboring province of Ontario, where they will have a choice of languages; and hundreds of businesses have moved also. All Canadian government employees now have to be bilingual, including the Royal Canadian Mounted Police, postal workers, and airport workers. The Canadian government is the largest employer in the country, and civil service employees make up a larger portion of the work force in Canada than in the United States, so requiring bilingualism is not an insignificant change.

In December 1988 the Canadian Supreme Court struck down a part of the Quebec language law that prohibits the posting of signs in any language but French, saying that this law violates the guarantees of freedom of expression in the province's Charter of Rights. The Supreme Court, while upholding Quebec's right to give the province a French "linguistic face" by having French appear on all public signs, held that the province could not at the same time ban the simultaneous display of English and other languages.[11] The reaction of the Quebec premier, Robert Bourassa, a few days later was to invoke a clause in the charter that allows a province in some circumstances to override the charter's guarantees, a move that angered civil rights advocates as well as proponents of bilingualism. Bourassa claimed that he understood the clear obligation in the court decision to allow other languages to be displayed in public, but that his responsibilities as Quebec premier gave him a unique duty to promote and protect French culture. He appointed a commission soon afterward to study the kind of signs that may be permitted in other languages *inside* of buildings sometime in the future.[12] This affair of the signs may seem trivial to outsiders, but it is a graphic indicator of the powerful pressures to keep Quebec purely French-speaking.

Quebec has rejected bilingualism, allowing only the use of French in every sphere of public life, at the same time that the federal government has imposed French/English bilingualism on the rest of the country from coast to coast, even though French-speakers constitute less than 5 percent of the population outside the provinces of Quebec, Ontario, and the Maritime Provinces. These language mandates, coupled with the threat of secession by Quebec, have been noted with alarm by some U.S. citizens. The Canadian experience has been at least partially responsible for the national movement in the United States for English as the official language, a lightning-rod case that I discuss fully in chapter 7.

The active promotion of bilingualism in Canada for twenty years has evidently not, however, increased the total number of bilingual citizens. In the 1981 census 15 percent of the respondents identified themselves as able to carry on a conversation in the two official languages—a proportion that has not changed in over twenty years. One reason may be that as the number of English-speaking people learning French has increased, the number of French-speaking citizens in Quebec who have a command of English has decreased, since there is no incentive for bilingualism in that province. The bilingual impasse may partly be due, as well, to the fact that people simply do not learn foreign languages easily or quickly on a mass scale. English-speaking Canadians tend to feel that they have been given the worst of both worlds, with their language rights almost nonexistent in Quebec and French/English bilingualism increasingly promoted by the government in the rest of the country. I find even the official terms the government uses for the major language divisions unappealing: French-speakers are Francophones, English-speakers are Anglophones, immigrants with other mother tongues are Allophones, and Indians and Eskimos are Endophones.

Signs of a renewal of separatist demands in Quebec have appeared since the last general election. It is unlikely that this movement will entirely prevail, for there are still many Quebecois who see their future clearly related to Canada even though they continue to support the so-called French-language fact. Nevertheless, some still fear the secession of Quebec from Canada in the next fifty years. The former premier, Pierre Elliot Trudeau, who championed the French language but not the separatist movement, may not have used the best judgment in the long run when he chose to appease the Parti Quebecois. The battle is not over, and although language is the conspicuous issue, much more than language is at stake.

Language, Culture, and Identity in Multicultural Settings

Controversy over the role of language in cultural preservation or revival will continue. Reviving languages that are no longer being actively used in a community is very difficult, if not impossible, to achieve. It is true, of course, that in countries where different languages exist side by side over a period of time, some languages will inevitably die out as they become less useful. I am not referring to any of the dozens of world languages but to some of the isolated languages of the indigenous peoples of the United States, Canada, Australia, Africa, and even some of the European languages such as Gaelic and Welsh. Since the formation of the Republic of Ireland in 1916 there has been a persistent effort to increase the use of Gaelic, and it is taught to all schoolchildren. Nevertheless, Gaelic is used less today than before any government measures were employed. The prime reasons, once again, involve practicality: the language has little use in everyday life, and it is not crucial to the political movement in Northern Ireland. Even the communiqués of the Irish Republican Army are in English.

The Welsh language is likewise dying out. Throughout the schools and in other settings its use has been vigorously promoted in Wales in the past twenty-five years, yet its actual public use continues to decline. Such language movements seem to have public support but are quietly ignored in practice. The Irish and the Welsh have maintained profoundly distinct cultures even though the average person does not seem to see speaking the ancient language as an important part of feeling Irish or Welsh.

The Irish and Welsh examples point out once again that schools alone cannot do the job of maintaining or reviving a language. Community members must take other strong measures if they are serious about keeping the language and the ethnic character intact. Such efforts are very difficult to carry out, it seems, unless the community closes itself off from outside influences as much as possible. Self-segregating religious communities that are also economically self-sufficient and have their own schools may succeed. The Hasidic Jews in New York and the Amish in Pennsylvania are the examples always cited because they are successful in maintaining entirely protected enclaves in the midst of our multicultural mixture. Both groups control their schools, allow the learning of English only for economic purposes, and very carefully control contact with the world outside their communities. They maintain stable bilingualism and biculturalism by keeping the two languages and cultures entirely separate. English is excluded from home or religious use and is only allowed for certain prescribed occupations.

Few minority groups in the United States would be able or even willing to go to such extremes. Instead, it is more often the case that groups will organize their own voluntary "Saturday schools." I have seen the Chinese in my own community providing one day a week of instruction in Mandarin language, as well as in Chinese music, dance, and poetry. Indeed, there is a national association of voluntary Chinese language and culture schools in the United States. The Japanese weekend school in a nearby suburb offers reading, writing, and other school subjects taught in Japanese. Their purpose is to maintain native-language skills for those children who will return to Japan. Hebrew schools abound in the Boston suburbs for teaching language, culture, and religious concepts. They are organized by parents and teachers and are, therefore, free to transmit whatever values they choose. These are but a few examples of the voluntary efforts made by different language communities to promote ethnic solidarity through language and culture classes.

Valuing Ethnic and National Identities

Here, then, we encounter several basic cultural questions for the United States: Have we largely lost our ethnic identities and our languages in the United States? Do we want to reinstate them? Might bilingual/bicultural education revive them? Amazingly, we have not lost those identities, according to sociolinguist Joshua Fishman. While many immigrants have forfeited some of their cultural and linguistic traits, the United States has not become a homogeneous or bland society—quite the contrary.[13] Ethnic groups have retained their foods, traditions, religions, and regard for their countries of origin for many generations. The impulse to embrace American culture is a practical one and stems less from self-hatred, as is sometimes suggested, than from an unembarrassing need on the part of minorities to feel a part of their adopted society. Multicultural diversity seems to be alive and well in the United States today in spite of the shrill chorus of ethnic writers who, says Gunnar Myrdal, "concentrate on an abstract craving for historical identity, but they have not clarified by intensive study what cultural traits are implied, who wants this identity, who should want it, and why, and how it should and could come about. I am afraid, therefore, one must characterize this movement as an upper-class intellectual romanticism."[14]

In the years since the end of World War II the United States has not only experienced a period of very heavy immigration but has also seen the rapid weakening of ethnic boundaries. As a specific example, forty years ago only one in ten Jews married outside of their group; now it is one in three. More generally, one-third to one-half of the people in our country now marry across ethnic lines.[15] With this level of mobility and intermarriage, preserving distinctive ethnicity grows less and less possible.

Almost all of us are of mixed ethnic backgrounds and have our own "hunger of memory." A majority of the close friends I had in high school have married out of their religious and ethnic groups. I was told recently of a newly formed organization for professional women of Italian-American descent whose leaders jokingly said that they should call it "The Association of Italian-American Professional Women (Married to Jewish Men)." A friend in Newton enjoys telling his own story of the amalgamation of cultures. He went to a community breakfast where at different tables he was introduced to the relatives of various acquaintances. What Uncle Ziggy, Uncle Angelo, and Uncle Ivan all had in common was that they each had a son named Scott! That was several years ago. The postscript to that story is that since the ethnic revival, families have once again been choosing names with strong overtones of group loyalty—the Deborahs, Angelas, and Deirdres are back.

Costs and Benefits of Assimilation

The tension between assimilation, language, and cultural loyalty has been sensitively expressed by Richard Rodriguez, who chose, at the cost of losing fluency in the language of his family, to enter the larger American society by acquiring the majority language. The experience was at times painful, and Rodriguez has described it with moving clarity. Still, Chicano and other latino cultural purists have criticized Rodriguez for disloyalty to *la raza.* Marco Portales, for example, in a review of *Hunger of Memory: The Education of Richard Rodgriguez,* says that Rodriguez ought to have been intelligent enough to realize that this was too high a price to pay for his success in the larger society and that he should not hold himself up as a model for Mexican-American children.[16] Portales and others are dismayed that Rodgriguez does not support native-language-based bilingual education or other measures that enforce the language minority child's connection to his ethnic community. Portales and Rodriguez represent the sharp division of attitudes on language and culture maintenance so central to the current discussion.

Education and the Controversy over Assimilation.   Historically, groups have sacrificed aspects of their ethnicity in the search for economic advantage, and this choice has, to some degree, always been a painful one. Portales evidently believes that this need not be the case, that we should not have to give up anything—not any measure of our language or culture—in acquiring the necessary elements of a public persona. He simplistically asserts that the success of an educational system "is not measured solely on whether a student shows everyone that he is Ph.D. material, but rather on how well that person is made to feel wherever he is and whenever he or she has to deal with the world at large."[17] Rodriguez, on the other hand, contends that education's primary purpose is to teach the skills of numbers and words crucial to public survival and to help a child develop an effective public self, apart, if necessary, from family or ethnic community.

These two views of the goals of education for language minority children are necessarily much discussed among educators, but far less so by the public. One side is concerned with bringing the language minority culture into the classroom and focusing on it. The other side, more concerned with the persistent risk for these children of underclass status outside of school, wants to concentrate on making the mainstream language and culture more accessible to the underprivileged. The first group, sometimes labeled romantic, progressive educationists, supports ethnocentric approaches in the classroom. They promote use of the child's background as the subject of lessons and place emphasis on the emotional aspects in the curriculum, folk culture, and ethnic differences. The other group, fearing that such education entails the possibility that the emotionally sensitive will be controlled by the intellectually competent, emphasizes instruction in more demanding subject matter and stresses literacy skills over folklore and competence over self-actualization.

The desirable course, surely, is to combine these approaches by recognizing children's emotional needs and teaching mutual respect for differences but focusing strongly on literacy and cognitive development—*combining a tough-minded compassion with high expectations.* Not all kids will be Ph.D. candidates, but *some* will; and all, one hopes, will reach similar life-enhancing objectives in their workplace, their family lives, and their recreation. The choice between an upbeat self-image and academic achievement is a false one. We must be capable of achieving both in our schools.

Personal Growth and Independence

Is the desire for economic well-being or for some other goal beyond those recognized by one's immediate ethnic group somehow disloyal? Inevitably, the rights of the group to cultural maintenance work against the rights of the individual to cultural choice. A friend of mine who had a resoundingly middle-class upbringing often is the one, I must confess, who talks the most about preserving the culture of some group whose deprivations she has never experienced. Similarly, a prosperous Italian friend deplores the loss of the dialects of the most remote Sicilian or Abruzzi regions, and a well-educated Puerto Rican friend would like to preserve the charming dialect of the *jivaros* (rural people). Cultural anthropologists, of course, need to be concerned with the preservation of archaic speech forms; for other people, however, these goals represent irrelevant exercises in romantic ethnicity.

In the United States, perhaps more so than in less competitive societies, the chance to gain economic well-being is sometimes tied to freedom from the demands of tradition. The ability to break through the constrictions of ethnic group customs often has a bearing on one's ability to gain financial independence, or at least the means of earning a living. For the language minority child, however, rejecting some of the values of the home culture in the growing-up years is doubly difficult. Examples abound. The Care Center of Holyoke, Massachusetts, was established to help pregnant teenagers with counseling, high school classes, and housekeeping and parenting skills, in either English or

Spanish. A young latino woman who was interviewed about how the center was helping her made this remarkable statement:

The baby's father never even saw her. I left him when I was pregnant. Because of my culture everybody thought it was a mistake. But I was in an abusive situation and I didn't want to bring my daughter up where everybody was screaming and yelling. I grew up in that kind of atmosphere and it really did a bad effect on my mind. It made me feel like I couldn't do anything. So when the baby's father started abusing me, I felt I had to get away. My family said, 'You shouldn't do it because you chose it,' you know. When I came here, I started getting support that I didn't make a bad choice.[18]

The young woman was asked whether the center pro-vided for the cultural diversity of the women there with her, and she answered, "Here at the Center nobody labels any-body. Everyone is treated with respect and love. My Span-ish culture is something I'd never take away from my daughter. We spent time looking at Puerto Rico, how they became Americans, the history . . . I didn't know that until I came to the class."[19]

The opportunity that this young woman has been given, and that she has grasped, may mean not only survival but attainment of a better life than her family has had so far. But it means daring to risk the solitary disconnectedness of shedding certain community values for others that offer hope. She has been fortunate to get help at a crucial time. Rather than rejecting her culture, she has tried to detach herself from the destructive aspects of it.

My own perspective has profoundly personal roots. My family was poor, so the first necessity was for us to gain the economic means to survive. We children did not enjoy the middle-class luxury of a choice of schooling or careers. The thought of taking time to "get in touch with myself" did not exist. I was fortunate that my mother convinced my father to let me finish high school and not leave school at sixteen to work in his grocery store. Because I was the oldest of five children and a girl, I did not think to question my fate: I should help my mother after school every day, and when I reached the age of sixteen, I should leave high school and help in the store. In fact, my father would have preferred that we stay closely attached to the family and neither attend school nor learn English. Mandatory attendance at school saved us! For me, convention dictated that family bondage would not end until I married—and married within the ethnic group and preferably in the neighborhood, when I would then no longer be my father's but my husband's responsibility.

School, however, opened up my horizons, and the English language gave me the entry not only to the excitement of academic advancement but to friendships with children from very different families, other ethnic groups, and other religions. I began to want to learn, with a desire for a range of experiences, and, yes, a desire for material things and an interesting job.

Of course, my experience was not unusual. I wanted to be free from what seemed the restrictive customs and language of my family and community, free from the burden of being "different." The desire is common to young people of various ethnic groups, and it is not surprising, therefore, that this liberation is the enduring subject of a large body of literature and drama, in novels such as *The Fortunate Pilgram, Call It Sleep,* and *Goodbye, Columbus* and films such as *West Side Story, Hester Street,* and *Crossing Delancey.*

It is daunting for anyone to cross the ethnic divide, but for women the voyage has been and continues to be even more difficult. To move out of poverty and beyond ethnicity requires individual motivation and strength of purpose *and* the reinforcement of outside help from the schools, job opportunities, and the presence of achievable role models.

I saw with renewed immediacy the clash of cultures and the hardship it imposes on the young in the case of three refugee women from Afghanistan who were in the Newton North High School ESL program for two years. They had learned English fairly well and completed a good part of their high school graduation requirements. They longed to enroll in a local community college, but the families arranged marriages for all three, finding them Afghan husbands instead. The teacher who knew the students and their families and had been an advisor to the young women was deeply disappointed. It is often just not possible to effect such change in the first years of residence in a new country.

The language and culture shift in my own immigrant family took an unusual twist. Oldest of the children in a family of three sons and two daughters, I have moved the farthest from my family geographically and in terms of assimilation into American middle-class life. My brothers and sister, who have all completed college degrees and achieved economic success, live near my mother and have, unlike me, married within the ethnic group and the religion of our upbringing. Yet I am the only one of us who has maintained and expanded her knowledge of Italian, which I speak and write fluently. None of the others is the least bit interested in the language, but they are still very close to the customs. Paradoxically, I am closer to our "roots," to our country of origin, because I travel to Italy frequently and have a husband and three sons who are all Italophiles. My sister and brothers, however, are more closely involved in Italian-American culture. We have each chosen the degree of ethnicity we wish to maintain. I am not convinced of the inevitability of guilt over some loss of ethnicity, the sort that Mario Puzo depicted in *The Fortunate Pilgrim*, when he wrote, "They spoke with guilty loyalty of customs they themselves had trampled into dust."[20] It is not that I am without sentimental feelings, but I cannot honestly wish that I or my family had remained immersed in our original language and ethnicity. We are immeasurably richer for having that background and for having added to it some of the achievements that American life offers.

Emphasis on a Desire for Betterment

I do not care to engage in a lengthy consideration of the importance of education in different cultures as part of the stereotyping of ethnic groups. The question of whether certain immigrant groups had to make economic progress first and then acquire a respect for book learning and whether other groups revered education and were then able to succeed economically because they persisted in gaining literacy and academic skills in the new country is strenuously debated by sociologists. In my reading there seems to be more support for the class theory—economic success before academic success—than for the culture-first theory that certain groups' reverence for learning inevitably leads to economic success, but the discussion has advanced little beyond the chicken-or-egg argument.

The sensitive question comes up in bilingual education regarding the relatively high level of success of Asian students in learning the English language and mastering school subjects within a few years. Are we to attribute these results mainly to cultural values, family child-rearing practices, group attitudes toward assimilation, the work ethic, or something else? I am not willing to draw conclusions, even in view of the evidence I have seen of consistently higher school achievement for Asian students as a group compared to white, black, and hispanic students nationwide.

A few examples illustrate the motivation of Asian students and the attitudes of their families. In the Berkeley Public Schools an after-school homework assistance program was started a few years ago to offer extra help three afternoons a week to limited-English refugee students, mainly from Southeast Asia. About 100 children from grades one to twelve attend these tutorial sessions regularly and are helped by paid tutors from the local university and community volunteers. The program was later expanded, with local funds, to include children from the Spanish-speaking families. The opportunity has not been taken up, and for whatever reasons, children from the Spanish-speaking community do not attend. The day I visited the after-school program, I walked around, observing and chatting with a number of the children and the tutors, and I could not help but see that every one of the eighty-five children there was Asian.

In the early stage of the Newton program the Chinese parents formally stated their desire that we teach their children in English as much as possible and not use Chinese in the classroom any more than 20 percent of the school day. Their attitude is consistent with other Asian groups surveyed across the country, as noted in chapter 2. Additional evidence of this attitude is the fact that families are known to move, if they can, to towns where they believe their priorities will be respected. I have interviewed a number of Vietnamese families who mentioned that they were leaving the Boston school system because their children were pressured to take part in bilingual programs where they were being taught most of the day in Vietnamese. At some personal sacrifice, since they had to move in with relatives and live in very crowded quarters, they were placing their children's chance to get a better education ahead of other considerations.

I had an eye-opening talk one day with a man from Southeast Asia who moved to Newton to enroll his four children in our schools. He admitted that he works for the Boston Public Schools as a bilingual teacher aide, but he was determined to take his children out of the native-language program in Boston. He had heard that in Newton his children would learn more English and have a better chance to do well in school. He was prepared to endure a difficult and long commute to work every day to give this opportunity to his children. The few examples I mention are meant to illustrate a long experience with many such cases over the past ten years.

Different groups may have different attitudes toward education and the role it plays in fulfilling their needs, but the desire for betterment is basic to all. Surely there is no community that does not prize its children and their abilities to achieve a better life than their parents. This desire must be common to all groups, but especially to the disadvantaged, who have to be the most concerned that their children be saved from disastrous circumstances. It is the one sentiment expressed to me consistently by parents, literate or not—whether Puerto Rican, Chinese, Italian, or Greek. They hope that the schools will enable their children to have more fulfilling lives, and they strongly desire respect for their identity, the ethnic and linguistic culture that the family represents. I do not see evidence that the current ethnic groups want the maintenance or revival of their cultures in substantial or complete ways, but they do want to see their cultures recognized, as a necessary measure of respect.

Perils in the Demand for Biculturalism

The ethnic revival of the 1970s has prompted widespread recognition of the incredible diversity of the United States

and has fostered a renewed interest in our various historical backgrounds—how we got here, what we have experienced, where we are today. Pushing cultural pluralism in-
sensitively, as in the demand for "bicultural" education,
disables the minority communities with the least power. The
critical question for multicultural societies like our own is
whether education policies that further the cultural identity
of minority groups at the same time enable minority children to acquire the knowledge and skills to attain social and
economic equality. As we have seen, school programs with
extended use of the native language and enforced preservation of the home culture are, by definition, segregative in
nature. James Lyons, counsel for the National Association
for Bilingual Education, recognizes the legitimate concern
that Transitional Bilingual Education tends to segregate pupils by language ability. He does not call this an invidious
form of segregation, but he observes that it "creates a tension, because the ethic of American society is integration."[21] Without sustained contact between majority and
minority children, there will be isolation of the minority
group, shamefully like the "separate but equal" policies that
kept black children's schooling separate and unequal.

The demand for biculturalism, we must recognize, creates tensions for the individual members of language minority groups. Other nations have been sensitive to this
conflict. In Sweden, the multilingual society that has enacted the most compassionate laws to protect minorities, the
national government provides every group with the choice
of being educated in its own language; supports retention
and development of the values, religion, and customs of the
original culture; and proposes that immigrants' cultures be
regarded as beneficial influences on Sweden's social development. Sociolinguists like Barry McLaughlin and Christina Bratt Paulston, who generally favor bilingual education, are skeptical of the Swedish policy. Although it

appears decent and humane, McLaughlin points out, it is difficult to realize in practice, "especially when Swedes are asked to appreciate the 'beneficial influence' of customs and habits of poor, rural Mediterranean cultures that are quite at variance with those of affluent, urban Swedish society."[22]

Paulston notes the difficulties that the demands of biculturalism impose on young women from very traditional Turkish village backgrounds who are growing up in Sweden: "It is difficult to see how those girls can internalize both their fathers' value system of women and that of Swedish society. In fact, they can't, and that situation casts serious doubt on the many glib statements of biculturalism as one objective of bilingual education."[23] This dilemma is unavoidable in countries where there are strikingly different cultures in contact and, perhaps, in conflict.

I do not believe that the bilingual child's best interests are necessarily served by large-scale institutional support for different cultures. But is such a policy ultimately in the best interests of the nation? In the case of Sweden, Paulston quotes an official who sees this danger in the official policy: "How can one encourage cultural freedom of choice without society splitting into numerous groups, all of which compete with each other?"[24] Paulston goes on to surmise that his question really concerns what is best for Sweden—not for individuals or ethnic groups, but for the country. She ends by saying, "It seems to me that the migrant children themselves have answered that question. By being allowed to assimilate and incorporate, they will with time become good Swedes, and Sweden herself will be infinitely the richer for enhanced cultural ties to the rest of Europe."[25]

Retaining ethnic boundaries inevitably reinforces existing inequality. Cultural pluralism in America is uncomfortably linked to ethnic inequalities and exclusion or alienation of certain groups. In fact, it can be argued that groups on the margin of the country's economy have kept their

ethnic distinctions because they have been isolated and excluded from the larger society. For these groups, however,
the retention of ethnicity is not the crucial issue. As Irving
Howe suggests, the central problems of our society have to
do, not with ethnic groupings,

but with economic policy, social rule, class relations . . . with
vast inequities of wealth, with the shameful neglect of a growing class of subproletarians, with the readiness of policy-mak-
ers to tolerate high levels of unemployment. They have to do
with 'the crises of the cities,' a polite phrase masking a terrible
reality—the willingness of this country to dump millions of
black (and white) poor into the decaying shells of once thriving cities. Toward problems of this kind and magnitude, what
answers can ethnicity offer? Very weak ones, I fear.[26]

Those of us who have experienced culture and language
shift—and we are many—have felt at different times both
the sentimental longing for a seemingly simpler past of
shared traditions, closer communities, and stable families
and the sharp sense that our cultural symbols from the past
cannot really shield us from the discontents of the modern
world. Overcoming the discontents of minorities will not be
achieved by having our schools emphasize biculturalism and
resegregating children along language and ethnic lines,
which are the realities in bilingual education classrooms.
Biculturalism will not make up for the years of neglect of
language minority children when they were invisible in the
mainstream classroom or out of school at an early age.

Social Strides and American Values

Finally, I want to highlight the unmistakably positive dimension of intergroup relations in the United States in the

past twenty-five years. Reading about the antistudent riots in the Peoples' Republic of China in late 1988 and 1989 and the strong animosity toward African students in that country made me reflect on the tremendous changes that have taken place here in the United States since 1963 when Bull Connor in Birmingham, Alabama, did to American blacks what the Chinese police are reported to be doing to African students. None of us who were young adults in the 1960s when civil actions to integrate buses or lunch counters were met with brutality could have imagined that in the 1980s black and white football players from southern colleges like Clemson and Auburn would be hugging each other joyously at the end of a bowl game, or that a black quarterback would lead a team nicknamed "the Fighting Irish" to a national championship. What we take for granted today has come about in a remarkably short time, considering the slow pace of integration before 1963.

It is difficult to imagine such radical changes in attitude and behavior taking place in China in a comparable period of time. For the Chinese, the sense of nationhood is closely tied to a people, a race, and an ethnic affiliation. In America, nationhood is based not on race or ethnic or tribal identity, but on a set of beliefs about liberty, equality, and individual rights. Americans want to be many things at different times—sometimes Jewish or black or Irish—but at other times they insist on being undifferentiated Americans. Self-identification and the ability to change that are basic to the dynamic of American life.

In race relations, important progress has been made in integrating our schools, housing, jobs, and professions, although much remains to be done to achieve a thoroughly just society. Likewise, a genuine start has been made in efforts to meet the needs of language minority children, as this book attests. Although we can at least take some satisfaction in the raised consciousness about the issues, we must take major steps forward to clarify alternatives and pre-serve individual choice. For all of our minorities we intend to see full realization of the "Promise of America," as Thomas Wolfe called it. Wolfe, despite what we of the 1980s call his gender-specific rhetoric, put it in the simple words characteristic of American public discourse: "To every man the right to live/To work, to be himself."[27] Unfortunately, individual choice in ethnic allegiance and individual achievement in language learning and school generally are all too often blocked by doctrinaire supporters of bilingual education.

7

Political Extremes Intensify the Language Debate

The 1970s produced opposing movements on the issue of U.S. language use. Cultural pluralists and bilingual education advocates on the one hand made much of the value of bilingualism to the individual, the community, and the nation. The melting pot diehards, on the other hand, calling for a more cohesive society through a single common language, began supporting the passage of legislation making English the official language of the United States. Proponents of these two opposing positions present us with the most extreme ways of coping with a rapidly growing language minority population.

Bilingualism on a societal scale is promoted, accordingly, as a reinforcer of ethnic solidarity, as a life-enriching asset, and, most of all, as the ideal way for language minority children to capitalize on a natural resource they already possess—knowledge of a language other than English. These prospects are appealing on the surface, but the goal of societal bilingualism is unrealistic and all too facilely proposed. It is the sobering complexity of actual bilingualism in the United States as a natural, achievable outcome of bilingual education that I take up first.

In the second part of this chapter I portray the other side of the language controversy, which is concentrated in the movement to declare English legally as the official language

of the United States. Proponents of the English Language
Amendment (ELA), as it is called, are against any officially
mandated bilingualism in this country. They are reacting in
part to the conspicuous social policies of the past twenty
years, notably bilingual schooling and bilingual voting ballots, that appear to be reversing the historic assimilation of
immigrants and threatening the common goals and social
cohesiveness of the country. Consequently, extreme, even
bizarre, positions have been taken both for and against the
ELA. The English-language movement clearly exists, and like
the language minority population it seeks to transform, it
will be around for a long time. The topic, therefore, needs
a clear, dispassionate explanation.

Social Reality versus Theories and Biases

Bilingualism is a relatively common social reality, since
more countries than not have within their borders people
who know two or more languages. In those societies, bilingualism is a natural state of affairs, that is, people routinely
grow up using two or more languages. This phenomenon,
centrally involved when different language populations as
well as class systems come in contact and political movements to advance or suppress certain languages or dialects
ensue, is a vast subject studied by linguists, sociologists, anthropologists, psychologists, and historians. I want to look
in particular, however, at the way such natural bilingualism
has become a misleading ideal for our educational goals
and to develop that discussion through a commentary on—
and in some cases a rebuttal of—the arguments advanced
in a recent, influential book, *Mirror of Language: The Debate
on Bilingualism,* by Kenji Hakuta.[1]

The book is important because it is the most recent ma-

jor publication in this field to present for a general audience the issues of bilingualism as a national condition and
bilingual education in the schools. Hakuta, an educational
psychologist presently at the University of California at
Santa Cruz, provides a comprehensive survey of the major
views on the effects and desirability of societal bilingualism.
He makes his information accessible to a general reader,
and I respect his work. Based on my accumulated research,
together with my experience and observations in the field,
however, I find him unconvincing on many crucial elements, inconclusive on the question of possible mental advantages to the bilingual person, and transparently political
on the supposed superiority of bilingual education.

Bilingualism—Reality or Fantasy?

Some countries have a long history of multiple languages
being used, officially and privately, by distinct groups of
people within their boundaries—in Switzerland, for example, French, Italian, German, and Romansch. In the United
States bilingualism has existed primarily as an intermediate
stage between an immigrant's use of the native language
and his or her acquisition of the language of the majority,
as noted in chapter 6 (see table 7.1). Groups become bilingual on the way to developing full proficiency in the
dominant language, English; gradually, over several generations, their use of the original language diminishes. For the
immigrant recently arrived, bilingualism is an uncomfortable, imperfect phase on the way to somewhere else. Knowing and using a different language at home have historically been seen as signs of being "lower class." Bilingualism
that is valued is the elite variety—full competency in two
languages among a small percentage of people for the purpose of scholarly work, diplomacy, foreign trade, or travel.
The attitude toward "folk bilingualism" in the United States

Table 7.1   Proportion of Persons Bilingual and Monolingual
in the United States (1976)

Language Background	Monolingual Non-English	Bilingual, Usual Language Not English	Bilingual, Usual Language English	Monolingual English
Scandinavian	2%	2%	16%	80%
German	3	5	24	68
Yiddish	2	6	26	66
Polish	4	5	24	65
Italian	5	7	28	60
French	4	7	31	58
Russian	15	5	22	58
Japanese	8	12	30	50
Filipino	5	17	36	42
Portuguese	17	13	30	40
Arabic	5	15	40	40
Greek	8	16	38	38
Korean	20	16	28	36
Spanish	12	23	37	28
Vietnamese	10	40	22	28
Chinese	20	25	35	20
Navajo	18	42	20	20

SOURCE: Barry McLaughlin, *Second-Language Acquisition in Childhood*, vol. 2. (Hillsdale, N.J.: Lawrence Erlbaum, 1985), 90.

has been negative, with each group that has acquired English tending to look down on the next group to arrive as foreign and inferior.

Changes in Theories on Bilingualism

Bilingualism was considered in the earlier part of this century to have a damaging effect on children's ability to learn. Two theories on the pejorative nature of bilingualism were widely accepted in this country. One held that immigrants were genetically inferior—except those from

northern Europe, of course—and the proof of their hered-
itary failings was their inability to achieve high scores on
tests administered in English. It has taken many years and
many studies to overcome the heredity theory.[2]

The other popular notion was that children raised in an
environment where two languages were used showed evidence of being mentally retarded in language development
and, consequently, confused. Psychologists and educators, it
seems, had to be convinced over and over that there is a
crucial factor of time—that the longer a person spent in
this country and the more he or she used the English language, the more fluent would be his or her command of
that language and the higher that person would score on
tests written in English. The so-called environment argument has still not been entirely dispelled. At the same time,
there is a body of research now claiming that bilingualism
has beneficial effects on thinking processes and on the
mental flexibility that knowing two language systems af-
fords.[3] But the unexamined belief that bilingualism detracts
from cognitive development is still apparent, as in the recent remarks of a researcher explaining poor test performance:

Among the reasons for [poor test performance] are the very
low socio-economic level of the Puerto Rican children, their
bilingualism which makes them deficient in both languages,
their extreme lack of test sophistication, and their poor emotional adjustment to the school situation. Insofar as this mal-
adjustment itself appears to have arisen from the children's severe language handicap during their initial school experiences,
a solution of the language problem would seem to be a necessary first step for the effective education of migrant Puerto
Rican children.[4]

Here, once again, we note how the complex causes of
poor school performance are reduced to the single matter

of language deficiency and that deficiency, in turn, is as-cribed to bilingualism.

The Influence of Hakuta's Claims

The basic neurological questions about the brain's struc-ture that underlie bilingualism are posed by Hakuta as he discusses the research addressing these issues. First, Is the bilingual mind somehow different? There is, according to him, no evidence to support such a thesis. Does language competence reside in the left hemisphere of the brain for speakers of one language, and does it span both hemi-spheres for people with two languages? Hakuta concludes that the answer is not known.[5] Despite studies that seemed to show hemisphere bridging to be the case, later evidence has not supported this conclusion. Are so-called compound bilinguals, those who use two languages from birth, differ-ent in their thinking processes from coordinate bilinguals, who start with one language and learn another one later? Hakuta ascertains here as well that there is no reliable evi-dence that conclusively demonstrates difference in brain ac-tivity. In addressing the questions of bilingualism and in-telligence, the nature of the bilingual mind, and how adults and children learn a second language, he stops short of stating his own position, overlooking the weight of evi-dence he has presented. He is scrupulous in pointing out flaws in the arguments of all sides and in deploring the generally poor quality of the research, but he leaves the reader without a clear sense of his own conclusions.

Hakuta's Support of Bilingual Education. The final part of his book concerns us most directly, however, because Hakuta abruptly shifts from his inconclusive survey of cog-nitive research to make a strong appeal for the support of, yes, bilingual education. To warrant this support he produces almost no evidence. In fact, in light of his earlier arguments, one is led to believe he will be at least as tentative about the value of bilingual education as he is about the linkage between bilingualism and intellect. Despite his surprising conviction, however, several instances that he cites actually contradict his advocacy of bilingual education:

- His case study of a five-year-old Japanese girl in the United States who advanced from no knowledge of English to full fluency and nativelike pronunciation within eighteen months is, in fact, evidence supporting early introduction of the new language.[6]
- The evidence of the steady decline in second-language-acquisition ability that accompanies advancing age, presented in his chapter on adult language learning, also argues for the earliest possible immersion in the new language.[7]
- Although he claims that adults and older children are faster at learning a second language in the initial phase of learning, he admits that young children, in the long run, are more successful learners of a second language.[8]
- He frankly admits the sober truth that evaluations of the effectiveness of bilingual education in helping students improve their English or math performance have not been favorable and concedes that "an awkward tension blankets the lack of empirical demonstration of the success of bilingual education programs."[9]

Hakuta's accumulated evidence points quite clearly—as does the evidence I have marshaled up to this point—to the conclusion that bilingual education would be the least effective model for second-language learning.

In his review of *Mirror of Language* for *The New York Review of Books*, Howard Gardner, the noted researcher on children's creativity, expressed pointed concerns similar to

my own that Hakuta, who has become a national spokes-
man in favor of bilingual education, is essentially partisan
rather than objective: "Where the evidence is weakest—on
the case for bilingual programs—he ends up drawing the
strongest, and least warranted, conclusions."[10] Gardner,
whose work on multiple intelligences is widely respected,
posed the basic cognitive question about bilingualism:

Suppose that it turns out that languages differ chiefly in su-
perficial ways and have relatively little differential effect on
basic thought patterns; the transition to a new language might
then present relatively few problems. By contrast, suppose that
both the differences among languages and imprints of each
language on mental processes are deep ones. In that case, the
risks of abandoning a native language would be higher and
making a successful transition to an unfamiliar language would
be more difficult.[11]

He proceeds to answer the question in this way: "I would
myself conclude that most differences among languages
(even those as remote as English and Chinese) are not deep
ones and that thinkers from different linguistic backgrounds perceive, classify, and reason about the world in
fundamentally similar ways."[12] One senses that Gardner, for
decent liberal reasons, would like to support Hakuta's ideal
of a carefully nurtured bilingual society but finds it an impractical prospect: "The deep differences among languages
that some theorists had anticipated seem not to exist. This
conclusion invalidates one potential line of argument in favor of lengthy transitional courses or of continued instruction in two languages. . . . Americans—whether old or
new—tend to be pragmatic and it is simply not practical to
sustain a variety of language communities in our country."[13]

Hakuta, one must observe, polarizes the issue of bilingual education along class and generational lines. In reporting on a survey he did with a group of his Yale students in New Haven, for example, he quotes a variety of extremely negative responses to support the facile conclusion that older Italian men are against bilingual education. We are not given the wording of the survey questions. He notes, furthermore, that in a national opinion survey Spanish-speakers who have acquired English and are better situated economically show only lukewarm support for bilingual education compared to Spanish-speakers who are limited-English and in poorer economic circumstances. From this comparison he blithely concludes that the young and poor whose children would be served by this program are most favorable to it.[14] Yet in my interviews with scores of latino families—as well as Chinese, Vietnamese, and others—over several years, I have heard a quite different response. Parents want equity and opportunity for their children and are not fundamentally devoted to a particular program. It may be that if latino families were asked questions that pose more options, they might look beyond bilingual education and home-language-maintenance programs in particular and toward comprehensive, skill-producing schooling.

Hakuta's examples of stable bilingual communities—a preliterate tribe on the Amazon and a Hungarian-speaking village in the Austrian Alps—and references to outdated (1961) information on Canada hardly begin to make a strong argument for societal bilingualism in the United States. Nevertheless, he seems to be using these examples in his advocacy for a Spanish/English bilingual United States. In my talks with Hakuta, I have found him to be impressively intelligent and appealingly idealistic and enthusiastic about his work. I surmise that his instinctive personal enthusiasm for latino culture and language is the strong impetus for his "leap of faith" toward bilingual education. For

Hakuta, bilingual education is an institutionalized political movement that, in his words, "gives some measure of official public status to the political struggle of language minorities, primarily Hispanics."[15] This baldly political stance has given a boost to the fans of bilingual education and has made Hakuta a favored voice of the bilingual education establishment. The major portion of his book—the thoughtful work on cognitive development and bilingualism and on the complex questions of the interlinking of language, mind, and society—is overlooked or ignored. In my view the fundamental problem with this book is its drift from an academic study—interesting but inconclusive—to a transparently political stand based on weak evidence.

—————— ◊◊◊ ——————

Bilingualism as an American Option?

Is bilingualism in the United States really an impractical dream? Not entirely, but we must have a clearer idea of what we mean by bilingualism—to what degree, for whom, in which situations, at what cost? Looking at the issue now with the fullest possible information and a more cautious eye will be more useful in the end than a naive belief that bilingualism/biculturalism is a simple matter, easily and widely attainable. Individual bilingualism up to the level of speaking, reading, and writing two languages well requires intensive, continuous effort by the practitioner—not merely personal motivation. The situational factor of close contact with native speakers is necessary and possible in parts of the United States with large concentrations of speakers of other languages. The practical benefits of using two languages, as in specialized careers in international commerce or comparative cultural scholarship, are self-evident.

Less demanding and more common is the case of passive

bilingualism. Most children who begin to learn the language of the dominant culture gradually lose their fluency
in the language of the home, but when they later find themselves in a situation where their native language is being
used, their skills can be revived. This is a familiar experience. At a recent Harvard conference linguist Barry Mc-
Laughlin described his son's early knowledge of German,
which he spoke for his first five years when the family lived
in West Germany. When the family returned to the United
States, the boy became fluent in English and rarely used his
German; but on their return to Germany a few years later,
the boy's German-language skills quickly returned.

Passive bilinguals, I have found, tend to be good learners
of a third language. In my own case, in my high school
years I studied Spanish because, for my generation, it had
much higher prestige than Italian. I became fluent enough
in Spanish (partly, to be sure, because of my early knowledge of Italian) to be employed as a bilingual secretary in
a New York export office. It is not unusual for a person
who has learned a second language to find the study of additional languages less daunting. Again, in my case, I came
back to my native language when I was in my early twenties
simply for self-enrichment. Many of the children I grew up
with never made the effort to develop the language of their
families, and in our current resurgence of ethnic sensitivity,
it is fashionable to mourn such a loss. My life, I know, is
richer in friends and cross-cultural experiences for my
knowledge of languages. I do not, however, judge others
who made different choices to be somehow stunted in their
lives.

To propose, one must conclude, that all language minority children or a substantial portion of the English-speaking
children in our country can or ought to become "balanced
bilinguals," capable of using two languages with equal confidence, is either naive or deliberately misleading. Com-

pared to other developed countries, the United States has a scandalously low national average on test scores in reading, writing, math, science, and history by American high school students who are using only one language. It is improbable that many of those students would be willing to invest the effort to acquire and maintain dual language skills. In the American context, the person who becomes bilingual will almost never be "balanced" unless he or she is working with two languages continually, and even then the one language of public life will be stronger.

Although it is unrealistic, given the circumstances, for American society to be fully bilingual, the conditions are present for varying degrees of bilingualism to be developed and supported. Keeping one's native language for informal, conversational use in the home and neighborhood and developing a high degree of English-language fluency and literacy for work and schooling and contacts outside the community produce a practical, comfortable combination for many language minority people. The individual in the United States who is motivated to keep or revive his or her home language may certainly do so, especially if that language is Spanish. These opportunities could very well be expanded in our public high schools, as I outline in the final chapter.

There will continue to be neighborhoods, and even entire cities, in which bilingualism flourishes due to geographical setting or the political circumstances that have evolved. Miami is currently 60 percent hispanic; many Texas cities, especially near the Mexican border, have a substantial hispanic population; and some Gulf Coast towns have sizable Vietnamese groups. California, like a mammoth Zabar's Broadway delicatessen, is the first state in which minorities, collectively, make up the majority of the population (see table 7.2). In this state, as in other areas with a mixed-language population, newspapers, radio, television,

Table 7.2   Ethnic/Racial Group
Representation in California
Public Schools

Ethnic/Racial Group	Percentage of School Population
White	49.2
Hispanic	30.7
Black	9.0
Asian	7.6
Filipino	2.2
Native American/ Pacific Islander	1.3

SOURCE: *Education Week*, 21 September 1988, p. 3.

advertising, and commerce routinely employ the multiple existing languages. In New York, where several Italian-language newspapers and radio stations existed fifty years ago, there is now one weekly Italian-language newspaper—along with several daily and weekly publications and a range of radio and television programs in Spanish. When languages are clearly useful and in demand, they survive.

Foreign Language Teaching

Inducting a modest number of Americans into the bilingual community is an attainable goal, as long as we see it in realistic terms. Our foreign language teaching programs should be vastly improved if we expect even a small number of our high school graduates to have the ability to *communicate* in another language and not just reel off isolated verb conjugations. It is time, to be sure, that Americans provided more instruction in the other major world languages—Chinese, Japanese, Russian, Portuguese—and

focused less on the European languages that were important a century ago. The only world language currently
taught in most U.S. high schools is Spanish. Offering these
options will require several concerted efforts toward change:
(1) a heavier financial investment in expanded foreign language teaching, (2) motivation of students to appreciate the
practical value of knowing another language well, and (3)
restructuring of the American high school schedule and
curriculum to allow a sustained and deeper focus on languages for motivated students.

Foreign language teaching programs now provide a large
number of students with a minimal competence in speaking, reading, and writing another language, and a slight
acquaintance with another culture. For many students that
is enough, because it serves to gain them admission to college courses in which foreign literatures are read and translated. We must do more, however, for students who are
genuinely open to the bilingual opportunity.

Whether it is the English-speaking student who wants to
acquire fluency in another language or the language minority student who wants to develop his or her own language as well as mastering English, the price of bilingualism is demanding work and the willingness to concentrate
on language study instead of on some other activity. It is a
worthwhile endeavor that I enthusiastically support, knowing the intense joy of being able to use more than one language. I am also aware that bilingualism will probably never
have mass appeal in the United States. As a realist, I cannot
defend the glib promotion of bilingualism as an achievable
national goal for all.

Bilingual Programs and Language Minorities' Needs

In the particular case of bilingual education and language minority students, the issues are practical and not to

House Joint Resolution 96, introduced by Representative Norman Shumway (Republican from California) and forty-nine cosponsors, is more specific, including four provisions:

1. The English language shall be the official language in the United States.
2. Neither the United States nor any State shall require by law, ordinance, regulation, order, decree, program, or policy, the use in the United States of America of any language other than English.
3. This article shall not prohibit any law, ordinance, regulation, order, decree, program, or policy requiring educational instruction in a language other than English for the purpose of making students who use a language other than English proficient in English.
4. The Congress and the States may enforce this article by appropriate legislation.

The ELA, despite the steady introduction of bills, is not given much chance of passage at the national level.

The bilingual voting ballot is the other major target of ELA supporters. A citizen's right to voting information in the native language was one of the extensions in 1975 of the Voting Rights Act of 1965 (PL 94–73, 89 Stat 400). In communities where 5 percent or more of the citizens are speakers of other languages and the district is petitioned by a representative of a language group, election materials must then be provided in that language as well as English. ELA proponents ask why a bilingual ballot is necessary, since all immigrants who become citizens and have voting rights must first have lived in the United States for five years and must also have passed an examination for naturalization given in English. (These residence and language requirements do not apply to Puerto Ricans, however, since they are U.S. citizens by birth.) Opponents of ELA argue that the bilingual ballot, like other civil rights won in recent years for minorities, was designed to put these groups on an equal footing with those who are fluent in English.

Official-English Efforts at the State Level

Efforts to effect the constitutional change, therefore, are being pursued through the state legislatures. Until recently, only two states had had a statute declaring English as the official language, Nebraska since 1923 and Illinois since 1969. Since 1969 fifteen additional states have adopted such an amendment, either by legislative action or by referendum petition, as shown in table 7.3.

The ELA movement across the states has prompted the full spectrum of responses. In New York the amendment was defeated by a strong coalition of different groups and the opposition of Governor Cuomo, who denounced it as repugnant, a renunciation of our multilingual national origins. In Ohio, where the measure, at this writing, is pending, the opposition is being led by Ramiro Estrada, state director of the Commission on Spanish-Speaking Affairs. Mr. Estrada hopes to convince the legislature that the amendment is unnecessary because, he says, "we do not have to declare an official language to create a common bond. This is America; this is the melting pot."[16]

Texas legislators came close to passing the amendment in 1988 with 88 votes in favor out of the 100 needed. Public opinion polls showed that 74 percent of the Texans interviewed in a broad-based sample favored official English.[17] In February 1986, Arkansas legislators, in sober concern for the public good, designated both an official state language—English—and a state vegetable but could not agree on an official state rock or a state fish. In Mississippi the amendment passed but was, alas, trivialized by some

Table 7.3   States with Official-English Legislation (January 1, 1989)

State	Year	Measure	Provisions
Arizona	1988	constitutional amendment	official language allows lawsuits
Arkansas*	1987	statute	official language repeals conflicting laws
California	1986	constitutional amendment	official language allows lawsuits
Colorado*	1988	constitutional amendment	official language
Florida*	1988	constitutional amendment	official language
Georgia	1986	resolution	official language
Hawaii	1978	constitutional amendment	2 official languages (English & Hawaiian)
Idaho	1986	statute	all official documents in English
Illinois	1969	statute	official language
Indiana	1984	statute	official language
Kentucky	1984	statute	official language
Mississippi	1987	statute	official language
Nebraska	1923	constitutional amendment	official language
North Dakota	1987	statute	official language
South Carolina	1987	statute	official language
Tennessee	1984	statute	official language
Virginia	1986	statute	official language; English instruction only

*SOURCE: Deborah L. Gold, "Official-English Laws Win Approval in 3 States," *Education Week,* 16 November 1988, 10.

SOURCE: James Crawford, "Official-English Activity in State Legislatures," *Education Week,* 17 June 1987, 14.

legislators who wanted to add a provision that all their colleagues should be made to take an English-language test.

In Massachusetts, where the measure has been introduced in each of the last three legislative sessions, the response has been emotional and largely negative. On one occasion devoted to strengthening shared tastes, it was coupled with a resolution to declare the corn muffin the state muffin. Representative Chuck Silvia supported the language proposition with an unassailable observation on culture: "When I was stationed in Germany, Germany didn't change for Chuck Silvia. I was expected to know the language and make my own way. I don't see anything wrong with that." Another representative, Robert Correia from New Bedford, countered by saying, "My Portuguese immigrant father was embarrassed by his accent and the proposed law would reinforce that reaction among new arrivals in this country." State Attorney General James Shannon said that while the bill "appears on the surface to be deceptively benign, it is likely to cause legal chaos."[18] The amendment is given almost no chance of passage in Massachusetts.

The success of the ELA in California in 1986, through the referendum question known as Proposition 63, drew the attention of the national media, since California often leads the country in social legislation. Proposition 63 has three provisions embodying the explicit intent of preserving and strengthening the English language:

1. English is the official language of the State of California.
2. The Legislature shall enforce this section by appropriate legislation.
3. Any person who is a resident of or doing business in the State of California shall have standing to sue the State of California to enforce this section, and the courts of record of the State of California shall have jurisdiction to hear cases brought to enforce this section.

This referendum question received 73 percent approval by California voters, many of whom are language minority citizens. A strong campaign against the ELA was waged by educational and civil rights groups. Voting information was provided in Spanish and Chinese in the counties with large non-English-speaking groups. Accounting for the referendum outcome in a state that has the largest language minority population in the country is still a riddle. Is it, as some ELA opponents contend, a matter of the voters not truly understanding the issue, even though information was provided in the appropriate native languages? I am reluctant to concede this. If voters do not vote in predictable ways, we recognize that action as one of the chastening virtues of an open society and of democratic decision making. It may be that we sometimes do not vote in our own best interests, but it is the very essence of our democracy that we trust the people, for the most part, to make the choices that, in practical terms, advantageously affect their lives.

Fueling Fears and Divisiveness

U.S. English, the organization that has placed the language measure on the agenda of many state legislatures, has declared its goal to be national unity through a single common language designated as the medium of communication in a multilingual society. The most critical observers believe that one motive of U.S. English in promoting the ELA may be their strong opposition to bilingual/bicultural education.

Few people will argue that a common language does not have pragmatic value or that English is not the common language in the United States—not because it is beautiful or better but because it is, in fact, the established medium of communication and has been so since the seventeenth century. Minority languages and cultures, history shows, gradually diminish in use through attrition .in an open society that needs and welcomes newcomers into its schools, industries, and organizations. Yet what is troubling to some ELA supporters is the growing ethnic visibility in the United States in the past twenty years that appears threatening to their nationalistic values. This extremist stance, it should be noted, is not an element of the policy of U.S. English.

The United States is experiencing a period of very high immigration—refugees and legal and illegal immigrants are entering the country in unprecedented numbers. The same period has produced legislation protecting minority languages in the schools and in government institutions on a scale never before attempted. As we have seen, the era of ethnic revival and the passionate rhetoric of cultural pluralism, which rejects the melting pot metaphor accepted in earlier times of high immigration, began in the 1970s. Vociferous promotion of cultural diversity has made many Americans feel that it is racist and oppressive to expect newcomers to accept the nation's language and shared customs. The divisiveness of the language battles in Canada that I have already described and the population shifts and societal changes they have effected have not gone unnoticed in the United States. The convergence of these several events has produced fear, in parts of the country where ethnic populations are large, of being overwhelmed by foreigners and by foreign languages and customs. The nerve being touched by U.S. English is our sense of community, raising fearful concern for the further fragmentation of our society and the loss of a shared culture. The perception is that we no longer see ourselves as we are represented in the motto on our coins—e pluribus unum, or "one out of many." These fears are exaggerated but, given the population shifts, not totally without foundation.

For their part, recent immigrants hear a very negative message. To language minority communities, a law making

English the official language seems to signify animosity toward them, their language, and their culture. The feeling is especially strong among leaders in the latino communities that this legislation is aimed principally at the Spanish language and Spanish-speakers, since they make up the largest group of new arrivals. Some latinos fear losing the language rights gained so recently—the right to special education programs for their children, to voting ballots in Spanish, and to special services in their own language in hospitals, the courts, and other social agencies. Such fears are leading to the belief that the official-English movement must be an extremist initiative, since English, quite apart from any prescriptive legislation, is already not only the actual language of public life in this country but is growing as the major language of international communication. The question then is, Why agitate for an unnecessary act?

Suspicion, distrust, and outright scaremongering abound on both sides of this issue. On the far right, R. E. Butler, a former congressional aide, warned of these dangers: "Chicano . . . activists of the 1960s and 1970s resurrected the dream of a Hispanic homeland in the southwestern United States . . . (called Aztlan) . . . Indeed, forces outside our national boundaries could very well help Aztlan become a reality." Butler then goes on, in the same report for the Council of Inter-American Security, to quote the alarming assertion of a Dutch criminal psychologist: "There is a danger that the language situation could feed and guide terrorism in the U.S."[19] On a considerably more reasonable note, Gerda Bikales of U.S. English decries "the breakdown of institutional support for assimilation, symbolized by the growth of bilingual education and bilingual voting and the controversy surrounding seemingly innocuous congressional proposals to recognize English as the official language of the United States."[20]

In the 1988 elections official-English statutes on the ballot in Arizona, Colorado, and Florida were passed in all three states. Voters disregarded the opposition to the statutes by both presidential candidates and the majority of state candidates. Ugly incidents occurred. During the Arizona campaign, a 1986 memo written by the then chairman of U.S. English, John Tanton, was published, causing embarrassment within the organization at large and outrage among the public. Presented at a conference on immigration, the memo made clear that Tanton was looking for ways to reduce the influx of immigrants from Latin American countries. It asked, in part, "Does the heartland want to give up more [Congressional] seats to California, Florida and Texas just so immigration can continue?"[21] The incident caused such an uproar that the U.S. English president, Linda Chavez, resigned to show her disapproval. Suspicion that more than a language issue is at stake certainly has validity.

Sharp opposition to official English comes not only from latino advocacy groups but from the American Civil Liberties Union and other civil rights groups and a coalition of national and state professional organizations led by the National Association of Bilingual Education, the National Council of Teachers of English, the Linguistics Society of America, the Modern Language Association, and the international association for Teachers of English to Speakers of Other Languages. One of the harshest provocations in the battle over the ELA was a quote appearing in an English First publication and attributed to Humberto Garza, a public figure in Santa Clara, California. Garza commented on a rule requiring city employees in Los Altos to speak only English on the job: "Those council people from Los Altos should be made to understand that they are advocating their law in occupied Mexico. . . . They should move back to England or learn how to speak the language of Native Americans."[22]

Most critics of the ELA, as I have indicated, attack the legislation as nationalistic, xenophobic, racist, and bigoted. More thoughtful editorial writers across the nation are concerned that the law will have certain unforeseen and undesirable effects. Will it deny justice in the courts to non-English-speakers? Will it make the school dropout rates go even higher because special programs for non-English-speaking children will no longer be provided? Will it mean neglect of health and social services because medical personnel will be required to speak only English? Opponents of ELA are understandably not nearly persuaded by the arguments of U.S. English that its advocates are really supporters of integration and against the fragmentation of the U.S. into "linguistic ghettos."

Among my professional colleagues I have heard unexpectedly inflammatory opinions on the topic. At a meeting in Massachusetts of the executive board of the English as a Second Language Teachers state organization, one board member asked us to consider whether, in fact, the teaching of English is an act of cultural imperialism. Coming from a faculty member of the Department of English as a Second Language at our state university, it seemed a novel conjecture, that perhaps everyone involved with English teaching is engaged in political oppression. Elliott Judd at the University of Illinois suggests the possibility that an official-English policy will force us to "return to a philosophy of ESL as 'Americanization' . . . our goal being one of trying to assimilate our students into American culture as well as to teach the language. . . . We may have to choose between violation of conscience and violation of job responsibility. . . . We must go on record, both individually and collectively, opposing the ELA and other legislation that threatens us and those we teach."[23]

The logic in Mr. Judd's reasoning seems absurdly inverted. Should we who teach our students the English language and the customs of our country be conscience-stricken about what we are doing? When we succeed in helping our students use the majority language fluently and feel comfortable with the customs of the place in which they are living, I would argue, we are empowering our students rather than depriving them. I believe that we are preparing our students for life in a thriving multicultural society in which they can dance a Polish polka, eat a Japanese meal, watch a Spanish-language television show, or sing in a Ukrainian choir, preserving whatever customs they wish to preserve while sharing fully in the English-speaking common society. I am afraid I lose my patience with academic friends whose reactions are narrowly ideological and remote from the practical concerns of the people they teach. And, of course, I marvel that so many stay on in the field when they believe they are oppressing the young.

Significantly, no discriminatory effects have yet been found in the states where English-language legislation has been approved. Illinois, with an official-English law on the books since 1969, has not had any challenge to its large-scale bilingual education programs or to its municipal services in other languages for the substantial language minority population. In California, where minority groups make up the new majority of the population, no lawsuits have been brought, in the three years the law has been in place, to restrict or abolish language services in education or social services. California has, in fact, allocated even greater funding to English as a Second Language classes to help illegal immigrants to prepare for citizenship proceedings through the amnesty program.[24]

The potential for citizens' lawsuits to attempt to dismantle a variety of native-language programs, however, is real. If challenges occur and bilingual programs are threatened, other citizens' groups made up of language minorities are prepared to sue for their rights under federal law Title VI.

Bilingual programs in California continue to operate and to be funded as fully as ever.

In light of the impassioned disputes, we must commend the calm tone and common sense of Joshua Fishman, who says, "Intergroup problems will not disappear merely because sidestream languages are not recognized, nor are they caused merely because such languages are utilized for governmental services to minorities."[25] If it were possible to view this issue neutrally and with the information available, one could reasonably argue that affirming English as the language of our country would be a minor, innocuous act. It would bring on neither the salvation nor the destruction of our communal well-being. For reassurance, we may look to the many modern industrial societies that have official languages—France, Germany, Japan, Italy—and to the many emerging countries that have one or more official languages.

On balance, however, official-language enactment is basically unnecessary and is, in spite of the good intentions of some of its supporters, inevitably provocative of some very negative attitudes. Such libertarian attitudes, as the examples below indicate, are worth applauding when they express basic truths. As long ago as 1915, Horace Kallen, professor of philosophy at the University of Wisconsin, called for an open-ended vision of the American experience and urged against the attempts to impose immigration quotas, exclusionary laws, and literacy tests for immigrants. He argued that "democracy involves not the elimination of differences but the perfection and conservation of differences."[26] In 1985, Richard Rodriguez argued persuasively against the English Language Amendment with this forthright appeal:

What bothers me most about defenders of English comes down to a matter of tone. Too shrill. Too hostile. Too frightened.

They seem to want to settle the issue of America's language, once and for all. But America must risk uncertainty if it is to remain true to its immigrant character. America is not finished. We are not complete in our destiny. I am asking America to remain vulnerable. . . . We must remind the immigrant that there is an America already here. But we must never forget that we are an immigrant country, open to change. If we lose our public generosity, we will protect our language, certainly, but we will have lost our reason.[27]

Formulating Goals for American Society

Here, then, in this chapter is the spectrum of positions, including the polar extremes, on linguistic and ethnic identity in U.S. society. The extremist camps—the doctrinaire official-English supporters and the strident proponents of full bilingualism—have attracted strongly partisan advocates for their views on where our society should be heading. There is a very wide ideological and political distance between them, yet the sides appear to be promoting such beneficial goals as equal opportunity, social justice, multicultural understanding, and social integration of early and late immigrant communities. The questions posed by the sharp differences between these two advocacy groups are surely basic to the present and future well-being of language minorities: Are their educational and economic opportunities helped by one officially designated common language? Should public funds be concentrated even more on the effort to teach the majority language to children or shifted toward maintaining their different native languages? In our desire to re-spect differences, are we actually moving away from the ideal of a just, integrated society with shared values? There is no question that crucial changes in government policy and in our educational practices are needed to meet the di-vergent needs of our growing minority populations.

8
Decisions for the Future

In the foregoing chapters I have examined the pressing issues involved in the education of a large and growing population of children for whom English is not the mother
tongue. I have strongly criticized the development over a
twenty-year period of policies and practices that have fallen
far short of their stated goals. My reaction to the wide gap
between the doctrinaire rhetoric of the bilingual advocates
and the observable reality impelled me to call attention to
the crippling disparity as it affects language minority children. My views clearly run contrary to what has been heard
most often from the advocates on both sides of the debate.
I am calling for a place in the public dialogue for a boldly
pragmatic viewpoint that neither accepts the political
agenda of the far right that would do away with bilingual
education entirely, denying the need for any special help
for language minority children, nor agrees with the other
extreme that demands native-language instruction as the
only viable option and native-language and culture maintenance as a civil right. My low tolerance for extreme positions, I am sure, has been apparent throughout.

Bilingual education need not be regarded as the tool in
a conspiracy to force Spanish on this country as a second
national language, as some advocates of the English language amendment seem to fear. But bilingual education has

created a bureaucracy that, like many government institutions, is intensely committed to maintaining its power and control and strongly resistant to change. Twenty years of experience have demonstrated the fundamental fact that bilingual education just doesn't work. The obligation is on us to provide the kinds of special, proven programs in the schools that will succeed. This final chapter outlines the legal and educational changes that are required if we are to help our language minority children in the *next* twenty years to become full participants in the life of the United States.

Legislative Change

Recent legislative changes in federal laws affecting language minority children are pointing the path to the improvement of educational programs. Supporting the choice of educational alternatives in the local schools with a better funding formula at the federal level is a definite advance. Improving interagency cooperation among the separate programs for limited-English students needs closer scrutiny by the U.S. Department of Education. Opening up the choices of schooling through changes in state laws, however, would have the greatest beneficial impact on local school districts.

Efforts at the National Level

Federal legislation on behalf of language minority students, while it does not specifically require one type of education program, is still too heavily committed to native-language teaching programs. In practical terms, the federal government, through the Office of Bilingual Education and Minority Languages Affairs (OBEMLA), denied choice to school districts until now by allocating 96 percent of its budget to a single method, Transitional Bilingual Education (TBE) programs. The revised Bilingual Education Act of 1988 now allows up to 25 percent of the budget to be spent on alternative programs. This welcome change will finally begin to bring about more flexibility in program choice. I strongly urge that, as soon as possible, the formula be revised even further so that more funding—without attached program restrictions—will be provided for improving the education of language minority children.

The federal contribution is exceedingly small as it now stands, amounting to only 7 percent of all education funds spent. The sharp rise in the arrival of legal and illegal immigrants and refugees in the 1980s, especially from the Caribbean, Central America, and Southeast Asia, imposes an inescapable obligation on the federal government to bear a larger burden for the necessary social services, especially schooling. Specific court decisions, moreover, that have commendably confirmed the right of the children of illegal aliens to be enrolled in our public schools have added dramatically to the costs of public education in several cities in California, Texas, and Florida. The extraordinary local expenses in the most heavily impacted areas where new immigrants and refugees are settling should be assumed by the federal government.

Change is needed in the funding operation of OBEMLA, the office that administers bilingual education funds under the U.S. Department of Education. The fiscal year 1989 budget for OBEMLA was $198,625,000.[1] The major part of that funding is distributed on the basis of grant applications from school districts that want to start up bilingual programs, to universities for teacher training, to funding a few research studies each year, and to supporting sixteen Multifunctional Resource Centers across the country. These centers employ specialists who carry out in-service training programs for teachers, organize conferences on aspects of bilingual education, and provide assistance to local school districts and institutions of higher education. All school districts with limited-English students, it should be noted, do not receive funds from the federal government. When bilingual education started in 1968, the annual funding was an extremely modest $7,500,000, and the law specified that money was to be awarded, for one to three years, to districts specifically to start up programs that would then be supported by local funds. Years ago this practice of providing seed money was localized, and the amounts were adequate. Now, despite the hugely increased need in additional locales, some of the same "seeded" districts in only a half dozen states are funded most often.

The overall operation of OBEMLA ought to be radically restructured. Funding should no longer be parceled out to grantees, but instead should be distributed as entitlements to all districts with limited-English students. The new formula should provide for a block grant (a lump sum) to each state with limited-English students, based on an annual census count. The major portion of the OBEMLA budget then would go to the states to distribute proportionally to the appropriate school systems. Finally, for improved effectiveness in the longer term, OBEMLA's research activities ought to be transferred to the Office of Educational Research and Improvement, where they properly belong for improved administration.

These basic changes would result in equitable use of federal bilingual education money, because its distribution would follow the census-based procedures used in distributing federal refugee and immigrant funds. As a specific instance, since 1978 the federal government has earmarked money to help all school districts that have an influx of new arrivals, either refugees or immigrants, when that number exceeds 5 percent of the total student enrollment. Each state receives a block grant, according to the immigrant-refugee pupil count, and distributes it to specific schools for supporting the educational needs of these students. The advantages of this plan are several: (1) districts have direct receipt of money that can be used at local discretion for additional teachers, teacher aides, books, computers, and staff training; (2) fund disbursements are monitored by the nearby state authority and not from Washington; (3) the elaborate grant application process is replaced by a simple, rationalized written plan for the use of the funds. I am not alone in urging this legislative change. In the 1987 Annual Report of the National Advisory Council on Bilingual Education to the U.S. Congress, the council members unanimously recommended the change in allotment and administration.[2]

OBEMLA, in addition, must lobby not only for greater funding for language minority programs in general but for early childhood education in particular. Important as the office's other responsibilities—adult literacy, dropout prevention, vocational and job training, and bilingual/special needs—are, early education for language enrichment and school preparation is almost surely the most crucial element in school success and reduction of the dropout rates.

The most successful and widespread early education program, Head Start, began as a federal program in 1965 to give four- and five-year-olds from poor families a chance to compete in school with children from more affluent backgrounds. A persistent shortcoming, however, is that only 16 percent of the eligible children are in Head Start. The goals for the children participating—higher scores on intelligence tests and improved nutrition—are being met admirably. However, not nearly enough children are being served overall, and language minority children, as a special group, should also be afforded this early opportunity. Members of Congress must be enlightened to recognize the mag-

Table 8.1   States with Laws Mandating Bilingual
Education, 1985–1986

Alaska	Massachusetts	Washington
Arizona	Michigan	West Virginia
Connecticut	New Jersey	Wisconsin
Illinois	Texas	Guam
Iowa		

SOURCE: National Clearinghouse for Bilingual Education, *Forum*, March 1986, p. 7.

nitude of the problems of language minority children and to give their needs a higher priority. Educators know well that it is far less costly, socially and financially, to prevent the onset of educational and social problems than to treat them after they have become deeply rooted.

As I reflect on the research I have done in this field, I realize that, in many cases, it is not federal law that needs changing so much as the application of existing law. I have observed, in fact, that it is often easier to change policies than actual practices. Once established and staffed, programs work to sustain themselves and are strongly resistant to change. More broadly, still, the perceptions of legislators, judges, educators, and parents need to evolve toward a shared recognition that language minority children need special attention; that to be most effective, special help can take a variety of forms; and that precisely focused programs must be better funded and more carefully monitored.

Efforts at the State Level

Existing laws in twelve states and one territory that mandate only bilingual education and allow no other type of program ought to be revised (see table 8.1). The freedom of choice allowed by federal law is nullified by state mandates that are narrowly restrictive. This disabling restriction is a problem of both legislation and implementation. In California and Florida, where there are no language instruction statutes whatsoever, the bilingual education lobby is so powerful that little variety in program choice is possible. As particular school districts experiment with new approaches and report successful results, as in the cases I described in earlier chapters, their success will encourage others to try out new ideas. It is the nature of this evolution, however, that change will be neither easy nor rapid.

There is, of course, much at stake for the educators involved when changes in mandated programs are considered—jobs, union contracts, budgets. In this most politically sensitive of all areas of education, it is especially difficult to envision program changes that are based on neutral, enlightened considerations of effective instruction alone. I am not optimistic, even though Colorado and Rhode Island did liberalize their bilingual education laws recently, that legislative changes elsewhere at the state level will come about easily. The trend I see beginning, thus far on a small scale, is change at the local district level, and I earnestly hope the spread of information about successful local alternatives will eventually produce a groundswell for state legislative change.

Coordinated Support for Effective Programs

The director of the Center for Applied Linguistics at Georgetown University in Washington, D.C., G. Richard Tucker, who is one of the staunchest and most articulate advocates for native-language-based bilingual education, nevertheless gave his strong endorsement of program choice in his testimony before a congressional committee considering bilingual regulations. The heart of his testimony was this:

The Center for Applied Linguistics unequivocally supports the role and utilization of bilingual education. . . . The Center does not, however, believe that it is appropriate or useful to prescribe only one educational option for all youngsters. . . . The important point is that the local school system, working together with teachers and with parents who must be given an active voice in educational decisions, is best able, in our view, to develop effective educational programs to meet the needs of a rapidly changing student body.[3]

Fortunately, Dr. Tucker's advice was heeded at the federal level when Congress rejected the attempt by the Carter administration to pass the so-called Lau Regulations, which would have imposed only bilingual education nationwide. Tucker's view, pragmatic and free of ideology, has had little effect on politically ambitious state legislators, bureaucrats, and partisan professional advocates.

The overarching concern by which federal and state education departments could effect significant improvements has to do with the disconnectedness of services for language minority children. The proliferation of separately funded programs has, in some cases, resulted in duplication of services, fragmentation of curricula, and conflicts among educators. The effect on an individual student who is eligible for more than one program, such as Chapter 1 (remedial math and reading) and Special Education (learning problems), can easily be a disjointed, even contradictory, educational experience. Because of the independent funding and curricula of these programs, a student may be taken out of class three or four times a day for unrelated special instruction. The reverse sometimes happens instead. A student with multiple needs may be completely neglected because each special teacher thinks the child is someone else's responsibility. Interagency cooperation is needed at the federal and state level to define and eliminate the areas where their services overlap. At the classroom level, much more systematic coordination among teaching staff needs to be undertaken to accomplish a coherent daily learning pattern for students.[4]

Advocacy

An unorthodox appeal must be made to the individuals and groups that advocate on behalf of language minority children. Much commendable, necessary work has been done by legal aid societies and other advocacy groups in class action suits pressing for the rights of language minorities. Yet these groups often bring pressure to bear exclusively to impose the strictest form of native-language teaching as the one non-negotiable remedy for the improvement of school progress. Their position is unnecessarily rigid and even counterproductive. When these advocates direct their energies toward promoting effective programs with improved outcomes for language minorities, and for accountability of school districts, they are admirably serving the needs of these children. Too often, though, they narrowly and wrongly advocate only a program heavy in native-language use, and they insist that this feature alone is the measure of civil rights compliance.

One of the most prominent advocacy groups, Multicultural Education, Training and Advocacy, Inc. (META), has successfully initiated actions in a number of states on behalf of language minorities. One laudable example is their work in the recent Lowell, Massachusetts, case in which they obtained a court order mandating a wide range of improvements for the language minority children who make up 40 percent of the 13,000 students in the district. The new plan will correct a flagrant case of negligence and segregation. In Berkeley, California, however, META filed suit on behalf of twelve hispanic students against the Berkeley Unified School District to enforce and expand the strict bilingual instruction already provided. In this instance, the case was brought *not* to correct a situation of negligence or segregation—Berkeley has provided an impressively successful and well-funded program for fifteen years—but to obtain a judicial mandate for extended instruction in the native language, a mandate that is not present in federal law, in the Supreme Court's Lau decision,* or in California state law.

The lawsuit itself has cost the city of Berkeley over a million dollars in court costs and untold hours of teacher time for providing depositions and gathering documentation. The trial in federal court lasted five weeks—staff time and district money taken away from the students. Judge D. Lowell Jensen's comprehensive, incisive decision in San Francisco Federal District Court on February 14, 1989, was in Berkeley's favor, a full endorsement of the school district's practices and of the underlying freedom to choose that parents and schools must have. META, attorneys for the plaintiffs, did not make a convincing case that Berkeley was either neglecting language minority students' needs or providing inappropriate services. The judge found that the Berkeley schools are neither denying the civil rights of these children nor impeding their access to equal educational opportunity.[5]

Strong and vigilant advocates for language minority children are essential, but their focus—if they care about educational outcomes—should be on implementing strong, adaptable school programs and not on imposing the polit-

---

*Regulations drafted by the U.S. Department of Education to implement the Lau decision were considered so restrictive that they were never adopted. The Lau decision stands but no federal regulations are in place dictating exact procedures.

ical ideology and programmatic narrowness of bilingual education in all communities.

Educational Improvements

Specific, precisely targeted changes in our schools will have an immediate effect in increasing opportunities for language minority children. I acknowledge at the outset, however, that more factors influence our students' learning capacity than just the teacher, the school, or the program. The disabling conditions of urban poverty, family instability, adjustment to an alien language and culture, high mobility, the traumatic childhood experiences of refugees, and, most destructive of all, the spreading drug epidemic all affect our students' ability to benefit fully from their formal schooling. Comprehensive improvement of these societal ills continues to be a daunting challenge. Our attention here is on the part that education plays in giving each child the best possible chance to grow, to achieve, and to become a productive and self-confident adult. No quick formulas exist for this immensely complicated task. Rather, as I outline now, an array of changes are called for, ones that derive from my research, my professional experience over two decades, and, not least, my personal experience in living through some of the same difficulties that our students are encountering now.

These recommendations comprise a tough, demanding campaign that includes curricular improvements specifically for limited-English students, general recommendations for school restructuring, teacher-training needs, collaboration between public schools and business associations or universities, and innovations in foreign language learning for English-speaking students.

Early Childhood Education

One of the most powerful factors in a child's future school success is an early learning opportunity, at age three and four, for language enrichment, for acquiring rudimentary social skills, and for beginning to understand some of the abstract concepts that will later be taught in the classroom. For limited-English students the early program is an ideal time to involve parents in their children's schooling. Parents, in fact, can be brought into the school as volunteers or as paid assistants. At this impressionable time, school staff must demonstrate through their behaviors respect for all the languages and the cultural backgrounds of the children. Besides building the parents' self-esteem and helping them understand an unfamiliar education system, frequent communication between parents and staff establishes early the crucial home–school connection, which is especially vital for minority families.

From Kindergarten to High School Graduation

The strongest recommendation possible applies here: limited-English children must be placed with specially trained teachers in a program in which these students will be immersed in the English language, in which they have as much contact as possible with English-speakers, and in which school subjects, not just social conversations, are the focus of the English-language lessons from kindergarten through twelfth grade. For all of the reasons presented thus far, I have found this approach to be the most effective for children of any language background and of any age when they first enter our schools. Delaying the early learning of English while teaching subject matter in the native language clearly will inhibit the students' later development of the English language. Nothing seems to be more basic to the school performance of our students or to their self-confidence and sense of belonging than their firm control of the standard spoken and written language of their school community.

In the specific case of Spanish-speaking children, the evidence leads me to be even more outspoken in opposing the assumption that the use of Spanish in the classroom is necessarily helpful. Many of our students, as I demonstrated earlier, speak a nonstandard Spanish or a mixture of Spanish and English. We know that the more different the home dialect is from the standard, the greater is the difficulty in using standard Spanish as the language of instruction. To begin instruction, therefore, by doing extensive remedial work in vocabulary and grammar in Spanish before attending to English-language development makes little sense, if the goal is to learn English. In some cases, as I have indicated, there may not even be much reinforcement for the Spanish language at home if there are not books or newspapers in Spanish on hand or if our students' families do not routinely listen to Spanish-language radio or watch Spanish-language television.

Important insights into school and home language use are found in a 1988 study conducted by the National Assessment of Educational Progress of the U.S. Department of Education. It is the most extensive national assessment to date of Asian and hispanic student achievement. The researchers found that Asian students, who tend, as we have seen, to take more rigorous coursework and to have more affirmative attitudes about schooling, outperform their white and hispanic peers in reading and mathematics at all grade levels tested. The study also found that hispanic students who claimed competence in English performed relatively well on the tests, *even if they spoke Spanish at home.* "It would appear that whether or not one comes from a home where a [different] language is frequently spoken is not an important issue in itself, but whether or not one is competent in English is," the study asserts. "While frequency of use of one's non-English language in the home is not a variable that can be easily manipulated, the development of English competency is manipulable and should be of high priority within school systems."[6] In addition to developing students' English competence, the report recommends that schools help ensure that hispanic students take more rigorous courses and emphasizes the importance of preparing and encouraging hispanic students to enroll in these courses. The last piece of good counsel in the report is that schools should develop among students the belief that effort, not merely ability, contributes to achievement.

Bilingual education advocates constantly remind us that we should not waste the natural resource of the native language already possessed by our bilingual children. But if we do not give these students the indispensable tool of a high level of competency in the language of the country, we will lose an even greater resource—the ability of large groups of citizens to earn a living, to surmount class barriers, to become upwardly mobile, and to succeed at whatever they are determined to do. The basic decision for school districts is a matter of priorities. Our first responsibility in public education, surely, is to see that all our students acquire the basic competencies for life in the public sphere. A desirable, but secondary, goal is to support the interests of specific groups in maintaining the home language.

Concurrent with these priorities, a carefully structured school day stressing the major subjects is essential for our students. They need as much time as possible on mathematics, science, history, geography, reading, writing, art, and music as the school day can provide. This emphasis is not easily managed in the average American school, which has crammed many additional activities into the curriculum while keeping the traditional schedule of hours and days.

These additions are not without value—discussions of bicycle safety, driver education, handicaps, death and dying, drug abuse, AIDS, and bus safety, for example—but the school hours are limited. Given approximately twenty-four hours of instructional time per week, we have steadily reduced the amount of time devoted to teaching the essential subjects and skills.

Two Promising Approaches

New ways of teaching abound and must be pursued as well. One new approach that brings students of different ability levels together in academic projects, called Cooperative Learning, is demonstrably successful in helping students at all levels make greater progress in academic learning and in improving social and racial relations in the classroom. In the past ten years many teachers have been trained to use this approach, which has these salient features: (1) groups of students of different ability levels—perhaps one or two of the top students, two or three in the middle range, and one or two at the lower end—are assigned to work together on a learning task in a particular subject; (2) the students learn to plan the work and assign different parts of the task to different members; (3) all, individually and collectively, are responsible for the quality of the finished work. The Cooperative Learning approach is effective when implemented at any age level. Deceptively simple sounding, it actually requires that teachers be retrained to abandon their traditional role as the purveyors of knowledge and instead organize the students to take charge of their own learning. The approach benefits all students but especially minority and language minority children, promoting as it does student interaction across ability, class, and racial lines. It stimulates students to motivate each other in the same way that members of an athletic team do, stressing cooperation among individuals as well as competition between groups.

American Educator magazine recently published a study of the inner-city Köln-Holweide School in West Germany that reports exceptional student progress as a result of using the Cooperative Learning approach. The significant aspect is that while the school's population is composed of a fairly equal mix of high-, middle-, and low-achieving students, it also includes a one-third proportion of Turkish students of limited competency in the German language. The school's directors credit their success to the creation of a "school community" through the Cooperative Learning strategy with these results: (1) only a 1 percent dropout rate, compared to a national average of 14 percent; (2) a 60 percent rate of student acceptance in four-year colleges, compared to a 27 percent national average; and (3) no truancy and only minor discipline problems.[7]

A unique university–school collaboration also bears watching. The daring approach that has received attention in the national press is the joint endeavor between Boston University and the city of Chelsea, near Boston. The university proposed to Chelsea that it take over the Chelsea school system for ten years and be held accountable for raising student achievement. The same bold proposal was offered to the city of Boston some years ago and rejected. Chelsea is a city with one of the lowest average incomes in the state, and its students score very low on subject matter achievement tests. By entering this long-range partnership, Chelsea expects to accomplish goals that are not otherwise possible: the university will have a free hand to train staff, revise curriculum, restructure the schools, and involve the parents in understanding and supporting the renewed educational efforts. The university also plans a community-wide public health program, including nutrition and prenatal care, teen pregnancy prevention, parenting classes for new mothers, and adult literacy classes, with the expectation of federal funds and private foundation grants for the project. It is an unprecedented venture, the first of its kind in the United States, and its outcome will be watched carefully.

The Dropout Problem

The percentage of minority students, principally black and hispanic, who leave school before completing a high school education remains unacceptably high. Accurate figures are difficult to obtain. U.S. Department of Education statistics in early 1989 reported that the dropout rate for hispanic youth nationwide was 29 percent in 1985, down from 34 percent in 1982.[8] Our job is to make the improvement a steady trend. The partnerships between schools and businesses—like the Boston Compact, which motivates students to complete their high school diploma with the incentive of jobs and funding for college—have resoundingly succeeded but exist on a discouragingly small scale. Partnerships between universities and high schools to inform black and hispanic students about higher education possibilities, such as the one established between Middlebury College in Vermont and DeWitt Clinton High School in New York City, are worthwhile but at present reach only a tiny number of inner-city students.

The challenge is twofold: to steer minority students toward college and at the same time, at the minimum, provide them with the entry-level skills necessary for stable employment that pays a living wage. The president of the Associated Industries of Massachusetts, John Gould, has given us an unvarnished assessment of the current situation:

While industry is generally getting more scientific in its orientation and more numerical in its requirements, the nation

to enter a field that will take them out of poverty. This is just one example of on-the-job English-literacy and skills-training opportunities that industries are providing. Alan Natapoff at MIT cites not only the immigrants' work ethic but the early start of their own math training as the two important elements in their success. "If you want childen to speak a language fluently, you teach it at an early age," he asserts. "If you want them to be comfortable with mathematics, you teach it early."[12]

I must stress that the effort to keep students in school until they have acquired a high school education, with good job skills or the qualifications to pursue higher education, needs much more decisive attention and resources at the local, state, and national levels. By the time students from disadvantaged backgrounds reach the secondary schools, attitudes have already been formed. For students who have not been prepared well enough in the elementary school years to perform competently in high school courses, the risk of a self-defeating attitude and poor behavior is in place, and there may be no catching up. The language minority student who has not yet achieved the ability to use the English language is, then, doubly at risk of dropping out. In the urban schools, minority students with an early record of poor school achievement are at the greatest risk of all when they reach junior high school. Our schools clearly must do a much more systematic and comprehensive job in the earlier grades.

Setting High Standards and Encouraging Achievement

The federal report entitled *A Nation at Risk*[13] is the most visible of numerous recent studies that have called attention to the poor quality of the American education system and to the alarmingly high percentage of Americans who are functionally illiterate—that is, unable to read with understanding even at the eighth-grade level and unable to do simple math for everyday life. Outspoken on this disastrous lack of competence, John Shannon, a thoroughly frustrated citizen who is perhaps more representative than we care to believe, wrote this in a letter to the *New York Times Book Review* on various compensatory pursuits of our illiterate population:

Three out of four kids appearing in juvenile court are functionally illiterate. Ninety-nine percent of the spoon-benders, U.F.O. abductees and crystal people are functionally innumerate. The kids turn to crime because they can't make it in a literate world; the New Agers turn to Shirley MacLaine and L. Ron Hubbard because they can't make it in a 20th century world. Our problems, from ozone to overpopulation, come from people who can't face facts, won't accept responsibility, and deny cause and effect. Crystals, channeling, creationism and political committees won't solve the problem of hypodermic syringes on the beaches of New Jersey or AIDS in our hospitals. We need literacy, we need numeracy.[14]

Shannon's testy remarks dramatize what we know from the 1989 results of the International Mathematics and Science Test. U.S. students at age thirteen, compared with students from five other countries and four Canadian provinces, rank at the bottom in performance. Our students rank low in scientific knowledge and in the ability to apply mathematics learned in school to real-world problems. The news is alarming, but not entirely surprising. Educators know that science and math are not taught well partly because many elementary school teachers are not sufficiently prepared in these subjects. Albert Shanker, president of the American Federation of Teachers, points out a telling irony in the comparison of student attitudes: "When the tested students were asked whether they thought they were good at math, only twenty-three percent of the Koreans—the highest achievers—said yes (perhaps due to cultural modesty). But sixty-eight percent of U.S. students—the lowest achievers—answered yes! (We scored highest on immodesty.)"[15] Perhaps we learn from this self-deception that we need to place more emphasis on actual achievement and less on unjustified praise and encouragement of students to feel good about themselves without reason.

Let us be clear on the scope of the problem: If the education system is failing students in general, then it is even less helpful to students who start out with greater needs. As noted in earlier chapters, one of the best predictors of successful learning is time on task, that is, students who spend one hour a day on mathematics will learn more math than students who spend only one-half hour a day. This measurable relationship between time spent on study and success in learning is a well-known phenomenon that is not peculiar to bilingual classrooms.

Rethinking the School Calendar

If U.S. students are achieving at the lowest level compared to students in other developed countries and U.S. students are receiving the least number of hours and days of schooling, a cause-and-effect relationship seems likely. Our 180-day school year looks meager next to the 240-day one of Japan, China, and Korea. European children routinely attend school six days a week. Our school calendar was originally developed for an agrarian society when children were needed to help on the farm in the spring and summer. We can no longer afford the culturally irrelevant practice of giving our children so little time in school. Even if one defended this school calendar for the lucky ones who have long, enriching summer experiences in libraries, museums, and summer camps, it is still not appropriate for our minority students whose needs are not met by the abbreviated school year. We cannot, I suspect, continue to justify a four-year high school schedule in which students are in school only from 8:30 A.M. to 2:30 P.M.

A strong case, then, can be made for extending the school calendar to provide more weeks of instruction in the regular school year, giving our students a minimum of 200 days of schooling, with frequent and shorter vacations rather than the ten-week summer break. Students would derive measurable benefits, as would teachers. Salaries would have to be increased proportionately, relieving some teachers of the need to work at two jobs and take on summer employment.

The superior accomplishment of students in other countries is undeniable, not just in Japan, which is an unusually homogeneous nation, but in countries such as Sweden, Germany, and Canada, which have multilingual, multicultural populations such as ours. Two telling complaints are addressed to me over and over again by immigrant parents: (1) their children are not given enough homework, and (2) they are not in school enough hours. Breaking out of the traditional school-year calendar will be difficult, but solving our serious problems demands radical departures.

For language minority students the need for more hours of schooling is not disputed. Newton, Berkeley, Fairfax, and other school districts are already providing hours of after-school tutorials and an extra month of summer school for limited-English students. These efforts are directly reflected in better student progress. But participation in these programs is necessarily voluntary, and often the students who need them most do not attend. A longer school day or an extended school year for all language minority students will provide not only more instruction in English language and in the school subjects but time, as well, for native-language classes for students who are motivated to maintain and develop their native language. Federal and state money, as well as grants from private foundations, is needed at the outset to enable a number of forward-looking demonstration districts to extend their schedules.

Teacher Training and Qualifications

The improved training of teachers and others who work with limited-English children is already strengthening the professional standards in the field. Twenty years ago, almost anyone who spoke English, regardless of credentials or experience, could be an English as a Second Language teacher, and just about anyone with teaching credentials (and sometimes without!) who was fluent in Spanish was assured of a job as a bilingual teacher. Universities now offer degree programs in second-language and bilingual teaching, and several states have established standards for professional certification. Although there is a central corps of competent teachers in the states with large bilingual populations, with the rapid growth of bilingual programs there are still not nearly enough qualified professionals to staff them fully. Also, there continues to be a shortage almost everywhere of trained Spanish bilingual teachers and, not surprisingly, of teachers who speak the less common languages such as Khmer, Cantonese, Vietnamese, and Korean.

Education critics rightly question the overemphasis on "techniques of teaching" and voice the general concern that teachers ought to have a better knowledge of their discipline—for instance, math, science, or history—to be effective teachers. There is, in fact, a movement to abolish the university undergraduate major in education in favor of requiring prospective teachers to complete a degree first in a particular discipline and later take the specified courses in methods of teaching.[16]

The effective staffing of bilingual programs is still hampered by a serious deficiency that undermines the established standards for teachers and directly affects children's learning: bilingual teachers ought clearly to be bilingual, but that is sometimes not the case. Hakuta notes, for example, that some of the newly arrived teachers from Puerto Rico who were assigned to bilingual classrooms in New Haven, Connecticut, "sometimes had limited English [so] . . . they had to go through the process of learning English, with varying degrees of success."[17] In the current rush to recruit staff for the growing number of bilingual classrooms, teachers who speak little or no English have been hired from Spain, Portugal, and other countries. This eager, but faulty, recruiting is not confined to one part of the country but has occurred in New York, New Jersey, Connecticut, Massachusetts, Illinois, Texas, and California. It is important, surely, to insist that, for effective bilingual instruction, teachers must be able both to communicate with their students formally and informally in English and to teach in the native language. When students in the elementary grades spend most of the school day with a teacher who is uncomfortable in expressing himself or herself in English, there will be an overreliance on the native language by teacher and students alike. Some schools have pairs of teachers in bilingual classrooms, one English teacher and one native-language teacher. That arrangement diminishes the problem, but it is an expensive staffing strategy that not all school districts can afford. I noted in chapter 2 that for a period of years bilingual teachers in Massachusetts were tested for accreditation only in Spanish and not required to take an English test. That officially endorsed imbalance is not unique. In New Jersey, the state teachers' union actually went to court in 1981 to overturn a state rule requiring that teachers in bilingual programs be able to speak English. Wisely, the federal court in Trenton dismissed the appeal and upheld the state rule.

The reverse form of the problem exists in California's

practice of imposing on ordinary classroom teachers the obligation to become bilingual. The shortage of Spanish-speaking staff is cited as the reason for imposing this obligation. Thousands of teachers have been put on "waiver," a conditional notice that they must take courses in Spanish after school hours to become competent in using the language in their classrooms. But, as with other schemes I have noted earlier, to expect large numbers of adults to learn a new language well enough to teach in that language is unrealistic. California teachers have protested against the waiver rule, but their union has remained quietly neutral on the issue.

As urgent as it is to train special staff for bilingual programs, it is equally important that regular teachers, principals, and administrators receive additional training to give them a fuller awareness of the nature of the second-language-acquisition process and of the different learning styles and cultural backgrounds of language minority students. Because of the essentially segregative nature of bilingual education, teachers of the standard subject curriculum often view the bilingual students as the "property of the bilingual program." When these students leave the bilingual program and begin to work in regular classrooms, teachers may have unrealistic and even contradictory expectations, either too high or too low. Regular teachers need to know that bilingual students are as capable as any other group of students and that the transition from one language to another is a continuing process that is not perfectly accomplished in a single period of time. That process need not keep students from working well and learning the subject matter in a regular classroom among English-speakers. The students' inclusion will, to be sure, require the teacher to make an extra effort, to adapt the classroom operation, to give a little more explanation of a word or concept and, on occasion, to rephrase and repeat instructions.

The entire school community—the librarian, the custodian, the principal, the music teacher—must help language minority children become integrated with their English-speaking classmates. The more communication these students have with adults and other students in the school, the more welcome and comfortable they will feel, the faster their English-language skills will develop, and the more positive will be their attitude toward school and learning. These children "belong" to the whole school, not only to the bilingual program staff, but the longer they are kept out of the mainstream life of the school, the less sense of community they are likely to develop.

Bilingual teachers, I want to stress as well, need to assume other important roles in the life of the school besides teaching their limited-English students. They should be the *culture brokers* between the bilingual children and the majority school population. These special teachers are the adults who bridge two languages and cultures, and they must help create cross-cultural understanding, making the bilingual students comfortable with the majority culture and promoting understanding of the bilingual students' history and culture for the school at large.

Improved Foreign Language Teaching for English-Speaking Children

Bilingual teachers are now needed in the new Two-Way bilingual programs, where they will teach Spanish (or another language) to English-speaking children. Two-Way programs, as described in chapter 5, are now offered in at least three dozen school districts in the United States, and they appear to be a valuable development in education. Most appealingly, they offer mutual benefits to language minority and majority students—for each to learn the other's language and for students to work together naturally as equals instead of being separated by language. This type of intensive language-teaching program would no doubt enrich the foreign language teaching field generally by bringing together bilingual and foreign language teachers in a cooperative way they do not now enjoy.

Our foreign language teaching efforts for English-speaking children, as all interested observers know, have not been accorded enough importance. In the wake of the widespread cancellation of the foreign language requirement at many colleges in the 1960s, the teaching of languages in our high schools was even further diminished. It seems that only in times of war or of heightened national self-scrutiny such as the post-*Sputnik* period is the rigorous study of foreign languages emphasized. National commissions and task forces are appointed periodically to study the decline of foreign language learning, and our national leaders make pious statements about the importance of the knowledge of other languages for world trade; but rarely is there enough serious and sustained attention or money allocated to this goal. If there were a national or even regional consensus on the urgency of improving foreign language study—making it a high priority with sufficient funding—we in the United States could look to the various successful exemplary programs in other countries, as I have described, that we might profitably duplicate.

Early Total Immersion programs, like those in Canada, have proven very effective with average American children in places such as Culver City, California, which has had a Spanish Immersion program for fifteen years; in Holliston, Massachusetts, which has had a French Immersion program for ten years; and the Oyster School in Washington, D.C., described in detail in chapter 5, to name a few outstanding examples.

The Holliston program represents what is possible. Initially funded as an experimental project by a three-year federal grant in 1979, it begins in kindergarten with one class of twenty-five new French Immersion students every year and now extends up to the high school. I have visited the Holliston schools, observing kindergarten, third-grade, and seventh-grade classrooms, and I have found them an absolute marvel! In kindergarten within a month children are using words and phrases in French among themselves and with the teacher. In grade three I observed an hour-long mathematics class conducted in French, and the students were completely at ease. Although they sometimes struggled with the math, the students did not fumble with the French. In grade seven the class was reading Canadian literature and having a fairly sophisticated discussion, complete with the teasing and kidding around that is typical of that age group—all in French, with no visible awkwardness and with a firm control of syntax and pronunciation. Admission to this program is by parent application, not by test scores. Nevertheless, this heterogeneous group of American students with wide-ranging levels of ability and motivation is— in an otherwise unremarkable school district—completely fluent in French and working comfortably and successfully in two languages!

If an Early Immersion program is not feasible, then starting it at the secondary school level still provides a more concentrated program than the current U.S. high school schedule allows. Exciting possibilities are readily apparent, for example, in the models of Late Immersion language schools that I have observed in Bulgaria and Turkey. At the seventh-grade level, students in the special language schools temporarily interrupt their regular schedule of classes to spend one year on intensive language study. Their high school courses from then on are almost all taught in the second language—English, Russian, French, German, or whatever language is available to the students. High school students consequently develop a high level of competence in the second language, which they can use in employment (tourism, commerce, banking, government) or in higher education, especially in the fields of science and technology. On a lecture tour in Bulgaria in 1988, I visited several of the special English-language high schools and had discussions with students both in and out of the classrooms. Their fluency in a language not much used in their country was impressive. There are no English-language newspapers, radio stations, or television programs; only a small number of English-speaking tourists; and an even smaller number of English-speakers in residence. Of course, this type of program adds an extra year of schooling, a major financial consideration. We could establish "language academies" on the magnet school model in the United States to attract students from a whole city instead of just a neighborhood, as we have organized magnet schools stressing science, drama, or computers.

A less radical and less costly plan for deepening the acquisition of a foreign language at the high school level is the linking of language, literature, and history courses into an integrated block of study: the history and literature could be taught *in the foreign language*. This integrated program can be offered in a two-hour period daily for a two- or three-year period. The Dodge Foundation has provided funding for Chinese-language and -culture classes of this sort to be started in a number of public and private schools. The Brookline, Massachusetts, High School has provided such a program, with Dodge Foundation support, for the past five years. Again, it is the employment of the new language in the teaching of other subjects that solidifies its use.

Innovations of the type just described will bring bilingual and foreign language teaching together in productive new ways. Inviting bilingual teachers who have native fluency into the regular school curriculum will not only improve foreign language teaching but enhance the status of bilingual teachers in our public school systems. Bilingual programs suffer because they are perceived as being separate, remedial efforts only for the disadvantaged. Indeed, there has not yet been enough of a dialogue between the bilingual and foreign language professionals, as both sides harbor suspicions over territorial encroachment. Not to capitalize on the natural resources of our multicultural population is surely wasteful, but the merging will require a change in the perception of teachers' traditional roles.

———————— ◇◇◇ ————————

Administrators, Parents, and Teachers—Courage!

Finally, the need for courage on the part of school administrators, members of school boards, superintendents, and others in decision-making positions must be stressed. Legal choice of program type is possible in many states, but school administrators are often reluctant to take a risk that might elicit critical, even militant, reactions. California is a stark example of such a paralysis of will. In spite of the public disagreement about whether bilingual education programs can ever meet the needs of different language groups in all situations, very few districts have been willing to resist the pressure for conformity from the state bilingual education bureaucracy and from militant latino activists, even when teachers and parents agree that a different type of program would meet their goals better. The fear of lawsuits is a powerful disincentive to innovation.

The Berkeley School District, however, because it was able in court to demonstrate conclusively that its students compare favorably in school achievement with students in other California cities, will no doubt have an encouraging and enabling effect on districts that want to institute different educational approaches. But even if a school district believes that its cause is just, mounting a defense in a civil rights suit is risky and potentially very expensive. If an advocate sues an institution on the grounds of denial of civil rights, he or she, as plaintiff, is not liable to pay court costs or the defending district's legal fees even if he or she loses. But if the defendant loses, the institution must pay all court costs and legal fees of the plaintiffs. This arrangement is, of course, a powerful and necessary incentive to encourage the filing of suits to correct injustice. If Berkeley, a proud, liberal community, had been less courageous, it might have settled out of court by allowing unwanted program demands to be forced on it.

Educational advance in the schooling of language minority children needs to be energetic, informed, and courageous. Schools alone cannot change damaging social realities, but a better-educated minority community active in its own economic, social, and political advancement is a primary ingredient.

In calling for a common, practical goal and a united educational effort, I am bucking a current tide of politically exploited divisiveness and intergroup tensions. Yet my rebel voice speaks for the teachers and parents whose voices are not otherwise heard—the many who have confided their concerns that the experts are misleading us, that the children are not being served.

We live in a time of growing contentiousness regarding race, gender, class, and ethnicity. We want societal integration—interdependence—at the same time we cherish cultural pluralism and the preservation of separate group identity. My purpose in *Forked Tongue* is to reduce the harmful manipulation by doctrinaire bilingual advocates and to increase opportunity for minority children. I am calling for their freedom of individual choice of identity within the communal aspirations of their cultural group.

This freedom begins with the children and the way we educate them. We call for equality of access and equal treatment, but these goals cannot be met unless we give higher priority to the rights of children and less weight to the bureaucratic and political agenda of community leaders.

There is a clear view emerging that the very policies we have promoted to help language minority children are in many cases working to their disadvantage. From the basic perspectives provided in this book—language acquisition research, the examples of other multilingual societies, and the rapidly changing demographics of the United States—I believe the new approaches we must pursue are self-evident. The experimental idea proposed twenty years ago called bilingual education has not attained the goals this society determinedly seeks. In many cities, the old bilingual programs are being modified in consonance with new insights on language learning. But the broader changes that are needed are strongly opposed by the bureaucracy that has grown up around the bilingual education program. The hidden agenda of the bureaucracy—preserving hispanic language and culture at the price of social integration and advance—is ideological; the political agenda—garnering jobs, power, and community control—is predictably self-serving. In short, the nobility of the publicly stated agenda of educational improvement is deceptive: our leaders, to use the familiar metaphor, are speaking with forked tongues.

Without competence in the standard language of the society, immigrants, refugees, and migrants are at a disabling disadvantage, unable to share in the economic opportunities or to participate fully in their responsibilities in a democratic society. The sooner this enabling skill is acquired, the sooner children can join in the full life of their school and community. The pragmatic benefits of starting early to learn a second language cannot be ignored, except as an act of self-delusion. And the choice is not a matter of either learning English well or retaining cultural identity. Both goals can be accomplished, but they are distinct and should not be blurred. A conscientious public debate based on the kind of information I have presented will help school districts, parents, and communities make informed decisions about their priorities and about what the schools ought to be doing to meet agreed-upon educational needs effectively.

My concern has been to raise the level of the public debate and to get at the reality behind the doctrinaire rhetoric of bilingual education. It would be refreshing and surely productive to generate a rational discussion of the issues without name-calling. The quotation of Sir Kenneth Clark on my office wall captures the ideal: "I prefer gentleness to violence, forgiveness to vendetta. On the whole I think that knowledge is preferable to ignorance, and I am sure that human sympathy is more valuable than ideology."[18] Surely it is possible to debate basic differences in societal values and aspirations and still complete the job of educating our children.

Epilogue

The issues raised and discussed when *Forked Tongue: The Politics of Bilingual Education* was first published in 1990 have not been resolved, but substantial change is evident. The information brought together in this new chapter is not easily accessible anywhere else in the country. It is the sum total of five years of advocating, consulting, speaking, writing, and agitating to improve the education of language minority children—and no one else can provide such a comprehensive report. The section in chapter 4 on language education policy in the Soviet Union is entirely out of date, since the unanticipated breakup of the USSR, but remains an interesting historical note on the complexities of multilingual societies.

In the United States, however, the efforts being made and the money being invested in the special programs to help immigrant, migrant, and refugee school children who do not know the English language when they enter U.S. schools are still largely misguided. The current population of limited-English students is being treated in ways that earlier immigrant groups were not. The politically righteous assumption is that these students cannot learn the English language quickly and must be taught all their school subjects in their native language for three to seven years, while having the English language introduced gradually. Twenty-seven years of classroom experience with this education policy and a growing body of research show no benefits for native language teaching either in better learning of English or better learning of school subjects. These facts have hardly dented the armor of the true believers in the bilingual education bureaucracy.

Yet some changes and improvements have occurred in this most contentious area of public education. *Forked Tongue*, in fact, has played some small part in promoting positive changes in the education of limited-English students in dozens of school districts across the country—by supporting the efforts to modify bilingual education laws in several states; by heightening the public awareness of the grossly ineffective education policies and programs for these students; and, most important of all, by giving courage to hundreds of teachers in U.S. public schools who daily see the failure and futility of bilingual programs. Research reports contribute additional evidence on the poor results of native language instruction as the superior road to English language competency for classroom work. But the successful results from programs emphasizing intensive English are beginning to appear, now that some small measure of funding is being allocated to these so-called alternative model programs.

What *Forked Tongue* has not succeeded in doing is improving the character and tone of the public dialogue. All too often, it remains almost impossible to voice criticism of bilingual education programs without being pilloried as a hater of foreigners and foreign languages and of contributing to the anti-immigrant climate. Another area in which little positive change has occurred in the past few years is in reducing the established power of state education departments to impose education mandates on local school districts. The power of the bilingual education bureaucracy has hardly diminished, even in states like California where the state bilingual education law expired in 1987. However, there are counterforces opposing the seemingly settled idea that native language programs are the single best solution for limited-English students and these challenges are growing at the local school level.

In reviewing the contents of the original *Forked Tongue,* I decided that the most useful information to give readers is an extended description of recent developments in these particular areas: national research on effective programs for language minority students, changing demographics, program costs; descriptions of a representative sampling of school districts that are substantially revising their approach to the education of limited-English students; legislative initiatives to reform bilingual education laws at the federal and state level; and revisiting the movement to make English the official language of the United States. My personal reflections on the future of bilingual education will conclude this section.

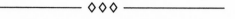

Updating the Research

The basic questions posed in the early years of bilingual education still have not found clear-cut answers. Are there measurable benefits for limited-English students when they are taught in their native language for a period of time, both in their learning of the English language for academic achievement and in their mastery of school subjects? Has a clear advantage emerged for a particular pedagogy among the best known models—transitional bilingual education, English as a Second Language, structured immersion, two-way, dual immersion, or developmental bilingual programs? There is no more consensus on the answers to these questions than there was five years ago. However, there is growing evidence of an almost total lack of accountability in states that have invested most heavily in bilingual education for the past fifteen or twenty years and have not collected data or evaluated programs to produce answers to the questions raised above. The research that has been published in recent years includes these major reports.

The GAO Study

Every year since the late 1970s, the school enrollment of limited-English students has increased at a faster rate than the rest of the school population and the costs of special programs nationwide are beginning to be tallied. The U.S. General Accounting Office (GAO) published a study in January 1994 titled *Limited-English Proficiency: A Growing and Costly Educational Challenge Facing Many School Districts* at the request of the Senate Committee on Labor and Human Resources. The GAO study provides an overview of the serious problems confronting U.S. public schools in meeting the needs of limited-English students, new demographics on where these students are concentrated, and a detailed description of five representative school districts with rapidly growing LEP populations.

Briefly, the GAO report highlights these problems in the five districts that are common to all public schools with LEP students:

- immigrant students are almost 100 percent non-English speaking on arrival in the United States
- arrival of LEP students occurs at different times during the school year, which causes upheavals in classrooms and educational programs
- some high school students have not been schooled in their native lands and lack literacy skills in any language
- there is a high level of family poverty and transiency and a low level of parental involvement in students' education
- there is an acute shortage of bilingual teachers and of textbooks and assessment instruments in the native languages.

The information gathered by the GAO study is valuable to educators, researchers, and policymakers. An alarming fact reported in this study is mentioned only in passing and never explained: *immigrant children account for only 43 percent of the*

Table E.1   Limited-English Proficient (LEP) Students in Five
Districts and Their Proportion of the Total Enrollment,
1982–1992

District	TOTAL ENROLLMENT		LEP ENROLLMENT				NUMBER OF LANGUAGES 1992**
	1982	1992	1982	%	1992	%	
A	193,701	197,413	24,021	12.40%	39,569	20.0%	7***
B	12,963	11,998	1,256	9.90	1,427	11.8	12
C	46,752	73,647	3,092	6.60	20,937	28.4	88
D	24,565	28,739	4,395	17.80	7,108	24.7	57
E	57,498	74,084	7,815	13.50	24,093	32.5	37

* Percentage of the total enrollment
** Number of languages present in 1982 was not available for the most part
*** District A reported 60 additional languages but documents specifying those languages were not available. They reported 94% of LEP students as Spanish speakers and 2400 students speaking other languages.
Prepared by R. P. Porter from data in GAO report.

SOURCE: *READ Perspectives* 2, no. 1 (Spring 1995).

limited-English students in our schools. Who, then, make up the other 57 percent and why are such large numbers of native-born children classified as limited- or non-English proficient and placed in native language instruction programs? In a private conversation with one of the GAO regional managers I was unable to get an explanation for the high percentage of native-born students classified as limited-English. I was told that the GAO had not found an agreed upon definition of what a "limited-English person" is and that they have included in this category children who speak English but may not read and write it well enough for school work. In that case, there surely are a large number of students who are wrongly enrolled in programs where they are being taught in another language when what they urgently need is remedial help in reading and writing in English.

Curiously, the GAO study does not provide any data on the costs of different types of bilingual education programs even though "cost" is part of the study's title. However, a report on costs and other issues of bilingual education in the United States was prepared by the American Legislative Council (ALEC) as a special supplement to its publication, *The Report Card on American Education 1994.*

The ALEC Study: Bilingual Education in the United States, 1991–92

The ALEC Study makes a bold attempt to unravel the mysteries of exactly how many students are served by special programs that aim to remove the language barrier to an equal education, what kinds of programs they are enrolled in, where these students are concentrated—by state, and how much is actually being spent in this special effort. As a former school administrator, I know firsthand that it is quite possible to account for special costs. In the Newton, Massachusetts, Public Schools annual budget there is an account for bilingual/ESL programs that covers all the costs incurred for the LEP students: teachers, teacher aides, books, materials, transportation, and administration. One knew what was spent each year, over and above the school costs for general education, and in Newton this averaged about $1,000 per student, per year, for LEP students. Not all school districts keep such information and it is not collected consistently by all state education departments because this is not required by the federal government.

Analyzing data from the National Center for Education Statistics, the Office of Bilingual Education and Minority Languages Affairs (OBEMLA), and various other federal and state sources, the ALEC study synthesizes the data to arrive at these conclusions for the 1991–92 school year:

- on average, all federal funding for education amounts to 6 percent—state and local sources provide roughly 47 percent each;

- federal funding for bilingual education, $101 million in 1991 and $116 million in 1992, was mostly allocated to native language instruction programs, giving only 20–30 percent to ESL programs;
- 2.3 million limited-English students were enrolled in U.S. public schools while only 1.9 million were enrolled in any special language program, leaving 450,000 LEP students without any special language help;
- of the 1.9 million students in special programs, 60 percent were enrolled in bilingual, 22 percent in ESL, and 18 percent in a category labelled "unknown," because states could not describe their special language programs;
- candidly explaining the difficulties of collecting strictly accurate data, the costs of programs for LEP students are estimated to be $5.5 billion (56 percent) for bilingual programs, $1.9 billion (20 percent) for ESL, and $2.4 billion (24 percent) for unknown programs, totaling $9.9 billion for 1991–92;
- projecting the same recent increases in enrollments, spending on special language programs would amount to $12 billion in 1993 (4–5).

The ALEC study draws some tenable conclusions from the data summarized above, while it admits that the approximate cost figures may be an over- or underestimation of what is actually spent. Both federal and state agencies do give preference to native language instruction programs over ESL in funding decisions by a wide margin, even though "there is no conclusive research that demonstrates the educational superiority of bilingual education over ESL" (3). Even if the ALEC cost estimates were overestimated, this is only one of several recent reports that point out the widespread lack of accountability in bilingual education. Twenty-seven years of heavy investment in mainly bilingual programs has not produced exact data on how much these programs cost or how successful they are in realizing their goals in student achievement.

The cost to adult immigrants of not having fluency in the dominant language has been reported by economists Barry R. Chiswick and Paul W. Miller. In a 1995 study, they published their analysis of the differences in human capital earnings in some of the largest immigrant receiving countries, between immigrants who have acquired dominant language fluency and those who have not. Earnings for immigrants with English-language skills were 8.3 percent higher in Australia, 16.9 percent in the United States, and 12.2 percent higher in Canada (Chiswick, 279). They also defined the factors that contribute to the development of fluency in the new language: exposure to the language, efficiency in second language acquisition (related to level of schooling and age), and perceived economic benefits from language fluency (Chiswick, 246). These elements are comparable to the factors contributing to successful second language learning and school achievement for LEP students: sufficient exposure to the target language, sufficient schooling in the new language, and an understanding of the benefits of second language acquisition for school success and complete integration with English-speaking, mainstream students. The research has yet to be done on differences in earnings for immigrant/migrant/refugee children schooled in the United States who do not acquire English-language proficiency as a result of their long years in bilingual classrooms.

Though cost should not be the determining factor in deciding on special language programs for LEP students, analyses of cost benefits inevitably do affect decision making on education policy. Some recent studies comparing native language instruction programs with intensive English language assistance provide indirect cost comparisons from the oblique angle of student achievement. In both the El Paso and New York City longitudinal studies, whose descriptions follow, students in the English language, structured immersion programs met program goals in three to four years and were assigned to regular classrooms without special help, while students in the traditional bilingual classrooms needed six to seven years to reach the same level of skills for mainstreaming. Although neither study set out to study costs, it becomes obvious that the expense of giving large numbers of students extra services for two to four additional years are formidable.

The El Paso Bilingual Immersion Project

An interim report on the first three years' outcomes in the El Paso experiment with English language immersion appears on pp. 68–69. In 1992, the Institute for Research in English Acquisition and Development (READ) published a monograph on the final results of the seven-year longitudinal study of the Bilingual Immersion Project by Russell Gersten, John Woodward, and Susan Schneider, which was later summarized in an article by Gersten and Woodward in *The Elementary School Journal* in 1995. This evaluation clearly demonstrates advantages for the immersion approach over the traditional bilingual education (TBE) model.

- the Iowa Test of Basic Skills (in English) results for grades four and five do show superior performance in all academic areas for students in the immersion program over students in the transitional bilingual program (1995, 236)
- by grade six, 99 percent of immersion students were mainstreamed; at end of seventh grade, 35 percent of TBE students were still in the bilingual program (1995, 232)
- well-designed bilingual immersion leads to more rapid, more successful, and increased integration of Latino students into the mainstream, with no detrimental effects in any area of achievement for students who took part in this program. The increased integration may lead to a decrease in high school dropout rates among Hispanic students. Subsequent research

is needed to explore the possibility of this effect of immersion programs (1992, 31)

- major strengths of the bilingual immersion program are its use of contemporary thinking on language acquisition and literacy development and its relatively stress-free approach to the rapid learning of English in the primary grades (1992, 31)
- teacher questionnaires revealed much greater satisfaction with the early, systematic teaching of English in the immersion program than with the slow introduction of English in the bilingual program (1992, 30)
- student interviews indicated no significant differences in reactions to the two programs. No evidence, from students, parents or teachers, that native language teaching produces a higher level of self-esteem or that early immersion in a second language is more stressful, two of the common beliefs promoted by bilingual education advocates (1992, 30–31).

Research such as that conducted in El Paso is invaluable in the ongoing debate on program effectiveness. Because the comparison was made between two radically different teaching methods in the same school district with the same population of limited-English students, this study provides incontrovertible proof of the benefits to students of early second language learning. More recently, the New York City public schools published a report that threw a metaphorical bomb shell into the bilingual education camp.

The New York Study

Educational Progress of Students in Bilingual and ESL Programs: A Longitudinal Study, 1990–1994, was published in October 1994 by the Board of Education of the City of New York. New York City invested $300 million in 1993 in bilingual programs where the instruction was given in Spanish, Chinese, Haitian Creole, Russian, Korean, Vietnamese, French, Greek, Arabic, and

Bengali—an investment that was not only misguided but harmful to the student beneficiaries, as can be seen when the results of the longitudinal study are examined (Dillon, 1).

The New York City study is important because, like the El Paso study, it examines student achievement in basically different programs in large, urban school districts, and it charts student progress over a period of years. The criteria of student success measured included: numbers of years served in a special language program before exiting to a mainstream classroom, reading level in English, and performance in math. The two groups of limited-English students whose achievement was monitored were: (1) Spanish speakers and speakers of Haitian Creole who were enrolled in bilingual classrooms where they received mostly native language instruction in reading, writing, and school subjects, with brief English language lessons, and (2) students from Russian, Korean, and Chinese language backgrounds who were placed in ESL classes where all instruction was provided through a special English language curriculum. Total enrollment of students in the study:

11,320 entered kindergarten in fall 1990
 2,053   "   1st grade   " "   "
   841   "   2nd grade " "   "
   797   "   3rd grade " "   "
   754   "   6th grade " "   "
 1,366   "   9th grade " "   "

(Board of Education of the City of New York, ix)

As any disinterested observer might have anticipated, there is strong evidence showing that the earlier a second language is introduced, the more rapidly it is learned for academic purposes. Surprising? Not at all, but it flies in the face of the received wisdom of Jim Cummins's theories that were developed to justify bilingual education, after the fact—the facilitation theory and the threshold hypothesis (chapter 3 of this volume). With appropriate teaching, children can learn a new language quickly and can learn subject matter taught *in* that language. Reading and writing skills can be mastered and math can be learned successfully in a second language and here is the proof from thousands of New York City school children.

The most riveting outcome of this research is the reported fact that, "At all grade levels, students served in ESL-only programs exited their programs faster than those served in bilingual programs" (Board of Education, ii). For students who entered school in kindergarten, second grade, and sixth grade, the three-year exit rates were as follows:

	Exit Rate *ESL-only*	Exit Rate *Bilingual*
Kindergarten	79.3 percent	51.5 percent
Grade 2	67.5 percent	22.1 percent
Grade 6	32.7 percent	6.9 percent

(Board of Education, ii)

The three-year exit rates for LEP students who entered kindergarten from different language groups, whether they were in ESL or bilingual programs was reported as follows:

- 91.8 percent for Korean
- 87.4 percent for Russian
- 82.6 percent for Chinese
- 58.7 percent for Haitian Creole
- 50.6 percent for Spanish
  (Board of Education, ix)

Differences among language groups remained steady even for students entering the New York schools in the higher grades. Critics of the study, including Luis O. Reyes of the New York City School Board, allege that Korean, Russian, and Chinese background students are from middle-class families and that the social class difference invalidates the study (Krashen, 1995). Socioeconomic data is not reported in the study. We do not know how many of the children in any of the language groups are from poor, working-class, or middle-class families and we should not make unwarranted assumptions. One could hazard a guess that most immigrant, migrant, and refugee children attending the New York City Public Schools do not come from affluent families. The undeniable facts are that children from Spanish- and Haitian Creole-speaking families are mostly funneled into bilingual classrooms and children from other language groups are mostly assigned to ESL classrooms. I firmly believe that the type of schooling these children receive makes a large differ- ence in their ability to achieve at their own personal best. I be- lieve, even more firmly, that Haitian and Latino children would succeed in mastering English language skills better and faster and, therefore, join their English-speaking peers in mainstream classes much sooner than is now the case *if they were given the same opportunity given to Russian, Korean, and Chinese students.*

Exiting the special program classrooms more expeditiously is not only a cost consideration but a matter of integration and opportunity. Remaining in substantially segregated bilingual classrooms for several years does not equip students to com- pete in the broader life of the school and community—in fact it has the opposite effect. The New York Study reports the high- est success in school achievement for students who were in the special language programs the shortest amount of time, one or two years. "Students who tested out of LEP-entitlement after one or two years of service generally performed above average on the citywide tests of reading (in English) and mathematics that were given in Spring, 1994. However, there were large dif- ferences in performance between those who had been served in ESL-only versus bilingual programs, and between those who exited after one or two years versus those who exited after three or more years" (Board of Education, ix).

Even more important than the time element is the perfor- mance of LEP students in regular classrooms, after they exit a special program, and, once again, we find that students who had been enrolled in ESL classrooms received better scores than those who had been in native language classrooms in both reading and math. This must be the ultimate measure of program effectiveness: how well are students able to perform, unassisted, in regular classrooms after they have received the special services, for a period of time, of one or another special program? The New York study answers this question most emphatically in favor of intensive English language programs.

This study substantially refutes the work of Virginia Collier at George Mason University who flatly asserts that LEP students who are in English language programs need five to ten years to reach English fluency but only four to seven years if they are in bilingual programs (Collier and Thomas, 1995). In their recent research, their criterion for fluency appears to be the ability to score at or above the fiftieth percentile on a standardized reading test in English. This is an inappropriate standard. Reading ability is *not* the only indicator of language fluency. Students may be quite fluent in English—they may, in fact, be native speakers of the language—and not do well on a reading test.

The latest sequel to the publication of the New York study is the filing of a suit against the State Commissioner of Education by the Bushwick Parents Organization, which represents 150 Brooklyn families. The suit makes two major charges, one that "tens of thousands of immigrant children in New York City have been permitted to 'languish' for up to six years in bilingual classes, learning neither English nor other subjects particularly well" (Steinberg, 19 September 1995). The second charge faults the State Education Department for "routinely granting waivers that permit school officials to keep children in classes taught in their native language—usually—beyond the three-year limit allowed by state law" (Steinberg, B-6).

As an expert witness in this lawsuit, I have reviewed the affidavits of the petitioners and respondents. The Bushwick Parents Organization specifically alleges that because the children of its members routinely remain segregated in bilingual education programs in excess of three years, and in some cases in excess of six years, contrary to S 3204(2) of the State Education Law, these children are not receiving adequate instruction in English, the crucial skill that leads to equal opportunity in schooling, jobs, and public life in the United States. (Memorandum of Law in Opposition to Respondent's and Respondent-Intervenor's Motions to Dismiss, 19)

The affidavits of some of the Bushwick parents and educators reveal the unremitting failure of New York State's education policy and its harmful effects on school children, as illustrated in the following excerpts:

My grandson was in bilingual education from kindergarten through fifth grade at P.S. 377 in Bushwick. He is now in seventh grade, and cannot read in either English or Spanish.... We and other people we know were pressured into keeping our children in bilingual education by school officials. We were told that because my grandson has a Spanish last name, he should remain in bilingual classes. My grandson attended Head Start in English, and did not speak any Spanish at that time...I am very frustrated with the failure of the bilingual education program to teach my grandson either English or Spanish. (Ada Jimenez)

My son is eleven years old, and is in sixth grade at I.S. 291 in Bushwick. He participated in a Head Start program in English but has been in the bilingual program for six years...I have spoken with his teacher to try to switch him into regular English classes.... My son is confused between English and Spanish. I am unhappy with what he has learned in the bilingual education program. (Maria Cruz)

My son is in Ninth grade at Bushwick High School, and has been in bilingual education since he entered the school system.... My son is confused between Spanish and English. I have never been consulted about whether I wished to remove him from bilingual classes. (Carmen Quinones)

As part of my duties as Assistant Principal, I was required to observe Social Studies class at Eastern District High School. I observed that English was rarely used in the supposedly bilingual classes. The ninth grade classes were generally taught entirely in Spanish, and even by twelfth grade the classes were still conducted approximately 85 percent in Spanish, with written material and exams in Spanish as well. I attempted many times to withdraw students from the bilingual education program when I thought that they no longer needed to be in all-Spanish classes...I was never once successful at withdrawing a student from a bilingual education program. In my experience, once a child was in a bilingual education program, he remained in such program and was never mainstreamed into regular English-speaking classes...many students graduating from Eastern District High School were illiterate in both English and Spanish. (Edwin Selzer, former assistant principal, Eastern District High School, Brooklyn)

Within the last two years, we have spent a great deal of time examining the bilingual program. We have found that children in the bilingual program have not been improving their English skills, as their entire class day is taught in Spanish and only one period each day is devoted to studying English. Many of the children in bilingual classes were born in the United States and attended Head Start programs in English, but were then placed in bilingual programs when they entered the public school setting. Parents...discovered that their children were not advancing in English and, in many cases, their children's performance on English language tests were declining.... Although many parents are aware of their right to remove their children from bilingual programs, many parents indicate that when they initiate the idea of withdrawing their children from bilingual programs, the individual teachers and principals inform them that the bilingual settings are the best environment for their children...many of the parents are unable to overcome the pressure put on them by these school officials.... Many of these students graduate from school having never fully developed their English language skills, and they are therefore unprepared for higher education or employment in jobs in which English language skills are used. (Sister Kathy Maire, educator and organizer of Bushwick Parents Organization)

These statements make abundantly clear what has been observed in school districts from Massachusetts to Texas to California: the temporary assistance needed by limited-English children has evolved into a long-term assignment to segregated classrooms and the denial of parents' rights to a choice in their children's educational opportunities. A positive outcome for the Brooklyn parents who are mounting this challenge to the state education bureaucracy is crucial for the city's students and, one hopes, will embolden parents in other districts.

The California Study and Others, in Brief

New York City's willingness actually to monitor the progress of LEP students and report the results to the public is much to be praised when we survey the lack of accountability in other parts of the country. The State of California, with 1.2 million limited-English students (43 percent of all LEP students in the United States) and a twenty-year history of involvement with bilingual education, commissioned an evaluation of educational programs for these students. *Meeting the Challenge of Language Diversity: An Evaluation of Programs for Pupils with Limited Proficiency in English,* the published report of a two-year study,

1990–92, shows generally poor results for bilingual education programs in California and essentially evades the legislature's requirement that it provide "information to determine which model for educating LEP pupils is most effective and cost effective" (*Meeting the Challenge*, 3).

Major findings of this study:

1. California public schools do not have valid assessments of the performance for students with limited proficiency in English. Therefore, *the state and the public cannot hold schools accountable for LEP students achieving high levels of performance.* (emphasis added)
2. Many schools do not reclassify students (exit them from the bilingual programs with appropriate skills to work in mainstream classrooms), keeping them in native language classrooms well beyond the time when they are fluent in English. "It is not surprising that many students may wait years to be formally retested for program exit and that many others may never be reclassified, going on to the middle school still bearing the LEP label." (p. 38)
3. Junior and senior high school LEP students do not have access to core academic subjects through Sheltered English or ESL. Long stays in bilingual programs in elementary schools delay the effective learning of English language literacy skills which are so important for secondary school work. (Rossier, 1995)

Meeting the Challenge presents a bleak picture of the disappointing results of twenty years of bilingual education in California. When the Chacon-Moscone Bilingual Bicultural Act of 1976 expired in 1987, the California State Department of Education sent notification to each school district that the intent of the act would still be promoted by state regulations, principally, "that the primary goal of all [bilingual] programs is, as effectively and efficiently as possible, to develop in each child fluency in English" (Honig, 1987, 14–15). *Meeting the Challenge* fails to tell us how or if this goal is being properly met but offers a variety of excuses for not fulfilling its mission. The weaknesses in this giant instructional system for limited-English students—one out of every five students in California—are of giant proportions. The fact that the State Department of Education has allowed school districts to evade their responsibility to assess and report on student progress shows an unconscionable lack of accountability by this powerful bureaucracy. If we cannot hold the schools responsible for program outcomes after twenty years, then perhaps the responsibility for this failure rests squarely on the state agency that has forcefully promoted the bilingual education policy.

California's high school dropout rates reported in June 1995 amounted to a statewide average of 5 percent per year, or a four-year average of 20 percent of students leaving school before graduation. Discouraging as that seems, the dropout rate for Latino students statewide is even higher—28 percent, compared to 10 percent for Asian students, and 12 percent for white students. The four-year dropout rate for the Los Angeles Unified School District, the district enrolling the highest percentage of LEP students in the state, is a shocking 43.6 percent (Colvin, 14 June 1995).

In 1993 the Los Angeles Unified School District embarked on a plan to improve its bilingual education programs, partly through expanded teacher training in the native languages of the students (actually, in Spanish only) (Chavez, 3–4 September 1993). Clearly, the increased emphasis on native language instruction has not had any positive effect on the dropout rates for LEP students in the Los Angeles schools. The latest Los Angeles figures on dropout rates by ethnic breakdown, as reported by the State Department of Education in October 1994 for the 1993–94 school year, are 44.4 percent for Hispanic students, *three-fourths of whom are enrolled in bilingual classes in the district* (emphasis added).

Robert E. Rossier, in a review of the California study (1995) argues that, "Young people of limited-English proficiency have the same right as their native English-speaking schoolmates to have their linguistic and academic performance evaluated periodically by measures which clearly indicate to them and to the schools the extent of their progress toward the goals set for all students" (46–47). Rossier ends his review with two powerful indictments of the California study and the system that it attempted to evaluate.

While the report presents no statistical data that would shed light on the effectiveness of current programs, it does provide several items of information that, read carefully, point to the conclusion that California's heavy reliance on native language teaching has not served LEP students well. The conclusion could be formed that the bilingual programs described as exemplary have instead resulted in delaying the learning of English, delaying the enrollment of LEP students in mainstream classes, and, in many cases, denying these students the opportunity to enroll in classes required for high school graduation. Not having access to classes available to their English-speaking classmates, LEP students are, in effect, denied an important civil right: the right to equal educational opportunity. (47–48)

...*Meeting the Challenge* has shown—as much by what it has avoided saying as by what it has said—that this opportunity will continue to be withheld from them until we are able to look truthfully at the havoc that the programs of the past twenty years have caused. (48)

Massachusetts Revisited

Ironically, the Commonwealth of Massachusetts, which passed the first state law mandating native language teaching in 1971, Chapter 71-A, has an even more dismal record than California in the area of public accountability. Efforts to reform the Transitional Bilingual Education (TBE) law have been successfully resisted, even though there can hardly be one legislator who has any documented proof for the effectiveness of bilingual education in Massachusetts. A state commission was appointed by Governor Weld to survey the status of bilingual education in the state, and in December 1994 reported this conclusion:

we do not know, on the basis of measured outcomes, whether TBE programs in Massachusetts produce good results or poor results. There are no comprehensive data that evaluate the performance of TBE pupils compared with pupils from other groups. This specialized program which accounts for 5 percent of all pupils in Massachusetts public schools and 17 percent of all pupils in Boston public schools is not held separately accountable for its performance. (Massachusetts Bilingual Education Commission, 41)

Apparently, the commission has recommended that the State Department of Education develop new guidelines on accountability as soon as suitable tests are developed. As a veteran Massachusetts educator who has seen many a set of "guidelines" arrive with a flourish and disappear without a trace, I reserve judgment on the latest pronouncements.

Massachusetts probably leads the country in zany educational experiments. I reported earlier (30–31) on the Cape Verdean project to try to encourage the use of a nonstandard dialect as the classroom language of instruction. The Boston Public Schools, in its infinite wisdom, now maintains a K-12 bilingual program in Kriolu, a dialect of Portuguese spoken in the Cape Verde Islands, which has no alphabet, no written language, and no books. Massachusetts is thought to be the only place in the world to have school rooms in which Kriolu is the language of instruction, with Kriolu programs in Boston, Brockton, and New Bedford schools. Portuguese is the official language of education in Cape Verde (de Jong, 7 May 1995)

Aside from the minor matters of alphabets, a written language, and books, there are these exquisite complications. Cape Verdean students may speak one of many dialects and not understand Kriolu, as explained by a science teacher in the Dearborn School, Boston, who says, "Sometimes a student gets upset because he's not understanding the Fogo dialect so you have to go back and help him in Kriolu or Portuguese." Communication between the schools and Cape Verdean parents is not improved either. Massachusetts law requires that all paperwork be sent to parents in the student's native language. A teacher at the Condon School, Eileen Fonseca, says it frustrates parents to receive a notice written in Kriolu. "When we send home report cards and matriculation papers in Kriolu, parents complain. This is new to them. They have to have it read three times, or they just ask for Portuguese or English, often so it can be read to them by family or friends." One parent made this comment, "They sent me a letter apparently to tell me something. I never understood what it was trying to say. I called to say that if the intent of the letter is to communicate, it would be better in Portuguese" (de Jong, A94).

The Kriolu Caper makes an amusing, now-I've-heard-everything anecdote, but the enormity of such folly in education policy is no laughing matter. This program neither helps students learn the language or acquire the literacy skills necessary for school achievement, nor does it facilitate communication between school and family. What it does do is foster resentment in the Cape Verdean community that does not feel respected or understood, a situation similar to the misguided attempt to make black English the language of instruction for African-American school children two decades ago. The Peoples Republic of Massachusetts is in serious need of a reality check.

The Special Alternative Instructional Programs (SAIP) Study

William Tikunoff and his associates, under the auspices of the Office of Bilingual Education and Minority Languages Affairs (OBEMLA), published the first survey of successful English-language intensive programs in U.S. public schools in 1991. Very little attention had been given until recently to programs that do *not* use native language teaching. From 1968 when the first Bilingual Education Act was passed until 1988, 96 percent of federal funding for demonstration projects and research studies went to native language teaching programs, with a meager 4 percent for programs concentrating on English language teaching. In 1988 Congress voted to revise the funding formula to allocate 25 percent to "Special Alternative Instructional Programs," as these English-teaching programs are labelled.

The SAIP report is a descriptive study of nine school districts in the United States, selected for their well-documented success in educating limited-English students. Through careful observation of classrooms and examination of school records, this study presents detailed data on effective teaching practices. How do these particular schools in suburban, rural, and metropolitan areas manage to teach their LEP students English rapidly and effectively and to teach school subjects *in English* to students from many different language backgrounds? The study supplies the answers to this central question by describing the program features in each school that contribute to positive outcomes for LEP students. It lays out a blueprint for building solidly efficient English language-based instruction for students from kindergarten through twelfth grade.

Russell Gersten and associates at the University of Oregon, in their review of the SAIP study (1995a), summarize the various ways that teachers of LEP students are effectively meeting the dual challenge of teaching English language literacy—speaking, reading, and writing—and the teaching of school subjects such as mathematics, science, and social studies in English. They emphasize the key lessons from the Tikunoff study: school programs must be restructured to respond more flexibly to LEP students' needs for higher levels of English proficiency, and more teacher training is needed in how to merge English language development with content area instruction.

The Rossell/Baker Review: The Educational Effectiveness of Bilingual Education

This section will conclude with the review of an unpublished work in progress by Rossell and Baker that summarizes the major studies on the effectiveness of bilingual education and analyzes those studies that are methodologically acceptable.

Social science research in education is, at best, an approximation of true scientific research. School children cannot be isolated in laboratory test tubes and studied under pristine conditions, controlling for minute variables. In the area of bilingual education research, the quality of the product is generally acknowledged to be especially low. The elements of a scientifically valid evaluation of a special effort must include, at the minimum:

- random assignment of subjects to avoid self-selection bias;
- a control group to compare with the group receiving the special program (treatment);
- pre-testing to establish that students in different groups are starting with the same traits, that is, all are limited or non-English speakers, or statistical adjustments are made for pre-treatment differences;
- post-testing to determine the effect of different treatments;
- assurance that one group does not receive extra benefits, aside from the difference in treatments, such as after-school programs, or a longer school day.

In the area of bilingual education research there is the added problem that the label is applied to a range of educational varieties from the classic model in which native language instruction is given 80–90 percent of the school day to the other extreme where the teacher may use a word or two of another language on occasion. This complicates the work of analyzing the effects of bilingual programs.

Rossell and Baker read over 500 studies, 300 of which were program evaluations. The authors found 72 methodically acceptable studies, that is, studies that show the effect of transitional bilingual education on English language learning, reading, and mathematics, compared to (1) "submersion" or doing nothing, (2) English as a Second Language, (3) structured immersion in English, and (4) maintenance bilingual education. The authors' overall finding, which is of crucial importance as this is the most current, comprehensive analysis of the research, is that, *"there is still…no consistent research support for transitional bilingual education as a superior instructional practice for improving the English language achievement of limited-English-proficient children"* (emphasis added) (14–15).

The table that follows provides a graphic illustration of the poor results for transitional bilingual education programs that prove to be either no better than other approaches or, in most cases, to be worse than other alternatives. In only a very small percentage of the studies does bilingual education show better results. The data comparing TBE assistance with classrooms where students are given no special help at all (submersion) are especially damning for TBE and are rarely reported. Here we see that TBE is better than doing nothing in only 22 percent of the studies in reading, in only 7 percent of the test results in language learning, and in 9 percent of the programs in math achievement (16).

How can state and federal education policy supporting transitional bilingual education hold up much longer in the face of such negative evidence? The reason for mandating bilingual education programs was the expectation that they would help limited-English students do *better* than if they were given no help at all. In fact, the U.S. Supreme Court's Lau decision of 1974 specifically requires that something special be done for these students. Hence, if bilingual education is no better than or worse than doing nothing, the advocates for this failed remedy have much to answer for.

Rossell and Baker discuss Cummins's facilitation theory and threshold hypotheses at some length, systematically refuting the particular studies supporting these ideas. Cummins's theoretical support for transitional bilingual education was pronounced after the fact, about ten years after bilingual programs had been started—not as an educational but as a civil rights initiative. No credible evidence yet emerges that children who are taught in their native language until they reach a certain threshold (about seven years of education) will reach a higher level of academic achievement than children who are taught in a second language from an early age. Neither is there any evidence for the notion that children must be taught to read first in their native language for they will then transfer that skill to reading in a second language very easily. The arguments advanced by Rossell and Baker disproving the validity of the studies (Collier, Skutnabb-Kangas, Burkheimer, Ramirez) that claim to support Cummins's hypotheses are valuable to an understanding of bilingual education's basic fallacy. The fundamental questions are clearly stated,

what knowledge transfers from the native tongue to the second language that cannot be learned simply from the second language learning process alone?...what particular mental processes or items of literacy related knowledge possessed by someone who learns to read in his native tongue enables him or her to surpass the child who learns to read or write in the second language?" (31)

Table E.2 Percent of Methodologically Acceptable Studies*
Demonstrating Program Superiority, Equality,
or Inferiority by Achievement Test Outcome

	*Reading***	*Language*	*Math*
TBE v. Submersion (Do Nothing)			
TBE Better	22%	7%	9%
No Difference	45%	29%	56%
TBE Worse	33%	64%	35%
Total N	60	14	34
TBE v. ESL			
TBE Better	0%	0%	25%
No Difference	71%	67%	50%
TBE Worse	29%	33%	25%
Total N	7	3	4
TBE v. Submersion/ESL			
TBE Better	19%	6%	11%
No Difference	48%	35%	55%
TBE Worse	33%	59%	34%
Total N	67	17	38
TBE v. Structured Immersion			
TBE Better	0%	0%	0%
No Difference	17%	100%	63%
TBE Worse	83%	0%	38%
Total N	12	1	8
Structured Immersion v. ESL			
Immersion Better	100%	0%	0%
No Difference	0%	0%	0%
Total N	3	0	0
TBE v. Maint. BE			
TBE Better	100%	0%	0%
Total N	1	0	0

* Studies are listed in more than one category if there were different effects for different grades or cohorts.
** Oral English achievement for preschool programs.

SOURCE: *Bilingual Education Reform in Massachusetts* (Boston: Pioneer Institute, 1996).

A graphic illustration of this point is presented in the following example:

while it is true that individuals who are literate in their native tongue are easier to teach a second language to, this tells us nothing about how non-literate individuals should be taught, nor the language they should be taught in. It is probably also true that a person who has been unable to learn to ride a bike is a harder person to teach to ski, but this does not necessarily mean that the best way to teach a non-bike rider how to ski is to spend years teaching them how to ride a bike. The bilingual education literature, however is rife with such unwarranted inferential leaps. (29)

The Ramirez study (1991), which Rossell reviewed at length in 1992, is routinely cited by bilingual education advocates as the strongest research evidence for the effectiveness of native language teaching programs. Briefly, Ramirez et al. studied and compared student performance in early-exit transitional bilingual education classrooms, all-English structured immersion classrooms, and late-exit maintenance bilingual classrooms, with a national sample of 1,054 students. Although the study is judged to be methodologically sound, its claims for the superiority of late-exit bilingual programs (six to seven years in native language classrooms) is not supported by the internal evidence. Students in the early-exit (three years) bilingual classrooms did better in reading than immersion students but not in language arts and math in the first two years, but the advantage of bilingual instruction had disappeared by the end of four years of schooling when immersion students did better in language arts and there was no difference between programs in reading or math performance (32). The Ramirez study does not show support for the facilitation effect since it shows that *students who stayed in bilingual classrooms the longest actually did the worst* (33). Nor does this study either provide a clear distinction between the three program models it described or make valid comparisons to support policy decisions, as was noted by the National Research Council (1992):

Although the study's final report claims that the three programs represent three distinct instructional models, the findings indicate that the programs were not that distinct. They were essentially different versions of the same treatment: immersion and early-exit programs were in some instances indistinguishable from one another.... The final designs of the longitudinal and immersion studies were ill-suited to answer the important policy questions that appear to have motivated them. (102–103)

Rossell and Baker's literature review, which will be published as chapter 3 of a book titled *Bilingual Education Reform in Massachusetts,* arrives at a few well-supported conclusions. Classroom teachers with some knowledge of the student's native language are more effective than teachers who are fluent in that language, presumably because the teacher who is fluent in Spanish will be inclined to teach in that language most of the time and the teacher with only low level skills in Spanish will use the language sparingly. A little native language teaching, when children just start school, is better than a lot. The teacher who was most successful in raising the English language achievement of Chinese students was one who taught 90 percent of the time in English, according to Fillmore (1980). In Austin, Texas, the successful bilingual program had teachers who used English as the medium of instruction 82 percent of the time (35).

The writers criticize my emphasis on the importance of time-on-task as the essential, though not the only, factor in effective second language learning. No argument put forward in this study convinces me otherwise. The reasons originally stated throughout this volume (pp. 83, 119, 125, 243) still stand in light of my observations of classrooms and my readings of the past five years. Immersion in a second language does not mean "teaching" the language but giving students the means to *use the language* in social and academic classroom situations. Any program, whatever its label, that employs a trained teacher who uses interactive teaching techniques, visual aids, educational technology, or other means to promote second language acquisition through learning of school subjects, is going to produce the best results in the short and long run. I believe the New York study bears this out. If the classroom contains students from only one language background and the teacher knows that language and can, in the early weeks, give a little help in the native language, all well and good. However, native language support is not crucial.

The writers propose two hypotheses for consideration: that bilingual education may be preferable to English immersion because it will give LEP students some time to be learning in their native language until the English becomes "comprehensible" and their time-on-task will be effective time-on-task. This is a very weak argument. There is no such thing as being in bilingual education only a little bit, it is like being only a little bit pregnant. True bilingual programs require all instruction in the native language, not just a little bit for comfort. Once engaged in this type of program, students will not acquire the English skills for literacy and for academic learning for years. A recent personal experience illustrates this point. I revisited the Armory Street School in Springfield, Massachusetts, in 1994, the school where I was a Spanish-English bilingual teacher for five years. After observing fifth and sixth grade students, I talked with one of their teachers about the low level of English language skills. She said, "No, these kids have not just arrived from another country, they've been in the Springfield schools for several years. But I'm only allowed to give them 45 minutes a day of English. The tragedy is that these kids will go to junior high school next year and they still will not have the skills to be in mainstream classes." Springfield is the classic example of why U.S. schools are probably not equipped to be "just a little bit bilingual."

The second idea advanced by Rossell and Baker is the "rest theory" of effective language learning. The "rest theory" seems to emerge from the studies on differences between massed versus spaced learning trials, that is, that subjects who were allowed interruptions for rest periods on repetitious tasks did better than subjects who had more practice but little or no rest. Their idea is that teachers should switch to the native language from time to time to give students a rest. This so-called theory reveals the enormous gap in the experience of the writers who clearly have never been classroom teachers of LEP students. Interactive, content-based language teaching does not consist of boring, repetitive drills, nor does it force children to spend all day studying grammar. Good teachers vary the pacing of activities to keep students interested and alert and there is so much variety in a school day, including opportunities for children to speak among themselves in any language they choose. As a former teacher and teacher supervisor, I find nothing of value in the "rest theory" for the education of limited-English students. Nor is there any documented evidence that young children will stay out of school because of the psychological strain of learning a new language.

There is a wealth of good material in the Rossell and Baker study, except for the wobbly theorizing, that will provide other researchers, educators, and policymakers with hard data and solid analyses. Perhaps this book, when it is published by the Pioneer Institute in Boston in 1996, will help forward the case for bilingual education reform in Massachusetts.

―――――――― ◇◇◇ ――――――――

The Local School Districts: The Grass-Roots Movements

The most promising development I have observed is the robust spirit in local school districts to question, reflect on, and finally reject the continuation of special programs that are not producing successful outcomes for limited-English students. Independent teachers, school principals, superintendents, and school board members in various cities across the country are braving the criticism of community activists and self-interested beneficiaries of the bilingual bureaucracy to reject the "facilitation hypotheses" now that it has been tested in their districts for years with nothing but failed results.

The message conveyed to me countless times in the past few years is typically this one:

We have been providing a transitional bilingual education program for ten, twelve, fifteen years, with instruction in the native language in all subjects including reading and writing, and some English lessons, with native language teachers and textbooks in the native language. We thought the students would be able to exit the program in three years or so with the skills necessary to work successfully in a mainstream classroom with English-speaking kids. But it isn't happening. Even after five or six years they have not learned enough English to speak, read, and write adequately. We're committed to spending the money but we must find a better way to educate these children. Can you help us?

One School in Massachusetts

In the fall of 1990, Frank Moriarty, principal of the Peter W. Reilly school in Lowell, Massachusetts, called me with exactly the complaint described above. In the working-class city of Lowell, home of the second largest Cambodian refugee population in the United States after Long Beach, California, there is a large Puerto Rican community as well. The Reilly School had been implementing a Spanish bilingual program for students in kindergarten to sixth grade for five years. Mr. Moriarty and his teaching staff were troubled by the poor results in student achievement in acquiring English language skills and in learning school subjects; they were also troubled by the segregative nature of their classrooms with Puerto Rican students substantially separated from their English-speaking classmates, most of the school day, for so many years. But what they found particularly disappointing was the fact that they were following the exact guidelines defined by the Lowell Bilingual Department and seeing nothing resembling the anticipated rapid second language learning or easy transfer of knowledge from the first to the second language.

I met with the entire school staff for a general discussion of their views on problem areas, visited classrooms to observe teaching strategies, reviewed the textbooks being used, and spent time with the bilingual and ESL teachers alone to discern their particular concerns. Interestingly, the bilingual and ESL teachers expressed two major concerns: that the approach they had been using with these students was not working and definitely needed changing, but that they feared job losses if the program were revised. Mr. Moriarty reassured the staff that their jobs were secure, that he was confident that each teacher currently in his school—with some additional training—would provide competent instruction in new ways, and that the professional staff would be involved in the redesigning of the school program for limited-English students.

In early 1991, a plan was developed for the start of the following school year, that would include revising the kindergarten and first grade curriculum to emphasize an English immersion approach with some use of Spanish, especially in the early months of school, for facilitating understanding of new concepts. All teachers at these grade levels were to participate in workshops on immersion techniques, content-based language teaching, and curriculum writing. These necessary activities were to be extended to grades two, three, and four in the second year of the plan and to grades five and six in the third year. Pre-testing and end-of-the-year testing on English language skills, classroom grades on school subjects, portfolios of classroom work, school attendance, and other data would be collected in order to be able to chart student learning over time and assess the value of the new program.

In late August of 1991, with initial planning completed and the first staff workshop scheduled, Mr. Moriarty received instructions from the then assistant superintendent that he was not to go forward with his project, that funds would not be provided to make the changes that he had outlined and that the school district did not approve of his plan, partly because of the involvement of Rosalie Porter. It was a bitter disappointment for Mr. Moriarty who had hoped to initiate a badly needed change of course in his school's inadequate teaching of limited-English students before taking retirement. He had earnestly wanted to close his long career as an educator in Lowell with a good gesture, but it was not to be.

I called the Peter W. Reilly School on 12 September 1995 and talked with the current principal, Mr. Vennochi. When he described the instructional program for LEP students, he confirmed my suspicion that nothing had been allowed to change. Students are still placed in self-contained classrooms (all Spanish speakers together) where the teaching is in Spanish 90 percent of the time, English 10 percent of the time, in kindergarten and first grade, on the orders of the Lowell School Department. In the second grade students are introduced to reading in English using the Ginn reading series and the principal said, in all seriousness, "It's very hard for these students to master reading in English because they haven't had very much preparation for it. And besides, they're still doing reading in Spanish and it becomes confusing for them. By the time these students reach grade four, the use of English in the classroom increases." In spite of the fact that Reilly school fourth graders had among the highest test scores in the city in most subjects, LEP students did not score at all as well as their peers in the mainstream classrooms. Since these students received the extraordinary services of the bilingual program for five years—from day one of kindergarten—and they clearly had not yet learned the English language or their school subjects well enough, it is reasonable to conclude that this approach is failing the students. Yet school principal Vennochi felt duty bound to pay lip service to the prevailing orthodoxy that is strongly promoted in the Lowell public schools about the benefits of native language instruction. The Reilly School story does not demonstrate support for this belief.

One Teacher in California

Not only are school administrators looking for new solutions for improving their teaching of language minority students, but teachers are eager to make changes in their own classrooms or, even more ambitiously, in their school districts. Dozens of individual teachers across the country have appealed to me directly or to the Institute for Research in English Acquisition and Development (READ) in Washington, DC, with which I am affiliated, for information on research, successful programs, and teaching methods. We have responded with various types of information and services to parents, teachers, and administrators in these localities: Los Angeles, Montclair-Ontario, Salinas, San Marcos, San Rafael, Santa Ana, and Westminster, California; Providence, Rhode Island; Mathis and Houston, Texas; Chelsea, Holyoke, Randolph, and Southbridge, Massachusetts; Atlantic City and Bay City, New Jersey; Dearborn, Michigan.

To convey the dismay and frustration of so many teachers of limited-English students and the actions they are beginning to take, the most moving and courageous example is from Salinas, California. Suzanne Guerrero, an elementary school teacher of limited-English students in the Salinas City School District called me a year ago to ask for advice and information on how to present her arguments for changing the bilingual program in her district. Suzanne related her total disillusion with native language teaching as a means of giving Latino students an appropriate education. She is Mexican-American and proud of her language and culture but fourteen years as a bilingual teacher have convinced her that the approach is not only ineffective but harmful to her students.

What distinguishes Suzanne from the dozens of others I have corresponded with or talked to is that she is willing to go public with her discontent. Most teachers, though critical of bilingual programs, are very reluctant to take a public stand and invite the inevitable personal attacks. Suzanne is a tenured, senior staff member in the Salinas schools and she knows that she cannot be fired for expressing her opinions. And that is exactly what Suzanne is doing. She is distributing articles and books to teachers and organizing group meetings to discuss the readings, in the face of a generally hostile response. Most recently Suzanne published an outspoken article in her local teachers' union newsletter. Here are a few electrifying quotes from Suzanne's article in *The Voice* of May 1995 in which she is responding to an earlier essay calling for salary stipends for bilingual teachers and complaining of racism in the community:

I am a bilingual teacher (and have been one for 14 years in this district) and certainly do not agree with you. Where is your proof, your evidence, to back up your accusations of racism? I have not experienced any racism toward myself. I am an American of Mexican heritage. Am I also racist because I oppose bilingual education—after personally observing that it just is not working? Definitely not!

...This is not a racial issue. In your article, you allude to the "research which clearly shows that students perform better when educated in a language they understand..." Nowhere has this been proven. In fact, the sooner a child begins to learn a second language, the more rapidly and effectively he will acquire that language for social purposes and academic learning. Also, the human brain acquires language more easily the *younger* a child is. There is no sound reason to delay the learning of English.

One School District in Pennsylvania

The Bethlehem Area School District encompasses five municipalities with 13,000 students, of whom 1,300 are limited-English, almost entirely Puerto Rican students who are native speakers of Spanish. In early 1992 the school superintendent, Thomas J. Doluisio, asked for my advice in remodeling the traditional bilingual education program then in place in the Bethlehem district. Dr. Doluisio voiced the frustration and disappointment that is not uncommon when a well-meant effort fails. The Bethlehem district had implemented a native language program of instruction for over ten years, with competent bilingual teachers following the classic model; with the busing of students to bilingual schools to make up entire classrooms of Spanish speakers; and the sum total of these special efforts had not achieved salutary results.

Pennsylvania does not have a state law requiring bilingual programs, which saved Dr. Doluisio from the need to defy state law to change his program, but he did have to confront the bilingual community and the bilingual professional staff in his school district. Apparently Dr. Doluisio was up to the task. Patiently but firmly he won acceptance for initiating what the district labels its English Acquisition Program. As I was leaving the country to take up a Fulbright Lectureship in Rome for a year, I referred the Bethlehem administrators to Dr. Esther Eisenhower for professional guidance in program revision. Dr. Eisenhower led the planning of curriculum revision and staff training and arranged for Bethlehem teachers to visit ESL classrooms in the Fairfax County Public Schools, one of the largest and most respected ESL programs in the country. One year of planning and preparation, public relations efforts in the community, and retraining and reassuring of staff in the school district, paved the way for the English Acquisition Program that started in September 1993.

The Board of School Directors stated the goal of the new program "to have all limited-English-proficient students become fluent in English in the shortest amount of time so they may experience maximum success in school" (Bethlehem Plan, 1993). The essential elements defined by the planning committee of thirty teachers and administrators are the following:

Elementary Schools

- limited-English students will be educated in their neighborhood schools, with few exceptions
- language minority students will be tested for English language skills on entering the Bethlehem schools; all LEP students will be classified as beginner, intermediate, or advanced level English learners, or as fully fluent in English and needing no special language services
- all LEP students will be heterogeneously grouped with native English speakers in regular classrooms, will be taught all school subjects in English through an adapted, regular school curriculum
- progress in oral proficiency, reading and writing in English will be assessed twice yearly
- special approaches for LEP students includes a literature based reading program, writing workshop, seventy-five min-

utes daily of ESL instruction for beginner level students, and additional tutorial support, when needed.

Middle and High Schools

- beginner level LEP students are assigned to an ESL center for intensive English language instruction by a team
- intermediate and advanced level students are assigned to their neighborhood schools and receive two periods daily of ESL instead of regular language arts; are integrated into regular math, social studies, and science classes; are given tutorial help, if needed, and may also participate in a daily after school program for extra help
- high school students receive the same services as are provided in the middle schools, with a mentor program adding extra, one-on-one assistance when needed.

Year One in the English Acquisition Program

In the fall of 1994, after the English Acquisition Program had been in place for one school year, St. Joseph's University professor Judy Simon Turner administered two surveys that were designed with the help of Ann Goldberg, English language program coordinator in Bethlehem. One survey was addressed to teachers and administrators in the Bethlehem Area School District, and one (printed in English and Spanish) to the parents of students enrolled in the program. The goal of the surveys was twofold: to be a general indicator of the degree to which the program is supported by teachers, administrators, and parents, and to gain information on the strengths and weaknesses of the program and specific recommendations for improvements (Turner, 1994).

An analysis of these surveys highlighted the following results to the Board of School Directors from teachers and administrators:

- 39 percent said all or most students made substantial progress towards the main goal of the program; 23 percent said more than half the students made substantial progress
- 50 percent of respondents registered a positive view of the new program and 44 percent gave it a mixed response with 4 percent giving it a negative reaction
- 83 percent said they anticipate the average LEP student to learn English well enough for social purposes in one to three years, while 53 percent said it would take an average of one to three years to learn English well enough for academic success in the classroom.

Turner adds a cautionary note on the question of number of years for English language acquisition,

It should be recognized that these responses are based...not only on the first year results of the English Acquisition Program but on the years in which some of the teachers worked in the former bilingual program.... it will be important to survey staff again in 3–4 years to determine if their response to this question has changed. (Turner, 3)

Two major recommendations from teachers were for reduced class sizes system-wide, not only in the English Acquisition Program, and for more teacher training, ideally through the services of a long-term training consultant to give a needed continuity to this effort.

On the parent survey, 276 responses were analyzed, with the following main conclusions:

- 81 percent of parents felt their child progressed well academically during the first year of the new program

- 82 percent of parents rated the program as good to very good
- 12 percent of parents reported their child's having academic problems during the year; 81 percent said they visited the school during the year while 53 percent said they had a conference with the teacher.

Parents recommendations for improvements focused mainly on more opportunities for English language learning, including after-school tutorials, a summer program, and more homework. A number of respondents suggested English classes for parents and that more information be sent home by the schools.

Turner notes at the end of the report that the high level of acceptance for the English Acquisition Program among teachers, administrators, and parents may be credited to the careful planning and sensitivity of the administration, and particularly Ann Goldberg. The evidence of positive attitudes developing in one year is particularly impressive considering the negative publicity in the community and the reluctant reception from teachers preceding the introduction of the program. Professor Turner recommended a longitudinal study be conducted over a period of several years to collect and analyze data on student achievement, which could not be reliably interpreted after only one year, and to maintain a descriptive account of successful teaching strategies, materials, and training.

Year Two in the English Acquisition Program

After two years of implementation, it is possible to examine early data on student progress. A brief report as of June 1995 on the achievement of all limited-English students, K-12, in the English Acquisition Program shows the following gains:

- 29 percent of those students classified "Beginners" at the beginning of the school year had moved to the "Intermediate" level by June

- 12 percent moved from "Intermediate" to "Advanced"
- 46 percent moved from "Advanced" level to exit from the program.

These classifications of English language proficiency cannot be considered scientifically accurate, but they are based on a carefully defined set of competencies that Bethlehem has developed as well as on testing and teacher evaluations. Considering the current state of the art in second language assessment, the Bethlehem standards are as adequate as I have seen in the numerous school districts I have studied.

Much more data must be collected, analyzed, and reported by the Bethlehem Area School District to substantiate any claims of success for this program. In the next few years, it will be possible to chart the achievement of students who entered the English Acquisition Program in kindergarten as limited-English speakers and determine how many years they were enrolled before mainstreaming. Were these students successful in the regular classroom after exiting the program; were they referred for special remedial services at a higher rate than native English speakers (Special Education, Title I, etc.)? Are they dropping out of school before high school completion at higher rates than other groups? When they graduate from high school, how many are going on to higher education? Bethlehem does not have a control group receiving a different treatment with which to compare the achievement of students in the English Acquisition Program. However, it would be of some value to dig back in the earlier records on Bethlehem students who participated in the former bilingual program to compare outcomes, if those records are still available.

One Lawsuit Against the Seattle School District

The Seattle, Washington, School District educates 45,000 students in its public schools, of whom 6,000 are limited-English proficient and represent ninety different language backgrounds. Three-fourths of the LEP students are Asian. As in many other urban school districts, the number of limited-English students swelled suddenly in the 1980s and the number of different languages and ethnic groups increased also. To accommodate this multicultural, heterolingual population of students and to remove the language barrier to an equal education, the school system tried a number of approaches, from a program focused largely on native language instruction to an intensive English language teaching effort, with various modifications in between. In reviewing the district's published documents and in discussions with school personnel, the rationale for Seattle's current approach became clear. The district cannot implement a dual language program for every LEP student. Thus, if it cannot be done for all language groups, then it would be unfair to do it only for some. It could very well create problems among ethnic groups. From my observations, the district is strongly committed to equity of opportunity.

Another problem with largely native language instruction is the higher cost and loss of flexibility in staffing. More bilingual teachers have to be hired who can only work with students from one language background; native language materials must be purchased in several languages, and neither teachers or materials are currently available in all the program languages. In the end, this type of program would be segregative and unfair to some students. Seattle School board policy was to establish a program that meets the needs of LEP students and helps them to assimilate.

In the early 1990s the district, which is divided into regions, prepared to initiate a system of school-based management that would give each school the autonomy to plan its own schedule, delivery of instruction, classroom organization, and strategies for meeting the needs of special students (limited-English, low achievers, gifted and talented, disabled, pre-literate, etc.). The decision making would rest not with a central administration but with the school staff, principal, and parents. The central administration essentially gave each school free rein in how it would use its budget but with the proviso that the school would be accountable for the achievement of its students.

In the 1993 school year, the Seattle district employed 230 qualified bilingual/ESL teachers and assistant teachers, plus 40 bilingual tutors. The district developed teacher preparation programs jointly with local colleges and universities, giving staff members the opportunity to take courses leading to an undergraduate degree in education, at district expense. It was anticipated that bilingual paraprofessionals would take these opportunities and become teachers in the Seattle schools on completing their degree requirements. Seattle has also invested in recruiting efforts to find qualified personnel to teach limited-English students.

Since 1992, a new inclusive approach called the "blended model" has been pioneered in several Seattle elementary schools, a coordinated approach that holds special promise for limited-English students. Concern for the long-term segregation of language minority students and loss of confidence in the bilingual approach of native language instruction, coinciding with the school-based management opportunity, led to the development of this new model. In essence, the elementary school assigns all students to regular classrooms, carefully controlling for an appropriate mixture in each, that is, of twenty-two students in a second grade classroom, five may be limited-English, three low achievers in reading or math (Title I), and two may have learning disabilities. Each classroom has a team-teaching setup, with a regular elementary teacher and one teacher who may be a Special Education, Title I, bilingual, or ESL specialist who is in the classroom all or part of the time. The central administration invested in the cross-training of the various specialist teachers so that they have some understanding of each other's specialties, and provided the funds for reducing class size in the schools implementing the blended model. Seattle has other innovative programs such as the Bilingual Orientation Center, which provides intensive English language classes and remedial academic work for students of high school age who arrive in Seattle with little or no English and, in some cases, with little or no formal education in their native land.

In September 1993 a suit was brought against the Seattle School District and the State of Washington in King County Superior Court by Sang Van et al. and the class of all Limited English Proficient students and their guardians, with Evergreen Legal Services, a public advocacy firm, as plaintiff's counsel. A number of complaints were alleged in the lawsuit, from the lack of credentialed native language teachers to the assignment of LEP students to particular schools, and the location of bilingual program schools, to the lack of sufficient materials in the native languages of the students, and other related problems. The applicable law in Washington state, Chapter 28 A 180, revised in 1982, requires transitional bilingual education programs when there are sufficient numbers of LEP students from the same language background, or, where use of two languages is not practicable, as established by the school superintendent, an alternative system such as ESL may be used to enable students to achieve competency in English. The Seattle district maintained that the variety of native languages and the district's desegregation goals made it impractical to do a full-time native language program but that students were better served in non-segregated settings with a special English language program supported by the use of the native language, whenever necessary, for clarification.

Seattle, in fact, could demonstrate several indicators of success for limited-English students in recent years. For students not completing high school, the dropout rate for LEP students is lower than for other students, system-wide. In the three school years from 1990 to 1993, the dropout rate for bilingual students averaged 10.9 percent while the dropout rate for the rest of the district averaged 16.2 percent (Seattle School District,

1993). A comparison of the numbers of high school graduates for the same three-year period follows:

Table E.3   High School Graduates—
Bilingual vs. Overall District Seattle Public Schools

		Number of Graduates	Average Senior Enrollment	Graduation Percent
1990–91:	Bilingual	210	249	84.3 %
	Overall	1954	2470	79.1 %
1991–92:	Bilingual	267	316	84.5 %
	Overall	1982	2498	79.3 %
1992–93:	Bilingual	300	367	81.7 %
	Overall	2153	2633	81.8 %

SOURCE: Seattle School District, 1993.

One additional indicator that the progress of limited-English students compares favorably with other groups in the district is the November 1993 Data Profile, which reports on the rate of students who are enrolled in Special Education programs. The district average is 9.4 percent, while the enrollment for Asian students who make up one-fourth of the student body and three-fourths of the LEP students is 4.1 percent. Nationally, the tendency has been to find higher percentages of LEP students than other groups erroneously placed in Special Education programs, not because of true learning disabilities but due to the temporary condition of being limited in their knowledge of the English language. Clearly, the Seattle district is not making that mistake.

Nevertheless, Evergreen Legal Services brought a class action suit against the Seattle School District. There is a strong suspicion that it was less for the complaints of the plaintiffs than to use Seattle as a test case to force it and other school districts in Washington to put in heavy duty bilingual education programs with native language instruction in all subjects, most of the school day, for several years. The district decided to fight for what it believed to be in the best interests of its students. As an expert witness on behalf of the Seattle district, I reviewed school documents, visited half a dozen schools, observed classrooms, interviewed teachers and administrators, and prepared to testify in court, along with other experts.

On 18 April 1995, a settlement agreement was signed by all parties to this suit which sets forth in detail the way in which the district will meet its legal obligations to LEP students, referring to monitoring of student achievement, recruitment and staff training, curriculum development, and other program features. This settlement does not essentially change the Seattle district's education policies or practices. Plaintiff's attorneys did not succeed in forcing the district into engaging in more native language teaching than it now provides. The settlement is a victory for the Seattle district and for its right to continue to give a range of different educational services to the limited-English students who are benefiting from this integrated, effective program. Seattle provides a wonderful example of sanity and strength prevailing against the threat of unreasonable demands. This case should give courage to other school districts facing similar threats.

Revisiting Newton, Massachusetts

The special program for limited-English students that I directed from 1980 to 1990 in the Newton, Massachusetts, public schools is fully described in chapter 5, pp. 126–41. Newton continues to enjoy its reputation as one of the most prestigious public school districts in the United States, both for the high quality of student achievement and for its commitment to high performance by racial and language minority students. It is worthwhile to describe some of the subtle changes that have

the highly educated student from Russia who has had several years of English but needs to master the American idiom and pronunciation to the underschooled, 15-year old Afghan mail order bride who has never learned a word of English, and everything in between."

McCarthy is introducing a number of innovations designed to enhance the opportunities for LEP students to maintain their first language and for native English speakers to begin learning another language early. In the middle school, a Russian language and culture elective is offered for eighth graders as well as a Chinese elective. Both classes enroll English speakers with native speakers of those languages. A kindergarten through third grade Spanish language and culture project is in the planning stages and is anticipated to start within the year in anywhere from six to nine elementary schools. McCarthy is working with the Newton Foreign Language Department to design a course in Russian for native speakers. These enrichment courses are valuable for native-born Newtonians and students new to the United States alike. But the rock bottom line for the limited-English students in Newton is the early and effective mastery of the English language for academic success and true inclusion in the school community, as it has always been.

At the end of our interview, I asked McCarthy how long it takes LEP students to achieve the goals of the program, on average, and be able to work successfully in a mainstream classroom. Her answer was, "Two years." One piece of research that she is conducting is to collect data and compare the performance of students who are receiving some native language instruction with those who are entirely immersed in the English language program, over the next three to five years. These groups are split evenly in grades K-6, about 50 percent in each type of program. The results of this research will add some useful information to the small pool of reliable research in this field.

—————— ◊◊◊ ——————

Legislative Initiatives

Bilingual education reform has been the focus of relentless activity in California, Massachusetts, and New Jersey, with very mixed results, while bills to modify or eliminate bilingual education entirely at the federal level are expected to be debated and, possibly, acted on in the fall 1995 session of Congress.

Massachusetts Strikes Out–Again

The Commonwealth of Massachusetts has seen the introduction of a succession of bills to reform the restrictive state law, Chapter 71-A. Every year since 1986, one or another of these bills has enjoyed a brief moment of public attention, a public hearing at the State House, and a hasty vote sending it to oblivion. On 25 January 1995, "An Act Relative to Bilingual Education" was submitted to the legislature by Governor William Weld which included these crucial improvements:

- local choice in program options (TBE, ESL, Two-Way Bilingual, Structured English Immersion)
- informed parental consent before enrolling students in special programs
- district accountability for monitoring and reporting student achievement
- bilingual teacher qualifications requiring fluency and literacy in English as well as another language.

Since the bill had been introduced by the governor, there was the reasonable expectation of a successful outcome. Yet, when the hearing on this bill was held on 30 March, the same old scenario of previous years was staged—hundreds of school children were taken out of school and brought to the State House to "demonstrate" against any changes in bilingual education (many of them students in the primary grades who had no idea what was going on). A reporter for the *Boston Herald* reported a grim irony on the current state of bilingual education:

hundreds of students in bilingual programs turned out—in the middle of what would have been a school day, we might add—to attend the hearing and protest.

But the saddest part of all was that most needed to have the hearing translated for them. Yes, high school students—many of them in bilingual programs for years—couldn't understand what was being said. When a Weld administration spokesperson got up to explain the changes being requested, the students applauded his remarks. Moments later, following a brief translation by an accompanying teacher, they booed. (Cohen, 12 April 1995, p. 29)

Once again, politicians reacted predictably, partly out of genuine ignorance of the issues and partly out of the craven cowardice that afflicts elected representatives when an organized interest group shows up in sizable numbers. In spite of testimony in support of the bill from Education Commissioner Robert Antonucci, Secretary of Education Piedad Robertson, and Professor Christine Rossell of Boston University, the House summarily voted against change by 124–30 on 11 April (Howe, 12 April 1995).

New Jersey Wins Two in 1995

The New Jersey legislature voted for two changes in its bilingual education law in 1995, after a year and a half of intense debate. The background to these changes is interesting. For several years, the State Department of Education had granted waivers to local school districts that argued hardship in meeting full-time bilingual program requirements, and they were allowed to provide some other type of educational help rather than native language instruction. However, in August 1994 the state Attorney General declared the waivers illegal, announcing that all districts must now provide full-time bilingual education, unless the law were changed. A number of bills were introduced, with Representative Raul "Rudy" Garcia leading the pro-bilingual camp and Senator Jack Ewing promoting the cause of bilingual education reform.

The first substantial reform bill, granting local program choice if it is justifiable based on local conditions and removing the legal mandate of full-time programs of native language instruction in every district in every language, was enacted in April 1995. On signing the bill, Governor Christine Whitman remarked, "The signing of the waiver bill (S.1474) provides a solution to an immediate and very serious problem. But I consider it only to be an interim measure. I believe that we must now achieve more comprehensive reform of the bilingual education law" (Mendez, 1 April 1995).

On 15 December 1995, an even more significant measure won approval. The Parental Consent Bill was unanimously passed by the state Senate after winning approval months earlier in the Assembly. Up to this point, New Jersey had been the only state in which the parents of limited-English students did not have the right either to decline the placement of their children in a bilingual program or to remove their children from bilingual classes for at least three years. The Parental Consent Bill gives parents the option to place their children in an alternative English language program, if they so desire, rather than having them automatically forced into programs where they are segregated by language and culture. Passage of this legislation owes a good deal to the efforts of Dr. Chiara Nappi of the Princeton Regional Board of Education who had argued for years that the New Jersey statute denied parents and children their civil rights (Nappi, 12 October 1994).

I strongly agree with the governor's statement on the need for comprehensive change. I worked on the drafting of these New Jersey initiatives and provided a good deal of research material to legislators, as I have done every year for ten years in Massachusetts. Although there is some measure of satisfaction in the passage of legal reforms, one can be only cautiously optimistic that many districts will be granted waivers. State Education Commissioner Leo Klagholz opposed the local choice legislation and his strong position in favor of native language programs could mean that the granting of waivers will be permitted in very few cases. Such has been the experience in California where, although the bilingual education law actually expired in 1987, only 20 of the 1000 school districts have permission to provide an alternative, English-language based program.

California–The Textbook Case

As mentioned earlier, the California Department of Education has pressured local districts to continue native language instruction programs even in the absence of a state law requiring it. This has been the continuing struggle for reform advocates in California: how to overcome an entrenched bureaucracy that dictates curriculum and testing standards to local districts and enforces its dictates through the power of public funds.

Two acts were drafted to change the education code in regard to bilingual education in 1995: Assembly Bill 955 (Member Knight) and Assembly Bill 1041 (Member Alpert). When I was invited to critique the two bills early in the year, bilingual education reform in California looked more promising than at any time since 1987. The basic provisions of either AB 955 or AB 1041 could make a major turnaround in the education of 1.2 million California school children—if enacted by the legislature and implemented by the State Department of Education and the State Board of Education.

In fact, enacting the legislation may be the easier part of the reform agenda. The harder part is crafting the bill carefully enough to keep the State Department of Education from thwarting the bill's purposes. It has not been possible so far to curb the power of this agency to intimidate school districts into providing unwanted and ineffective programs by falsely invoking federal and civil rights strictures. Neither the Lau decision of the U.S. Supreme Court, nor federal laws on education and civil rights require native language instruction—the stated intent is and always has been the removal of the language barrier to an equal education, by any sensible means. AB 1041 had these crucial provisions:

- repeal of the 1976 Bilingual-Bicultural Education Act
- *authorization by law* of local program choice, so long as "it has as its goal the development of proficiency in English for each pupil"
- strict accountability for student achievement
- parental notification and parental right to accept or reject placement of students in special programs.

AB 955 focused on these provisions:

- denial of power to the Department of Education to dictate which method to use in teaching LEP students
- local responsibility in designing programs
- school district accountability for measuring student progress in English language learning and academic achievement
- three-year limit on special programs for LEP students; other remedial services may be applied beyond that time
- funding provided to each district according to number of LEP students, *not* based on enrollment in a particular type of program.

After working on both bills, I believed that either one would make sorely needed changes in California. Alas, AB 1041 was handed over to the bilingual bureaucracy for comment in June and what emerged was an unrecognizable pastiche that would have ensured retention of the status quo. One outrageous provision of the revised bill was that any school district operating what is labelled an "innovative instructional services program" must demonstrate within a few years that at least 75 percent of the students are making adequate progress in English language development and academic achievement, comparable to their English-speaking peers. No such standard is held for bilingual programs! The revised AB 1041 could not muster support and was withdrawn. The Knight bill (AB 955) went into hibernation and is being prepared for reintroduction in early 1996.

Why is state legislation necessary, in the absence of a bilingual education law? To eliminate the remnants of the expired 1976 Chacon-Moscone bill and to spell out in concrete terms what the rights and obligations of school districts, teachers, parents, and students are, and what limits on the state education agency are in regard to special efforts for limited-English students.

The California Teachers' Association Urges Reform

One new and powerful ally has joined the bilingual education reform movement—the California Teachers Association (CTA). For the first time, a teachers' union has withdrawn its unqualified support and is publicly attacking the abuses of bilingual education programs. "Bilingual debate gets sidetracked by self-interests," was published in the union newsletter, CTA Action of May 1995. Considering that teachers' unions, lead by the National Education Association, have routinely paid lip service to bilingual education, the CTA stance amounts to a declaration of independence from doctrinaire positions.

New Policy from California State Board of Education

On Friday, 14 July 1995, the California State Board of Education announced a new policy in educating language minority children. Two major changes are emphasized—more concern for results in student achievement than in teaching methods, and removing the "preference" for primary language instruction by allowing maximum flexibility to local districts to choose their own program. Both of these changes will, if enforced, lead to dramatic changes in the adoption of English language programs. The Superintendent of Public Instruction, Delaine Eastin, vows that her bilingual staff will be reorganized, if necessary, to fortify the department's commitment to local control (Pyle, 14 July 1995).

If Eastin's new policy is not enforced, threats of litigation against the State Department of Education are already being discussed in several cities. The Westminster district is applying for the option of providing an entirely English immersion program, for which permission has been granted to only 20 out of 1,000 California districts. This appeal could force the first test of the Education Department's commitment to change (Pyle, 14 July 1995). Social changes seem to sweep across the country from west to east with California initiating and leading the movements to other states. One hopes this particular reform effort will be sustained and will spread to other states.

Federal Initiatives

Until the fall 1994 election that swept in so many new congressmen, the Bilingual Education Act—Title VII—had suffered few serious budget reductions. The federal budget for the Office of Bilingual Education and Minority Languages Affairs (OBEMLA) rose to its highest level, $155 million in 1995, since its modest $7.5 million start in 1968. But the budget-balancing, cost-cutting ways of the new majority rescinded $38 million of the 1995 funds in August 1995, and is in the process of reducing drastically the 1996 funding. From a budget of $195 million requested for 1996, the House appropriations bill passed in August reduces that amount to $53 million; the Senate bill that was expected to come to the floor in late fall proposed cutting the budget to $122 million. Differences in the two bills were to be resolved in conference.

One important amendment (S.1513/H.R.6) was added to the 1994 education appropriations bill by Senator Larry Pressler and passed in the Senate by a vote of 100–0. Wonder of wonder, it requires that bilingual teachers be fluent in English. That it would take a congressional action to make this clear must be amazing to people unfamiliar with the politics of bilingual education.

Efforts to modify, dismantle, or entirely abolish bilingual education at the federal level have been in the works for years. A convergence of propitious circumstances bodes well for this reform effort. The recent publication of new studies confirming poor results for bilingual programs, the increasing popularity of the concept of English as the official language of the United States and the importance to immigrant children of learning English to enter the mainstream, the mood of the new Congress to cast a skeptical eye on social programs of dubious value, and the budget crunch—taken together, these factors spell change. Two legislative initiatives on bilingual education were introduced in October 1995: the King bill (H.R. 1005) and the Roth Bill (H.R. 739), both of which abolish the Office of Bilingual Education and bilingual voting ballots. Both bills are tied to the official English language movement, which is discussed in the next section of this chapter.

Federal support for OBEMLA since 1968 has not been large in dollar amounts but has played an important role, symbolically, in legitimizing bilingual education. The disproportionate investment and the continual emphasis on native language instruction has had a strong impact on state legislation and local district implementation. Changing the course of the federal role in this area of public education to a neutral one or completely eliminating Washington's role in favor of state and local control are the two extremes. But change at the federal level is reliably predicted, the question being how extensive a change will be enacted at this time.

──────────── ◇◇◇ ────────────

Official English Movement

The campaign to make English the official language of government in the United States has been aggressively pursued in the past few years. Since I last reported sixteen states with official English laws, (pp. 207–220) five more have joined their ranks: Alabama, Arizona, Montana, New Hampshire, and South Dakota. A majority of voters approved the official English referendum in Maryland but it was vetoed by the governor. Official English campaigns are actively being promoted at this time in Connecticut, Missouri, Ohio, Oklahoma, Pennsylvania, West Virginia, Wisconsin, and Wyoming, largely through the efforts of U.S. English, the largest and best known organization connected with this issue.

The Commonwealth of Puerto Rico voted Spanish its official language, arousing concerns that if Puerto Rico voted for statehood in the 1993 election, the United States would be in the delicate position of having one state out of fifty-one with an official language other than English, conjuring up alarms about a Quebec-like situation. The issue was nullified when the citizens of Puerto Rico voted in favor of retaining commonwealth status.

To most people, the very idea that English is not already the official language of this country is shocking. State referenda on the language issue consistently receive overwhelmingly high voter support, even in states like California (73 percent) and Florida (84 percent), which have the highest proportions of

Figure E.1 U.S. ENGLISH/Luntz Research Survey Results*

Interviewers at the Luntz Research Companies asked 1,208 Americans:
"Do you think English should be made the official language of the United States?"

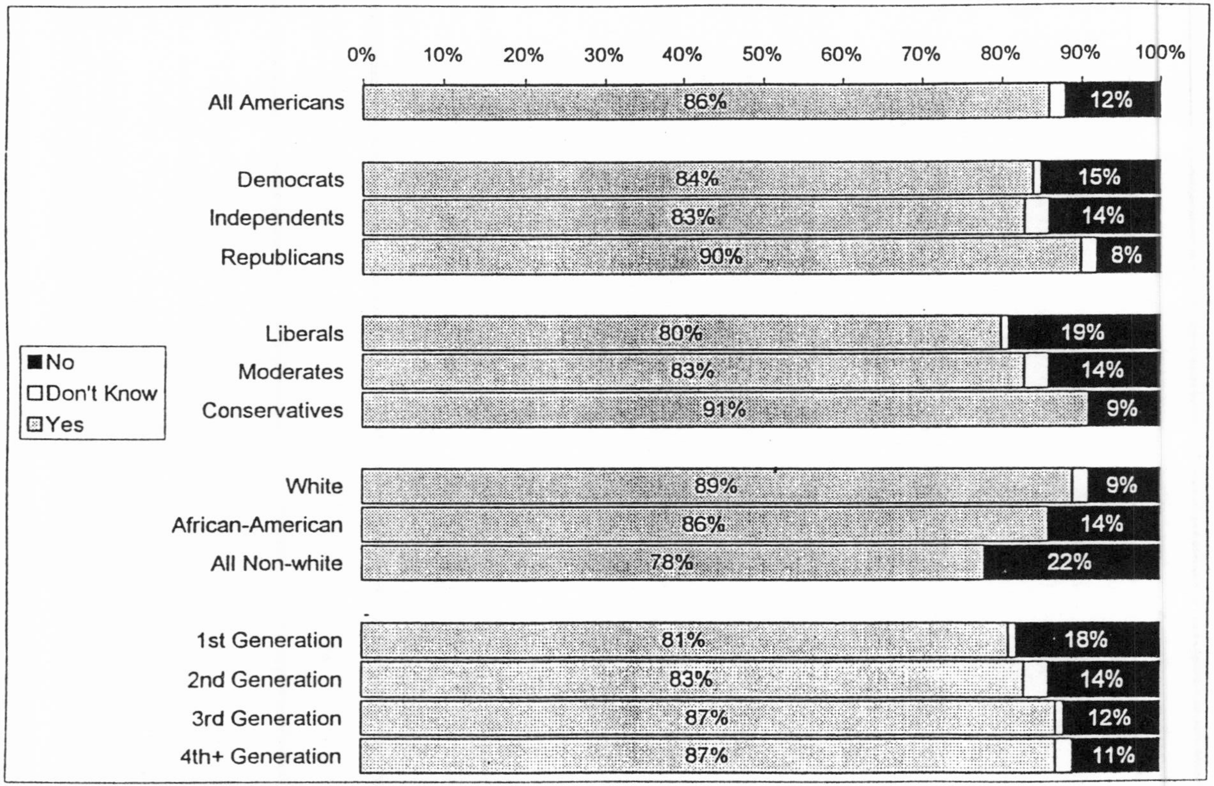

Legend:
- ■ No
- □ Don't Know
- ▨ Yes

Category	Yes	No
All Americans	86%	12%
Democrats	84%	15%
Independents	83%	14%
Republicans	90%	8%
Liberals	80%	19%
Moderates	83%	14%
Conservatives	91%	9%
White	89%	9%
African-American	86%	14%
All Non-white	78%	22%
1st Generation	81%	18%
2nd Generation	83%	14%
3rd Generation	87%	12%
4th+ Generation	87%	11%

*Survey was taken between August 2 - 6, 1995. Margin of error is plus or minus 2.8 percentage points.
SOURCE: Copyright © 1995 by U.S. ENGLISH, Inc.

new immigrants in the country and where the ballots are printed in several languages. Surveys conducted in thirteen states by U.S. English between 1993 and 1995 reported positive support averaging around 81 percent, from a high of 91 percent in Oklahoma to 71 percent in Wisconsin. The results of a survey taken in August 1995 can be seen in figure E.1.

Federal Activity

At the federal level, the introduction of Official English legislation or an English Language Amendment elicited a ho-hum reaction in the 1980s, but with the 1994 changes in the makeup of Congress the outlook for positive action has sharpened considerably. Politicians have been way behind the curve on this issue, in spite of the high voter support in state after state for official English. Suddenly, the two most powerful congressional leaders have dared to take public positions—Speaker of the House Newt Gingrich in his book, *To Renew America,* and Senate Majority Leader and presidential candidate Robert Dole in a major speech on 5 September 1995. Dole made two crucial points in his speech, one emphasizing the importance of a common language, "English is the language in which we still speak to each other across the frontiers of culture and race.... [Ensuring] that all our citizens are fluent in English is a welcoming act of inclusion" (Weymouth, 12 September 1995). He called for making English language classes available to new immigrants of all ages, a positive suggestion that is almost never mentioned. Dole's second point was a criticism of bilingual education, "fluency in English should be a central educational goal of every state" and that multilingual education should be abandoned, not employed "as a means of instilling ethnic pride or as therapy for low self-esteem" (Weymouth). The official language issue and bilingual education may very well be among the debating points in a presidential election campaign, for the first time, in 1996.

Table E.4   Official English Legislation 1995: A Side-By-Side Comparison

Rep. Bill Emerson (R-Mo.)
The Language of Government Act of 1995:
H.R. 123 -- A bill to amend title 4, United States Code, to declare English as the official language of the government of the U.S.
(Introduced 1/4/95)

194 Co-sponsors

■ **EXEMPTIONS:** Use of languages other than English for public health and safety, foreign language instruction, judicial proceedings, and tourism.

■ **DOES NOT:** Infringe on individual rights, nor does it prevent the use of languages other than English outside the government.

■ **REQUIRES:** English be the sole language used to declare policies, write laws and regulations, and make and enforce official acts.

■ **RECOMMENDS:** Savings derived by the Federal government from enactment of this act be used to teach English to non-English proficient individuals.

Rep. Toby Roth (R-Wis.)
Declaration of Official Language Act of 1995:
H.R. 739 -- A bill to amend title 4, United States Code, to declare English as the official language of the government of the U.S.
(Introduced 1/30/95)

94 Co-sponsors

■ **EXEMPTIONS:** Religion, training in foreign languages for international communication, and use of non-English terms of art in government documents.

■ **ABOLISHES:** Bilingual education and bilingual ballots.

■ **REQUIRES:**
-- Government promote use of English for communications among U.S. citizens (implies private sector);
-- Communications by officers and employees of U.S. government with U.S. citizens be in English;
-- All naturalization ceremonies be conducted solely in English; and
-- Government to enforce English proficiency standard for immigration.

Rep. Pete King (R-N.Y.)
National Language Act of 1995:
H.R. 1005 -- A bill to amend title 4, United States Code, to declare English as the official language of the U.S., and for other purposes.
(Introduced 2/21/95)

36 Co-sponsors

■ **EXEMPTIONS:** Religion, training in foreign languages for communication programs designed to encourage students to learn foreign languages, and persons over 62 years of age.

■ **ABOLISHES:** Office of Bilingual Education and Minority Language Affairs, and bilingual ballots.

■ **REQUIRES:**
-- All citizenship ceremonies be conducted in English;
-- Federal documents and publications be printed only in English; and
-- Recaptured funds (granted under Bilingual Education Act and not yet expended before enactment of Act) be deposited in the general fund of the Treasury.

SOURCE: U.S. English, Washington, DC., 1995

Three bills have been introduced in the House of Representatives for hearings in the October session, and the main provisions of each is described in the chart that follows:

Hearings were held on the three bills in the fall 1995 session of the U.S. House of Representatives on 18 October and 1 November by the Early Childhood, Youth and Families Subcommittee of the House Economic and Education Opportunities Committee. The first hearing was geared toward learning about the issue itself and did not focus on any one bill in particular, with testimony given only by members of Congress. The second hearing had the same focus and invited testimony from the general public at which time several speakers, including the Chairman of the Board of U.S. English, Mauro E. Mujica, and Linda Chavez of the Center for Equal Opportunity, spoke in favor of and Edward Chen of the ACLU spoke against the common language issue.

On 6 December the Senate Governmental Affairs Committee held a public hearing on S. 356, the companion bill to H.R. 123 of Representative Emerson. This is the only common language bill currently before the Senate. Several legislators testified for the bill, including Senator Richard Shelby (R.-AL), the sponsor, and Representative Toby Roth (R-WI), and a number of citizens. Although opponents had been invited to testify, they chose not to.

One additional bill was heard in January 1996, H.R. 351 sponsored by Representative John Porter (R-IL), the "Bilingual Voting Requirements Repeal Act of 1995." This bill amends the Voting Rights Act of 1975, which requires voting information and ballots to be printed in another language if there are sufficient voters in one county of the same language classification (5 percent) and they request it. Aside from the question of why bilingual ballots are necessary, since voters must be American citizens and naturalized citizens must have lived in the United States at least five years and demonstrate basic knowledge of English, there are other serious problems with this enterprise.

The costs of providing bilingual ballots are quite high when one examines the extent to which they are used. In the 1992 election, the city of Los Angeles spent $125,250 on bilingual voting materials that were used by 927 people. The city budgeted an additional $297,000 for the 1994 election in order to print ballots in Chinese, Japanese, Korean, Spanish, Tagalog, and Korean. In Hawaii, a state that has two official languages— Hawaiian and English—translation of voting materials in one election in 1992 cost the state $40,000. Two voters used the materials in the primary, and two in the general election, perhaps the same two (Eng. First document, 1995). The other large problem is the accuracy of translations. In a 1993 election in New York City, it was reported that "the city erroneously printed the Chinese character for 'no' as a translation for the word 'yes'" on one set of ballots (Dunn, 14 August 1994).

The Players

The activist organizations generating the various efforts to make English the official language of government in the United States are independent and feisty about their own turf. U.S. English, under the recent leadership of Chilean immigrant, Mauro Mujica, reports a growing membership approaching 600,000, and invests heavily in promoting state referenda and federal legislation. Mujica's organization takes the most moderate stand on bilingual education, advocating strongly for local choice in English language programs and for reforming bilingual education at the state and federal levels. His organization supports the Emerson bill on official English, which does not mention bilingual education, stating that "it is easier to pass legislation with one goal rather than several—that is why the Emerson bill has a better future and has gathered 182 co-signers" (Personal communication, 11 September 1995).

English First, the other national organization involved in the official language movement, concentrates its efforts mainly in the area of federal legislation. Their main thrust, in addition to official English, is to abolish bilingual education. The director, Jim Boulet, was quoted in the *Washington Times* (Price, 9 July 1995) as saying, "[the Emerson bill] doesn't do anything. It takes as much work to pass a bad bill as it does to pass a good bill, and you need one that really solves the problem."

Out in California, Stanley Diamond heads an organization called California English Advocates whose activities are concentrated on legislative and bureaucratic change to reform bilingual education in that state.

Arizonans for Official English, headed by Robert Park, waged the successful campaign to win voter support in a state referendum in 1988, only to have the law challenged, within hours after the election, in a major court case, *Yniguez v. Arizonans for Official English*. Mr. Park is the leading activist in the newly constituted English Language Advocates, an organization mainly concerned with supporting an appeal to the U.S. Supreme Court in the Yniguez case.

Courts Consider Challenges to English

Although there have been many court cases related to official English in recent years, two that have the greatest impact on the movements are the Spun Steak case and the Yniquez.

In 1990, the Spun Steak Company in San Francisco, California, established a work rule banning on-the-job conversation in languages other than English. Shortly thereafter, a group of workers filed a federal civil rights suit and an injunction preventing the company from implementing the rule was imposed. A federal appeals court ruled in 1993 that the decision did not violate the civil rights of bilingual or hispanic workers. This decision was appealed by the U.S. Equal Employment Opportunities Commission on behalf of the workers, but in 1994 the U.S. Supreme Court decided to let the lower court's ruling stand. It appears, then, that in private enterprise, employers can require that English be spoken in the workplace, in the interests of communication and worker morale.

The suit against the State brought on behalf of Maria-Kelly Yniguez alleged that the official English law of Arizona (voted by referendum in 1988) violated her First and Fourteenth Amendment rights. Ms. Yniguez was a first-year law student in 1988, employed by the State to evaluate medical claims against it. She had authority to settle claims of less than $10,000. Although competent in both English and Spanish, Yniguez would draft official documents in Spanish and knowingly admitted that her supervisor would not be able to read them. Her response, when asked why she did this was, "It's a solidarity thing." She claimed she could express some elements of malpractice claims in Spanish that are impossible in English. Yniguez noted that inexpressible concepts include her cultural heritage as a Hispanic, the sense of community and experiences shared by Hispanics, "and other feelings" (R. Park document, 1995).

In 1990 the federal court in Arizona found in her favor, ruling that she had a First Amendment right to use Spanish in her government agency work, knowing that neither her supervisor nor the auditing agency could read it. The governor of Arizona declined to appeal the decision. At that point, Robert Park petitioned the court for standing to appeal the decision, since he was the nominal head of the group that had mounted the Arizona English campaign. His petition was denied there, but he took his case to the Ninth Circuit Court of Appeals, which agreed to hear an appeal.

What Park is appealing is a set of new rights defined by the Arizona court that have never been in the U.S. Constitution: (1) that the choice of which language state employees choose to use in their workplace is protected by the First Amendment, (2) that governmental services must be provided in any other language if it is "normal" and the claimants wish it, (3) that non-English-speaking persons have a right to "receive" government information in a language other than English, and (4) that national origin minorities are protected by the government against discrimination.

As the Ninth District Court of Appeals covers a jurisdiction including Hawaii, Alaska, Washington, Oregon, California, Arizona, Nevada, Idaho, Montana, and Guam, the ruling in this case affects a wide area of the country. But its impact goes beyond the geographic area as it has relevance for challenges to the use of English for government purposes in all states and, therefore, to the legality of the official English laws in 22 states. The Ninth District Court of Appeals voted to hear this case *en banc,* that is, before a panel of eleven judges (one of only a dozen out of 8,000 cases that were selected for *en banc* hearings in 1994). It was heard on 20 July 1995 and the decision was announced on 5 October: by a 6–5 split decision the court ruled in favor of Yniguez, declaring Article XXVIII of the Arizona constitution (official English law) to be illegal. Judge Stephen Reinardt, writing for the majority, concluded that Arizona's official language law violated a government employee's First Amendment right of free speech by preventing the employee from writing government documents in any language he or she preferred. Judge Alex Kozinski, in a minority opinion, commented on the broad new language rights conferred on government employees by this decision,

Almost everything government does involves a communication of some sort, and those charged with carrying out government functions sometimes disagree with what they are ordered to say or do.... Today's decision [gives] bureaucrats the right to turn every policy disagreement into a federal lawsuit, arguing that their First Amendment free-speech rights take precedence. (Johnson, 6 November 1995)

This decision of the Ninth Circuit not only strikes down the will of the people of Arizona in a free election, but it opens a much broader question: if government cannot prescribe the language in which its employees are to do their work, can it require conformity on any other workplace policies? The case was appealed to the U.S. Supreme Court on 20 December 1995 by petitioner, Robert Park.

The Anti-Official English Lineup

English Plus, an organization promoting equality of all languages, has introduced legislation in several states. These resolutions are not legally binding and, in general, simply encourage the use of diverse languages. Such resolutions have been adopted in New Mexico, Oregon, Rhode Island, and Washington state, through the efforts of the American Civil Liberties Union (ACLU), the Mexican-American Legal Defense and Education Fund (MALDEF), La Raza, and TESOL, the professional organization for teachers of English to speakers of other languages. Ironically, not one organization working for official English is opposed to the use or study of other languages. In fact, the leaders of each of the groups are themselves fluently bilingual, as are their families.

The main accomplishment of the anti-Official English movement has been to label it firmly as "English Only," a pejorative label implying that no other languages may be spoken or studied in this country if the legislation succeeds, which, of course, is not the case.

Summing It All Up

Returning to the main themes of the first publication of *Forked Tongue,* many advances have been made in the public visibility of the plight of language minority students in our schools, in the increased willingness of school districts to strike out in new directions, in the expanded research base on educational alternatives. More is generally understood about the myriad factors that affect second language learning and academic achievement besides the school program—age, personality, motivation, family aspirations, culture, parents' educational level, family transiency, socioeconomic status. There will never be one school program that fits all language minority children in all school districts. What has changed the least is the political stranglehold on the public dialogue that is still powerfully weighted towards the status quo—blindly loyal support for bilingual education. "Doing the right (politically correct) thing" is still the fashion.

The politically righteous advocates for bilingual education, together with their well-meaning but often uninformed professional colleagues, publicly attack any deviation from the party line. Two brief examples make the point.

At the international TESOL Convention in Baltimore in March 1994, I attended a panel discussion with a large audience, and was startled to hear Dr. Jim Cummins, well-known proponent of native language teaching programs, state: "There is a growing anti-immigrant sentiment in this country, negative attitudes against other languages and against bilingual programs and it is being helped along by people like Arthur Schlesinger, Jr., Diane Ravitch and Rosalie Porter." When I was given an opportunity to comment, I confronted Dr. Cummins with this statement,

I am Rosalie Porter and I object to your characterization of my positions. I am familiar with the writings of Schlesinger and Ravitch and know that they have never expressed anti-immigrant sentiments, nor have I. I *am* an immigrant. I am fluent in four languages. I am proud of the multilingual, multi-ethnic makeup of this country. I am a critic of bilingual education programs but that does not make me an opponent of bilingualism.

Dr. Cummins limp response was, "Thank you for clarifying things."

More recently, a conference was organized in the Capitol Building, Washington, DC, on 18 September 1995, on "The Future of Bilingual Education," by the Center for Equal Opportunity (CEO), headed by Linda Chavez, long-time critic of bilingual education. A nation-wide search was made to invite scholars, teachers, and parents who have taken positions for and against bilingual education to participate in panel discussions to which congressman, staffers, and the media were invited. CEO's invitations were turned down by advocates for bilingual education—Steven Krashen, Virginia Collier, James Crawford. Instead, the National Association for Bilingual Education (NABE) and the Congressional Hispanic Caucus organized a counter-conference on the same day, at an earlier hour. No opportunity for the two camps to engage in civilized discourse. But this is the reality.

From its inception, bilingual education has not embraced diversity of educational ideas but fostered fierce protection of a single dogma, a panacea that failed. I am more committed than ever to the ideas first expounded in *Forked Tongue* in 1990, with even greater assurance that what I learned in my first sixteen years in this field has been reinforced many times over.

R. P. Porter
January 1996

References

ALEC. (1994). Bilingual Education in the United States 1991–92. *Report Card on American Education.* Washington, DC: American Legislative Exchange Council and U.S. English Foundation, Inc.

Berman, P., J. Chambers, P. Gandara, B. McLaughlin, C. Minicucci, D. Nelson, L. Olsen, and T. Parrish. (1992). *Meeting the Challenge of Language Diversity: An Evaluation of Programs for Pupils with Limited-English Proficiency, Vol. II, Findings and Conclusions.* Berkeley, CA: BW Associates.

Bethlehem Area School District. (1993). *English Acquisition Program Handbook.*

Board of Education of the City of New York. (October 1994). *Educational Progress of Students in Bilingual and ESL Programs: A Longitudinal Study, 1990–1994.*

———. (12 June 1995). "Chancellor Cortines Announces Gains in Citywide Reading and Math Scores." Press Release N-167.

———. (June 1995). Citywide test results in reading, Spring 1995.

———. (June 1995). Citywide test results in mathematics, Spring 1995.

Burkheimer, G. J., A. Conger, G. Dunteman, B. Elliott, and K. Mowbray. (1989). *Effectiveness of Services for Language Minority Limited English Proficient Students.* Raleigh-Durham, NC: Research Triangle Institute.

Bushwick Parents Organization vs. Richard P. Mills, Commissioner of Education of the State of New York, Respondent, and ASPIRA of New York, Inc., Respondent-Intervenor, Index No. 5181-95, Supreme Court of the State of New York, County of Albany.

California Teacher's Association. (May 1995). "Bilingual Debate Gets Sidetracked by Self-Interest." *CTA Action.* Sacramento, CA: California Teachers' Association, 12–15.

Chavez, S. (3 September 1993). "L.A. Schools' Bilingual Program Failing, State Says." *Los Angeles Times.*

———. (4 September 1993). "Schools Scurry to Overhaul Bilingual Teaching Program." *Los Angeles Times.*

Chiswick, B. R., and P. W. Miller. (1995). "The Endogeneity between Language and Earnings: International Analyses." *Journal of Labor Economics* 13, no. 2: 246–88.

Cohen, R. G. (12 April 1995). "Advocates Wage Campaigns of Fear." *Boston Herald,* 29.

Collier, V.P. (1987). "Age and Rate of Acquisition of Second Language for Academic Purposes." *TESOL Quarterly* 21, no. 4: 617–41.

———. (1989). "How Long? A Synthesis of Research on Academic Achievement in Second Language." *TESOL Quarterly* 23: 509–31.

Collier, V. P., and W. P. Thomas. (1995). *Research Summary of Study in Progress: Language Minority Student Achievement and Program Effectiveness.* Washington, DC: George Mason University.

Colvin, R. L. (14 June 1995). "Dropout Rate Twice the State Average." *Los Angeles Times.*

Cortines, R. (November 1994). *Message from the Chancellor on the Educational Achievement of LEP Students while Enrolled in Bilingual and ESL Programs.*

de Jong, C. (7 May 1995). "Only Place for Kriolu is Here." *Boston Globe,* A93-94.

Dillon, S. (20 October 1994). "Report Faults Bilingual Education in New York." *New York Times,* A1 and B4.

Dunn, A. (14 August 1994). "Bilingual Ballot Law Fails to Help Chinese-American Voters." *New York Times,* 39.

El Paso Independent School District. (1990). *Bilingual Education Evaluation: The Sixth Year in a Longitudinal Study.* El Paso Independent School District Office of Research and Evaluation.

English First. (1995). Letter to English First dated 25 October 1995 from Mazie Hirono, Lieutenant Governor, Honolulu, Hawaii.

Fillmore, L. W. (1980). "Learning a Second Language: Chinese Children in the American Classroom." *Georgetown University Round Table on Languages and Linguistics,* edited by J. E. Alatis. Washington, DC: Georgetown University Press.

Gersten, R., Woodward, J., & Schneider, S. (1992). *Bilingual Immersion: A Longitudinal Evaluation of the El Paso Program.* Washington, DC: READ Institute.

Gersten, R., T. J. Keating, and S. U. Brengelman. (1995a). "Toward an Understanding of Effective Instructional Practices for Language Minority Students: Findings from a Naturalistic Study." *READ Perspectives* 2, no. 1: 55-82.

Gersten, R., and J. Woodward. (1995). "A Longitudinal Study of Transitional and Immersion Bilingual Education Programs in One District. *The Elementary School Journal* 95, no. 3: 223-39.

Gingrich, Newt. (1995). *To Renew America.* New York: Harper-Collins.

Guerrero, S. (May 1995). "SETC Represents all Teachers." *The Voice... of the United Teaching Profession in the Salinas City School District* 4, no. 3.

Hakuta, K., and E. Bialystok. (1994). *In Other Words: The Science and Psychology of Second-Language Acquisition.* New York: Basic Books.

Honig, B. (26 August 1987). "Education Programs for Which Sunset Provisions Took Effect on June 30, 1987." *Program Advisory to County and District Superintendents.* Sacramento: California State Department of Education.

Howe, P. (12 April 1995). "House Rejects Change in Bilingual Education." *Boston Globe,* 50.

Johnson, Harold. (6 November 1995). "On the Scene: Speaking in Tongues." *National Review,* 28–30.

Krashen, S. (18 September 1995). "An Overview of Bilingual Education." Paper presented at NABE conference in Washington, DC.

Massachusetts Bilingual Education Commission Report. (December 1994). *Striving for Success: The Education of Bilingual Pupils.* Boston, MA: Executive Office of Education.

Mendez, I. (1 April 1995). "Whitman Signs Waiver of Bilingual Education." *Newark Star Ledger.*

Mujica, B. (1995). "Hard Evidence on Bilingual and ESL Programs: Findings of the New York City Longitudinal Study.: *READ Perspectives* 2, no. 2.

Nappi, C. (12 October 1994). Statement given in testimony before Education Committee, State House, Trenton, NJ.

National Association for Bilingual Education. (18 September 1995). *Bilingual Education: Separating Fact from Fiction.* Washington, DC: NABE.

National Research Council. (1992). *Assessing Evaluation Studies: The Case of Bilingual Education Strategies.* Washington, DC: National Academy Press.

Price, J. (9 July 1995). "Panel to Discuss Bilingual Schooling." *Washington Times.*

Pyle, A. (14 July 1995). "State Panel OKs Flexible Bilingual Education Policy." *Los Angeles Times.*

Ramirez, D., S. Yuen, D. Ramey, and D. Pasta. (1991). *Final Report: Longitudinal Study of Structured English Immersion Strategy, Early-Exit and Late-Exit Transitional Bilingual Education Programs for Language-Minority Children,* vol. 1. San Mateo, CA: Aguirre International.

Rossell, C. (1992). "Nothing Matters? A Critique of the Ramirez, et al. Longitudinal Study of Instructional Programs for Language-Minority Children." *Bilingual Research Journal* 16, nos. 1 and 2: 159–86.

Rossier, R. E. (June 1968). A study of graduating seniors who have been in the non-English speaking program of the Los Angeles city schools. Masters Project, University of Southern California.

———. (1993). "Second Language Teaching: A Theoretical Framework for Policy Makers." *READ Perspectives* 1, no. 1.

———. (1995). "A Critique of California's Evaluation of Programs for Students of Limited-English Proficiency. *READ Perspectives* 2, no. 1: 27–54.

Sang Van v. Seattle School District v. State ("State Case"), No. 92-2-28350-6 (King County Superior Court), and *Ledesma et al. v. Seattle School District v. State* ("Federal Case"), No. C92- 1970D (W.D. Wash.).

Seattle School District. (November 1993). "Comparison of Dropouts and Graduates, Bilingual Students vs. Overall District." Data Profile, Seattle Public Schools.

Skutnabb-Kangas, T., and P. Toukomaa. (1976). *Teaching Migrant Children's Mother Tongue and Learning the Language of the Host Country in the Context of the Socio-Cultural Situation of the Migrant Family*. New York: UNESCO.

Steinberg, J. (19 September 1995). "State is Accused of Overuse of Bilingual Classes." *New York Times*, B6.

Tikunoff, W. J., B. A. Ward, L. D. van Broekhuizen, M. Romero, L. V. Castaneda, T. Lucas, and A. Katz. (1991). *Final Report: A Descriptive Study of Significant Features of Exemplary Special Alternative Instructional Programs*. Los Alamitos, CA: The Southwest Regional Educational Laboratory.

Turner, J. S. (1994). "Analyses and Recommendations: Survey of Administrators and Teachers and Survey of Parents and Students." Bethlehem Area School District English Acquisition Program.

Turner, J. S., A. Goldberg, and M. J. Connelly. (1995). "The Bethlehem Area School District English Acquisition Program: The First Two Years." *READ Perspectives* 2, no. 2.

U. S. General Accounting Office. (January 1994). "Limited-English Proficiency: A Growing and Costly Educational Challenge Facing Many School Districts." Washington, DC.

Weymouth, L. (12 September 1995). "Bob Dole's Plain English." *Washington Post*, A-19.

Notes

Introduction

1. National Advisory and Coordinating Council on Bilingual Education (NACCBE), U.S. Department of Education; *Eleventh Annual Report to Congress* (Washington, D.C.: Government Printing Office, 1987), 29, 75, 76.
2. Jill McCarthy and Marlene Godfrey, "Follow-Up Study on Students with Extended Stays in the Boston Transitional Bilingual Education Program" (Wellesley, Mass.: Massachusetts Department of Education, Greater Boston Regional Education Center, 1986), 1.
3. Alfredo Mathew, Jr., "What Are the Perceived and Particular Problems and Needs of Students Whose Background Is Hispanic in the Desegregation Process?" (paper presented at the National Conference on Desegregation and Education Concerns of the Hispanic Community, Washington, D.C., 26–28 June 1977).
4. Quoted in Diego Castellanos, *The Best of Two Worlds: Bilingual-Bicultural Education in the U.S.* (Trenton, N.J.: New Jersey State Department of Education, 1983), 144.
5. See A. Covington, "Black People and Black English," in *Black English: A Seminar,* ed. D. Harrison and T. Trabasso (Hillsdale, N.J.: Lawrence Erlbaum, 1976). John Baugh, in *Black Street Speech: Its History, Structure, and Survival* (Austin, Tex.: University of Texas Press, 1983), 117, reports on William Labov's finding that "Black parents want their children

to learn norms for social assimilation and competitive, mar-
ketable skills."
6. Richard Rodriguez, "Unilingual, Not Unilateral," *Wall Street
   Journal,* 25 June 1985, p. 30.
7. Quoted in Noel Epstein, *Language, Ethnicity, and the Schools*
   (Washington, D.C.: Institute for Education Leadership,
   George Washington University, 1977), 69.
8. Ibid., 69.
9. Ibid., 69.

Chapter 1

1. Richard Rodriguez, *Hunger of Memory: The Education of Richard Rodriguez* (Boston: David R. Godine, 1982), 22.
2. Author's notes from Albert Shanker lecture in Harvard
   Graduate School of Education course, 8 February 1988.
3. Daniel Gonzalez, "Classes Educating Children in Their Native Languages," *Daily Hampshire Gazette,* 25 March 1988, p.
   25.
4. Christina Bratt Paulston, *Swedish Research and Debate about
   Bilingualism* (Stockholm: National Swedish Board of Education, 1982), 51–52.
5. Anna Uhl Chamot and Gloria Montanares, "A Summary of
   Current Literature on English as a Second Language"
   (Washington, D.C.: National Clearinghouse on Bilingual Education, March 1985), 32.
6. Ana Celia Zentella, "The Fate of Spanish in the United
   States: The Puerto Rican Experience," in *The Language of Inequality,* ed. Joan Manes and Nessa Wolfson (The Hague:
   Mouton, 1985), 47.
7. Deborah L. Gold, "Union Vote Downs Bilingual Method,"
   Education Week, 9 September 1987, p. 6.

Chapter 2

1. Dr. Gloria de Guevara Figueroa, personal conversation with
   the author, 12 April 1982. For several other accounts of
   Fuentes's offensive actions, mainly as a school superintendent on New York's Lower East Side, including colleagues'

depositions of his "outright bigotry," "anti-Semitic slurs," labeling Puerto Rican parents as "garbage," and other instances of racism and bigotry, see Albert Shanker, "Where We Stand," *New York Times*, 30 July 1972, p. 9.

2. Sarah Clayton, "Bilingual Program a Source of Pride," *Newton News-Tribune*, 12 January 1982, p. 8.

3. Robert K. Newman, "City Fails in Bilingual Ed," *Newton Tribune*, 15 May 1985, p. 6; Newman, "Crackdown in Newton: Bilingual Education Failures," *Newton Graphic*, 16 May 1985, p. 8; Nancy Matsumoto, "Language Barriers: State Cites Newton for Bilingual Violations," *Newton Tab*, 21 May 1985, p. 1; Howard Altman, "Board Boiling Over Bilingual Ed Report," *Newton Tribune*, 29 May 1985, p. 13; Lisa Rein, "Newton Responds to Criticism of Bilingual Program," *Newton Tab*, 2 July 1985, p. 1.

4. Author's notes, New England Bilingual Education Conference, Boston, May 1985.

5. Letter from Massachusetts State Department of Education to Newton Public Schools, 21 October 1986.

Chapter 3

1. Jim Cummins, "Educational Implications of Mother Tongue Maintenance in Minority Language Groups," *Canadian Modern Language Review* 34 (3 [1978]): 395. For additional readings of Cummins's influential works in this field see "The Role of Primary Language Development in Promoting Educational Success for Language Minority Students," in California Department of Education, *Schooling and Language Minority Students: A Theoretical Framework* (Los Angeles: California State University Evaluation Assessment and Dissemination Center, 1981); "Empowering Minority Students: A Framework for Intervention," *Harvard Education Review* 56 (1986): 18–36; and Cummins and M. Swain, *Bilingualism in Education: Aspects of Theory, Research and Practice* (London: Longman, 1986).

2. Tove Skutnabb-Kangas and Pertti Toukomaa, *Teaching Migrant Children's Mother Tongue and Learning the Language of*

the Host Country in the Context of the Sociocultural Situation of the Migrant Family (Helsinki: The Finnish National Commission for UNESCO, 1976). Related works by the same authors include: *The Intense Teaching of the Mother Tongue to Migrant Children of Preschool Age,* research reports 26 (Tampere, Finland: Department of Sociology and Social Psychology, University of Tampere, 1977); *Language in the Process of Cultural Assimilation and Structural Incorporation of Linguistic Minorities* (Arlington, Va.: National Clearinghouse for Bilingual Education, 1979); "Semilingualism and Middle Class Bias," *Working Papers on Bilingualism* 19 (Toronto: Ontario Institute for Studies in Education, 1979); Skutnabb-Kangas, *Bilingualism or Not: The Education of Minorities* (Clevedon, England: Multilingual Matters, 1984); Skutnabb-Kangas and J. Cummins, eds., *Minority Education: From Shame to Struggle* (Clevedon, England: Multilingual Matters, 1988).

3. Keith A. Baker and Adriana A. de Kanter, "Effectiveness of Bilingual Education: A Review of the Literature," Technical Analysis Report Series, U.S. Department of Education (Washington, D.C.: Office of Planning and Budget, 1981), 8.

4. Paulston, *Swedish Research,* 41–54.

5. Ibid., 55.

6. See Muriel Saville-Troike, *Foundations for Teaching English as a Second Language* (New York: Prentice-Hall, 1976), p. 12: "Given the complexity of language, it is no wonder that even adults with their mature intellects seldom attain native fluency in a new language. But children, with their limited memories, restricted reasoning powers, and as yet almost non-existent analytical abilities, acquire perfect fluency in any language to which they are consistently exposed, and in which they are motivated to communicate."

7. Kenji Hakuta, *Mirror of Language: The Debate on Bilingualism* (New York: Basic Books, 1986), 218.

8. Betty Mace-Matluck and Wesley A. Hoover, *Teaching Reading to Bilingual Children Study,* executive summary (Austin,

Tex.: Southwest Educational Development Laboratory, 1984), 29–34.

9. Keith Baker and Christine Rossell, "An Implementation Problem: Specifying the Target Group for Bilingual Education," *Educational Policy* 1 (2 [1987]): 263.

10. Office of the Inspector General, "Review of Federal Bilingual Education Programs in Texas" (Washington, D.C.: U.S. Department of Education, 1982), 21.

11. R. Berdan, A. So, and A. Sanchez, *Language among the Cherokee, Patterns of Language Use in Northeastern Oklahoma,* part I, preliminary report (Los Alamitos, Calif.: National Center for Bilingual Research, 1982).

12. H. Dulay and M. Burt, "The Relative Proficiency of Limited English Proficient Students," in *Georgetown University Roundtable on Language and Linguistics,* ed. J. Alatis (Washington, D.C.: Georgetown University Press, 1980).

13. Office for Research and Evaluation, *Interim Report of the Five Year Bilingual Education Pilot Project* (El Paso, Tex.: El Paso Independent School District, 1987), 51–59.

14. Ibid., 62.

15. Jim Cummins, "Linguistic Interdependence and the Educational Development of Bilingual Children," *Review of Educational Research* 49 (1979): 222–51.

16. Author's findings based on research in the following school districts: Berkeley, Fallbrook, and Paramount, Calif.; El Paso and Richardson, Tex.; Dade County, Fla.; Arlington and Fairfax, Va.; Oyster School, Washington, D.C.; and Brookline, Holliston, and Newton, Mass.

17. Tove Skutnabb-Kangas and Pertti Toukomaa, "The Education of Migrant Workers and Their Families," *Educational Studies and Documents* (UNESCO, 1987), 27.

18. C. Walsh and E. Carballo, *Transitional Bilingual Education in Massachusetts: A Preliminary Study of Its Effectiveness* (Boston: Massachusetts Department of Education, Bureau of Transitional Bilingual Education, 1986).

19. Christine Rossell, "The Problem with Bilingual Research: A Critique of the Walsh and Carballo Study of Bilingual

Education Projects," *Equity and Excellence* 23 (4 [1988]): 25–30.

20. Silvia Rothfarb, Maria Ariza, and Rafael Urrutia, *Evaluation of the Bilingual Curriculum Project: Final Report of a Three-Year Study* (Miami, Fla.: Dade County Public Schools, 1987), ii.

21. Author's notes, Massachusetts Association for Bilingual Education Conference, Boxborough, Mass., 14 November 1986.

22. Noel Epstein, *Language, Ethnicity, and the Schools* (Washington, D.C.: Institute for Education Leadership, George Washington University, 1977), 34.

23. Jill McCarthy and Marlene Godfrey, "Follow-Up Study on Students with Extended Stays in the Boston Transitional Bilingual Education Program (Wellesley, Mass.: Massachusetts Department of Education, Greater Boston Regional Education Center, 1986), 93.

24. K. Baker and D. Ramirez, *Becoming a More Frequent Speaker of a Second Language: Some Effects of Program Model on LEP Students and Their Teachers,* 2d. year report (Alexandria, Va.: SRA Technologies, 1987).

25. H. G. Widdowson, *Teaching Language as Communication* (London: Oxford University Press, 1978), 29.

Chapter 4

1. International Covenant on Civil and Political Rights, United Nations General Assembly, 21 U.N. GAOR, G. A. resolution 2200, Supp. (No. 16) 52, doc. A 6316 (1966).

2. Barry McLaughlin, *Second-Language Acquisition in Childhood,* vol. 2 (Hillsdale, N.J.: Lawrence Erlbaum, 1985), 40–41.

3. I am relying on the categories in McLaughlin, *Second-Language Acquisition,* 41–46.

4. Ibid., 42.

5. Ibid., 41.

6. Ibid., 45.

7. Ibid., 57.

8. M. N. Guboglo, "Factors Affecting Bilingualism in National Languages and Russian in a Developed Socialist Society,"

Language and Education in Multilingual Settings, ed. Bernard Spolsky (San Diego, Calif.: College Hill Press, 1986), 23.

9. Descriptions from McLaughlin, *Second-Language Acquisition,* 51–57, and E. G. Lewis, *Multilingualism in the Soviet Union* (The Hague: Mouton, 1972).

10. Guboglo, 23.

11. Ibid., 25.

12. Ibid.

13. McLaughlin. 30.

14. Ibid., 29.

15. Ibid., 30–36.

16. Ibid., 31.

17. Paulston, *Swedish Research,* 42.

18. Paulston, 49.

19. Ibid., 50.

20. Ibid., 53.

21. Ibid., 54.

22. Ibid.

23. McLaughlin, 76.

24. Bulletin, "Canada and the French-Speaking Community," (Quebec: Conseil de la langue française, 6 December 1973), 1.

25. John F. Burns, "Trudeau Emerges as Quiet Foe of Canadian Pact," *New York Times,* 17 May 1987, p. 8.

26. Ibid.

27. R. Grosjean, *Life With Two Languages: An Introduction to Bilingualism* (Cambridge, Mass.: Harvard University Press, 1982), 17–18.

28. W. E. Lambert and G. R. Tucker, *Bilingual Education of Children: The St. Lambert Experiment* (Rowley, Mass.: Newbury House, 1972).

29. Author's notes from interview with teachers in Holliston, Mass., French Immersion program, 1984.

30. Fred Genesee, "Scholastic Effects of French Immersion: An Overview After Ten Years," *Interchange* 9 (4 [1979]): 23.

31. McLaughlin, *Second-Language Acquisition,* 75.

32. Jim Cummins, *Bilingualism and Minority Language Children*

(Toronto: The Ontario Institute for Studies in Education, 1981).

33. Fred Genesee, "Bilingual Education of Majority Language Children: The Immersion Experiment in Review," *Applied Psycholinguistics* 4 (1983): 1–47.

Chapter 5

1. Bilingual Education Act of 1984, Title VII of P.L. 98–511, section 702, B-3.
2. Bernard Spolsky, "Speech Communities and Schools," *TE-SOL Quarterly* 8 (1 [March 1974]): 17. TESOL stands for "Teachers of English to Speakers of Other Languages."
3. Patricia Ruane, letter to the author, 30 March 1986.
4. Joan Baratz-Snowden, Donald Rock, Judith Pollack, and Gita Wilder, "Parent Preference Study," executive summary (Princeton, N.J.: Educational Testing Service, July 1988), ii–iv.
5. Ibid., v.
6. Data supplied by superintendent's office, Berkeley Unified School District, census report, 1 October 1987.
7. Christine Rossell, "The Effectiveness of Educational Alternatives for Limited-English Proficient Children in the Berkeley Unified District," report to the U.S. District Court in the case of *Teresa P. et al.* v. *Berkeley Unified School District* (San Francisco, Calif.: September 1988), 33.
8. Data provided by Fairfax County Public Schools ESL Department in telephone interview, April 1988.
9. Sarah Glazer, "Bilingual Education: Does It Work?" *Congressional Quarterly's Editorial Research Reports*, 11 March 1988, p. 137.
10. Walter D. Mallory and Puran L. Rajpal, *Follow-Up of Former ESL Students* (Fairfax County, Va.: Office of Research and Evaluation, Fairfax County Public Schools, April 1987), 15.
11. Mallory and Rajpal, 16.
12. Glazer, 137.
13. National Advisory and Coordinating Council on Bilingual Education (NACCBE), U.S. Department of Education,

11. Ibid.
12. Ibid., 43–44.
13. Ibid., 46.
14. Hakuta, 212–14.
15. Ibid., 191.
16. James Crawford, "37 States Consider 'English Only' Bills, With Mixed Results," *Education Week*, 17 June 1987, p. 15.
17. Ibid., 15.
18. Bruce McFarland, "Rep. Correia Opposes Making English 'Official Language'," *Herald News* (Falls River, Mass.), 5 March 1987, p. 1.
19. Quoted in Thomas Ricento, "The Framers Knew Best," *MATSOL Newsletter*, Massachusetts Association of Teachers of English to Speakers of Other Languages, Fall 1988, p. 1.
20. Ibid.
21. "English Spoken Here, but Unofficially," *New York Times*, 29 October 1988, p. A28.
22. Quoted in "Language War Heats Up Around Country," *English First* 1 (2 December 1986): 3.
23. Elliot L. Judd, "The English Language Amendment: A Case Study on Language and Politics," *TESOL QUARTERLY* 21 (1 March 1987): 129–30.
24. James Crawford, "Proposition 63: Much Talk, Few Effects," *Education Week*, 17 June 1987, p. 15.
25. Joshua A. Fishman, "Bilingualism and Separatism," *The Annals of the American Academy of Political and Social Science* 487 (September 1986): 169.
26. Horace Kallen, "Democracy Versus the Melting Pot," *Culture and Democracy in the United States* (New York: Boni and Liveright, 1924), 61.
27. Richard Rodriguez, "Unilingual, Not Unilateral," *Wall Street Journal*, 25 June 1985, p. 30.

Chapter 8

1. Personal communication from Office of Bilingual Education and Minority Languages Affairs, May 1989.
2. National Advisory and Coordinating Council on Bilingual

Education (NAACBE), U.S. Department of Education, *Eleventh Annual Report to Congress* (Washington, D.C.: Government Printing Office, 1987), 11.

3. "Research Center Criticizes Proposed Bilingual Regs as Based on Misunderstanding of Language Development," *Education Week*, 22 September 1980, p. 7.

4. National Advisory Council, *Annual Report to Congress*, 17–27.

5. *Teresa P. et al.* v. *Berkeley Unified School District*, U.S. District Court, Northern District of California, 1989.

6. Robert Rothman, "English Fluency Attainment Linked in NAEP Study," *Education Week*, 9 November 1988, 1.

7. "The Remarkable Impact of Creating a School Community," *American Educator* (Spring 1988), 10.

8. U.S. Census Bureau, 2 February 1989.

9. M. Cohen and D. Ribadeneira, "Poor Math, Science Skills Seen Hurting U.S. Economy," *Boston Globe*, 5 February 1989, p. 18.

10. William Snider, "Hispanic Students Require Income to Remain in School, Study Finds," *Education Week*, 21 September 1988, p. 17.

11. Deborah L. Gold, "Legal Settlement in Bilingual Case Hailed as Model," *Education Week*, 11 January 1989, 12.

12. Charles A. Radin, "Here, Math + English = Success," *Boston Globe*, 17 October 1988, p. 2.

13. *A Nation at Risk: The Imperative for Educational Reform* (Washington, D.C.: Government Printing Office, April 1983).

14. February 2, 1989, p. 31.

15. Albert Shanker, "International Math and Science Test: U.S. Rock Bottom," *New York Times*, 5 February 1989, p. E7.

16. Ann Bradley, "Teaching Board Says Professional Degree Is Not Requirement," *Education Week*, 2 August 1989, pp. 1, 26.

17. Hakuta, 9.

18. Sir Kenneth Clark, *Civilization* (New York: Harper & Row, 1969), 367.

Index

$\diamond \diamond \diamond$

343